W9-CZT-859

CYBERSPACE TEXTUALITY

Cyberspace Textuality

*Computer Technology
and Literary Theory*

Edited by Marie-Laure Ryan

INDIANA UNIVERSITY PRESS

Bloomington and Indianapolis

This book is a publication of
Indiana University Press
601 North Morton Street
Bloomington, Indiana 47404-3797 USA

www.indiana.edu/~iupress

Telephone orders   800-842-6796
Fax orders   812-855-7931
Orders by e-mail   iuporder@indiana.edu

The paper used in this publication
meets the minimum requirements of American National Standard
for Information Sciences—Permanence of Paper
for Printed Library Materials,
ANSI Z39.48-1984.

Manufactured in the United States of America

Library of Congress Cataloging-in-Publication Data
Ryan, Marie-Laure, date
Cyberspace textuality : computer technology and literary theory /
edited by Marie-Laure Ryan
p.   cm.
Includes index.
ISBN 0-253-33465-9 (cl : alk. paper). — ISBN 0-253-21242-1 (pa : alk. paper)
1. Computers and civilization.   2. Electronic publications—
Philosophy.   3. Literature—Philosophy.   I. Title.
QA76.9.C66R93   1998
303.48'34—dc21   98-43225

1 2 3 4 5   03 02 01 00 99 98

Contents

Contents

Acknowledgments

Early versions, foreign language translations, or excerpts of some of the essays gathered in this volume have been published elsewhere in electronic or print forms.

N. Katherine Hayles, "Artificial Life and Literary Culture," appeared in a French version titled "Vie artificielle et culture littéraire," *Théorie, Littérature, Enseignement* 12 (Fall 1994), 69–90.

A preliminary version of Christopher J. Keep, "The Disturbing Liveliness of Machines: Rethinking the Body in Hypertext Theory and Fiction" appeared in a French translation by Lara Fitzgerald under the title "Perdu dans le labyrinthe: réévaluer le corps en théorie et en pratique d'hypertexte" in *Littérature et informatique. La littérature générée par ordinateur*, ed. Alain Vuillemin and Michel Lenoble (Arras: Artois Press Université, 1995), 327–40.

Lance Olsen, "Virtual Termites: A Hypotextual Technomutant Explo(it)ration of William Gibson and the Electronic Beyond(s)," appeared in *Style* 29.2 (1995), 287–313.

An early version of Barbara Page, "Women Writers and the Restive Text: Feminism, Experimental Writing, and Hypertext," appeared in electronic form in *Postmodern Culture* 6.2 (January 1996).

Mark Poster's essay "Theorizing Virtual Reality: Baudrillard and Derrida" is appearing concurrently in CD form in Mark Poster, *The Information Subject* (New York: International Arts, 1998).

Jon Thiem, "Myths of the Universal Library: From Alexandria to the Postmodern Age," appeared in *The Serials Librarian* 26.1 (1995), 63–74.

I would like to thank the journals and individuals mentioned above for permission to reprint this material. The reproductions from the comic strip *Deathlok* in Thomas Foster's essay appear with permission of Marvel Comics in New York City.

CYBERSPACE TEXTUALITY

Introduction

Marie-Laure Ryan

No situation could be worse than that in which the cultured men and women isolate themselves in the territory of the alphabetical text and leave the language of tomorrow into the hands of technicians and salesmen.
—Pierre Lévy, "Toward Superlanguage"

Varieties of Computer-Supported Texts

Recent advances in computer technology, such as world-spanning information networks, virtual reality, multimedia communication, and the digitization of texts, have led to the development of a computer culture that is quickly becoming a major force in the humanities. The term "cyberspace" captures the growing sense that beyond—or perhaps on—the computer screen lies a "New Frontier" both enticing and forbidding, a frontier awaiting exploration, promising discovery, threatening humanistic values, hatching new genres of discourse, altering our relation to the written word, and questioning our sense of self and of embodiment. The purpose of this book is to explore the concepts of text and the forms of textuality currently emerging from the creative chaos of electronic technologies.

Computers were once thought of as number-crunching machines; but for most of us it is their ability to create worlds and process words that have made them into a nearly indispensable part of life. If computers are everywhere, it is because they have grown into "poetry machines."[1] The digital revolution of the last decade has let words on the loose, not just by liberating their semantic potential, as most avant-garde movements of the past hundred years have done, but in a physical, quite literal sense as well. Information patterns travel incessantly inside and outside the machine, from disk storage to active memory to output devices to other computer sites. At the end of their journey through cyberspace—each packet of information following its own itinerary—

1

bit patterns reorganize themselves into letters, words, and texts. Hopefully into meanings. Sometimes the words on the loose become malleable substance in our hands, as we grab them with a hand-shaped cursor, move them, erase them, banish and recall them, pull more words from under words, cut them out and paste them into a new context; sometimes they become actors and dancers on the stage of the computer screen, animated by the script of an invisible program; sometimes they fail to regroup at the end of their trip, and the screen fills up with garbage, dismembered text, visual nonsense, or surrealistic graphics. Whether we play with them or watch them perform for us, whether we control them or they rebel against us, electronic words never stand still for long, never settle down on a page, even when a copy is sent to the printer; for the printer merely outputs a lifeless replica, a still photograph of objects in motion.

The new forms of discourse and literary genres born out of computer technology can be classified into three categories, depending on the role of the computer. The machine can function as author or co-author, as medium of transmission or as space of performance—what Brenda Laurel calls the computer as theater. At the time of this writing, the genres of electronic textuality include the following:

The Computer as (Co-)Author

In the seventies and eighties, when Artificial Intelligence was the leading application of computing power—triggering the hope or fear that machines would soon replace humans—the potential contribution of computers to literature was generally envisioned as the production of text. This production does not necessarily mean that the human factor is excluded; as Espen Aarseth has observed (348), computer-generated literature is a collaboration between man and machine in which the computer can play three roles: output a blueprint for the human partner to translate into literary language, produce text in a live dialogue with the user, or perform various operations on a human-composed text. The human partner will be respectively post-processor, co-processor, and pre-processor. These projects may be intended as literary experiments, to be judged by the aesthetic value of the product, or they may be conceived as contributions to cognitive science. The output may be a standard print text, or exist exclusively in an electronic environment. (This last case is discussed under "Computer-modulated texts" below.) Here are examples of the three types of collaboration:

CLASSICAL ARTIFICIAL INTELLIGENCE: THE COMPUTER AS OUTLINE-GENERATOR. This category is illustrated by the story-generating programs developed in the seventies and eighties as contributions to AI. (The best-known is Tale-Spin by James Meehan.) What matters in these projects is not their output *per se*—usually mediocre imitations of standard types of narrative such as fables or fairy tales—but the reasoning power of the generative algorithm and its credibility as a simulation of human creative processes. In the most intelligent story-generating programs, the variety and quality of the output is out of proportion with the complexity of the algorithm. One of the most recent projects in the field, for instance, Scott Turner's MINSTREL, needs 10,000 lines of code to generate the plotline of a dozen different King Arthur stories of half a page each. These stories read like this:

> Once upon a time, a knight named Lancelot loved a princess named Andrea. Lancelot saw Andrea kiss a knight named Frederick. Lancelot believed that Andrea loved Frederick. Lancelot wanted to be the love of Andrea. But he could not because Andrea loved Frederick. This caused him to make a hasty decision. Later, he discovered that his hasty decision was incorrect. He wished he could take back what he did. But he couldn't. (Turner 183)

This story-outline poses little threat to win a Pulitzer prize, even if it is brilliantly rewritten by a human author, but the project is considered significant from a cognitive point of view because it begins with a small amount of knowledge, and is able to expand this database into stories through powerful logical and analogical reasoning.

ALTERNATIVE ARTIFICIAL INTELLIGENCE: TEXT PRODUCED IN A DIA-LOGUE BETWEEN COMPUTER AND USER. Here the prototypical example is ELIZA, a computer program written in 1966 by Joseph Weizenbaum. Its purpose was not to produce literature, but to "test the limits of a computer's conversational capacity" (Turkle 105) by simulating a dialogue between a patient (the user) and a psychotherapist (ELIZA). ELIZA was remarkable for its ability to carry on a reasonably coherent conversation without using any sophisticated language-parsing techniques. Rather than building a syntactic and semantic representation of the user's input, as do programs seriously aiming at language understanding, it relied on rather crude strategies, such as detecting key words, recycling the user's input, responding with canned formulae, or abruptly changing the topic. Yet despite the system's total lack of understanding of the human mind, ELIZA's conversation was clever enough to fascinate users. The program is now revered as the pioneer of a new brand of AI known as "alternative." In this new brand, faking intelligence and passing as human is more important than emulating thinking. The most advanced successor of ELIZA is Julia, a robot developed at Carnegie Mellon University who enlivens a MOO with her opinionated conversation.[2]

TEXT MANIPULATION: THE COMPUTER AS POSTPROCESSOR. The texts of this category are mostly intended as experimental literature. Their generation owes nothing to AI: words and textual fragments are manipulated as opaque objects, not as meaning-bearing units. A computer program fabricates text out of ready-made texts by searching a database for elements fitting certain patterns (rhymes, palindromes, anagrams) or by subjecting the input text(s) to various aleatory procedures, such as collage and permutations. In an automated version of the Mad Lib party game, words may be randomly selected from the database and pasted into human-made templates, thereby producing the surrealistic effect of "exquisite cadavers." The poetry of John Cage offers a good illustration of these various techniques. In a work titled *I-V,* which produces a print text, a program generates "mesostric strings" (internal acrostics) by selecting a word from a list and locating its individual letters in quotations randomly chosen from another list. In the output text, the capitalized letters of the mesostric string are centered in the middle of the page on the vertical axis, surrounded on the horizontal axis by the "wing words" of the quoted source texts (Perloff 208).

The Computer as Medium of Transmission

The texts of this group are not radically new forms of writing, but electronic implementations of already established genres. Though the computer functions primarily as channel of transmission, it is by no means a passive medium. As it facilitates certain operations, the machine fosters new reading and writing habits which can lead to significant stylistic and pragmatic differences between electronic genres and their print counterparts.

DIGITIZED PRINT TEXTS. Should the digitization of texts written to be printed—for instance, of the novels of Jane Austen—be regarded as a genre in its own right, or is it merely a new mode of storage? Some theorists of electronic culture (especially Lanham) have argued that the phenomenology of reading is radically altered when print texts are transferred to the electronic medium: "What happens when a text moves from the page to the screen? First, the digital text becomes unfixed and interactive. The reader can change it, become writer" (31). There is no denying that we can perform different operations on a digitized text than on a printed one: rewrite parts of it without leaving physical traces of this activity, reformat it, change its font, cut into it and paste the cuts elsewhere, establish electronic links with other texts, and so on. Some of these activities change the appearance of the text, others place it in a different context, and still others modify "the text" of the text. But is this still reading, or using the text for other kinds of games? Regarding the digitized text as generically different from its printed counterpart presupposes that "text" is not so much a collection of linguistic signs produced for the sake of being read as an activity kit, a set of possible operations including reading, among many others. According to this position, altering an electronic text does not create a different text, but actualizes the potential for transformation that results from its digitization.

ASYNCHRONOUS COMMUNICATION THROUGH COMPUTER NETWORKS: E-MAIL AND POSTINGS TO USER-INTEREST GROUPS. Here users do not interact live, in contrast to Internet chatrooms and MOO conversations (see below), but compose and send messages which will be kept in the semi-permanent storage of a bulletin board or an electronic mailbox. These texts are less durable and therefore less binding than handwritten and printed messages, yet they allow more time for planning and editing than live conversation. As they lessen the writer's sense of responsibility for the form and contents of the message, electronic mail and postings encourage informality, brainstorming, and the throwing of ideas on the forum for the pure sake of testing the reactions of the audience. Discussion groups are a stage for performance, where success is measured by the number of responses to a posting.

TREE FICTION AND COLLABORATIVE LITERATURE. Tree fiction is one of those ideas that can be realized in print or handwriting, but receives a boost from the ability of electronic telecommunications to establish contacts between physically remote people with common interests. Many tree fiction projects are currently being developed on the World Wide Web.[3] Like hypertext, tree fictions use electronic linking to join fragments of text and create forks in the plot, but their structure allows no returns to former decision points and no merging of paths. Since every branch in the plot is kept strictly separate from the others, it is relatively easy to maintain narrative continuity and logical coherence. In contrast to more densely linked forms of hypertext, every traversal of a story tree from the common root node to a terminal node should thus yield a well-formed linear plot with a definite beginning, and striving toward a definite ending. In the tree fiction projects of the Internet, more explicitly than in any other context, the purpose of reading is to become a writer. The user reads along a branch until he finds a suitable point for a contribution. Depending on the insertion point, his contribution may either initiate a new fork in the plot, or add text at the end of a branch. Collaborative literary projects can also take the form of a network of autonomous texts. This is the case in Robert Coover's literary MOO, the Hypertext Hotel.[4] Users are invited to add permanent texts to the system, and the rooms of the structure function as storage for their contributions, rather than as meeting places for real-time conversation.

ELECTRONIC SERIALS. This genre is exemplified by *The Spot*, a soap opera on the World Wide Web[5] which follows the daily lives of the five habitants of a California beach house. A new installment in the diary of the characters is posted every day. Each character is "played" by a writer responsible for his or her diary, but since the characters interact in the plot, the global coherence of the story line must be ensured through advance planning by the whole cast. Besides reading the entries, the visitor of the site can view pictures, buy merchandise, access summaries of past episodes, and send e-mail offering advice to the characters on how to live their life or suggestions to their writers on how to develop the plot. The writers/characters are supposed to respond personally to their fan mail. This interaction opens the possibility of a mild form of collaboration between writers and readers. It also leads to a transgression of the traditional ontological boundaries between readers and characters, since readers can write to characters.

The Computer as Theater

Here the text cannot be divorced from the electronic environment, because it exploits some of the specific features of its hardware and software support: fluid visual displays, interactive algorithms, structured databases, randomizing capabilities, and a "real-time" mode of operation which potentially turns every run of the text-animating program into a unique performance. In the following genres, electronic writing truly comes into its own:

HYPERTEXT. In this best-known of electronic genres, text is broken into fragments ("lexias," "textrons") and stored in a network whose nodes are connected by electronic links. A fragment typically contains a number of different links, offering the reader a choice of directions to follow. By letting readers determine their own paths of navigation through the database, hypertext promotes what is customarily regarded as a non-linear mode of reading. (Multilinear would be more appropriate, since reading always requires a sequential parsing.) Hyperlinks are not only used in experimental literary fiction, they can also build multimedia networks of autonomous documents relating to a certain topic (e.g., George Landow's *Dickens Web*). Since it facilitates access to information, the device provides an efficient searching tool through a database, such as on-line help files or the World Wide Web. Through its structured network of choices, hypertext stands halfway between texts that impose a strictly sequential reading order (traditional novels) and texts with a totally free mode of access (encyclopedias, texts written on cards that can be shuffled).[6] The "follow the links" idea can be implemented in print (*Choose Your Own Adventures* books; novels with multiple reading sequences, such as Julio Cortázar's *Hopscotch*), but these texts merely break the surface of a much deeper ground. The Codex book allows with great difficulty what comes easily for the computer: the bound format stands in the way of jumping around the text. This is why we should not categorize hypertext as the electronic implementation of a print genre, but rather, regard print texts with multiple reading sequences as the embryo of an electronic genre.

MUDS AND MOOS. Sherry Turkle calls them a "new form of collectively written literature" (11) but for John Perry Barlow they are "CB radio, only typing."[7] These diverging opinions concern multi-user computer games (MUDs) or social meeting places (MOOs) accessible through the Internet. On a MOO, users design and play a character through purely textual commands, interacting with other characters on a stage set up by the system or by the more experienced users. The MOO system relies on both permanent descriptions of the setting (typically a building consisting of many rooms furnished with various objects), and evanescent speech acts. These two types of discourse encourage two types of activity: exploring the setting by activating the textual descriptions stored by the system; and communicating in real time with other characters by typing dialogue or action-describing statements, which count as the live performance of these actions.

INTERACTIVE DRAMA. This term refers to applications of virtual reality technology (VR) designed for the entertainment of the participant. Interactive Drama allows a considerable range of variations. It can take the form of a multimedia version of the MOO (or conference room), in which physically distant users meet and converse in a virtual landscape under fictional identities; of dramatic performances placing the spectator in a computer-generated setting, where she listens to or interacts with live actors; or of an electronic theme park ride, during which the user explores a fantastic virtual world populated with computer-simulated characters. In its most utopian form, Interactive Drama would be a fully automated production, in which users would impersonate characters in a dialogue with AI-driven agents. The script would allow users to "choose what to do, say, and think at all times" (Kelso et al. 2), thus letting them influence the direction of the plot, but their actions would nevertheless be controlled by the system, so that every choice would result in an aesthetically pleasing and narratively well-formed dramatic action. This type of production, if ever implemented, would realize the age-old dream of abolishing the differences between author, characters, actors, and spectators.

COMPUTER GAMES. Computer games are not so much a new textual genre, as a new environment for the use of text. (The same may be said of all multimedia systems.) The textual dimension of computer games may involve the features of several of the categories listed above: as in Interactive Drama, the user is placed in the role of protagonist; as in hypertext, his progress traces a path on a hidden map of decision points; as in MOOs and MUDs, he may interact in real time with other players. (MUD stands for Multi-User Dungeon, and the earlier MUDs were in fact computer games based on the plot structure of *Dungeons and Dragons*.) In most games, however, the user receives a much more specific task than in the other types of computer-based textual activities. In the early eighties, computer games were either entirely textless (*Tetris*, *Pac-Man*, and most joystick-operated games) or entirely text-based (*Zork*). In the text-based forms, the computer displayed segments of an interactive fiction, and the user performed her moves by typing rudimentary verbal responses. The introduction of CD-ROMs allowed text to become a part of a multi-media environment. In recent games, such as *Myst* and the latest *Zork* episodes, the fictional world discloses itself though the spoken dialogue of characters and through written messages inscribed within the fictional world, but this mode of communication is not available to the user; his mode of action is point-and-click with a mouse rather than typing verbal commands. In an ironic revenge of the printed word, however, popular computer games tend to generate non-electronic texts, such as "cheat-books" offering strategic advice, or novels chronicling the history of the game world on fake antique leather-bound tomes artfully aged by chemicals (*Myst: The Book of Atrus*).

CD-ROM MULTIMEDIA WORKS. A variant on hypertext, interactive CD-ROM productions orchestrate text with sound, images, and animation.

The group includes two main subtypes: children's "Living Books," and artists' CD-ROMs. In *Arthur's Teacher Troubles*, a children's book produced by Brøderbund, the user moves page by page through an illustrated story, but every page offers hidden surprises: click on the teacher, and she turns into a monster; click on one of the students, and he makes a funny face; click on a mirror on the wall, and it is shattered by a baseball; click on the text under the picture, and it is read aloud. These activities are not forks in the plot, but the roadside attractions of a basically linear narrative. In artists' CD-ROMS—as in their more solid counterparts, artists' book-objects—the design of the user interface and the choreography of her movements through the work-world become an integral dimension of meaning. "As never before," writes Margot Lovejoy, "the creation of a work calls for an awareness of what is meant by reading and looking, and of how associative thought processes take place" (118–19). Here is how Lovejoy describes one of these works, Laurie Anderson's CD-ROM *Puppet Motel*: "[T]he participant can choose a theme to explore from a bank of images projected on the wall of what appears to be a mysterious tunnel containing animal tracks, clocks, and electric outlets. After exploring a chosen theme, the action shifts to an attic-like space full of images and forms. Clicking on these can call up excerpts from many of Anderson's poems, songs, and performances, and allows a level of choice. The more one visits this space, the more the forms change and increase in number" (120).

COMPUTER-MODULATED TEXTS (POETRY MACHINES, CYBERTEXTS). Cybertexts are a form of poetry that lives and breathes the fluidity of the electronic environment. They highlight the dynamic production of text, turning this production into a spectacle. Experiencing the text means watching words and meaning emerge and evolve on the screen, animated by the invisible code of a computer program. These "poetry machines" are the textual equivalent of the artificial life projects discussed in Katherine Hayles's contribution to the present volume: the user's occasional input is a random event which forces the largely self-regulating textual system to modify itself. According to John Cayley, creator of the cybertext series *Indra's Net*, "your selections will feed back into the process and change it irreversibly." Here is how Cayley describes his own projects: "Visitors to the installation will see the words of a generated text appearing on the wall before them. The computer itself is hidden, but there is a 'mouse' or other pointing device available . . . allowing the user to interact with the display. When a visitor ceases to control the installation, it will, after a short time, continue to generate text automatically, providing an intriguing, continually changing and visually engaging display."[8] Many of these productions are the electronic equivalent of conceptual art: texts that erase themselves after only one reading (William Gibson);[9] chaotic superpositions of pages on the screen that the reader peels off one by one to reveal a readable text (Rosenberg, *Intergrams*), texts that allegorize the incompleteness and selective character of the reading process by scrolling down so fast that the eyes of the reader can pick only some of the words (Bootz 242).

Rethinking Literary Language through Electonic Texts

For the literary scholar, the importance of the electronic movement is twofold: it problematizes familiar notions, and it challenges the limits of language. The emergence of a new form of writing has refined the concept of medium: we are now better aware that the medium (under this term I understand categories such as verbal language, music, painting, sculpture, cinema, or dance) is affected by its material support. Before the computer revolution, the question of the support of the literary text was reduced to a dichotomy of the oral and the written. Now the written has been exploded into at least three manifestations—manuscript, print, and electronic. Under this new taxonomy, the Codex book can no longer be considered the exclusive support of the literary text. One of the most significant effects of the development of electronic textuality on literary theory in general is that it has led to a rediscovery and critical investigation of print and the Codex book. Long taken for granted, the material support of the text and its expressive potential have now become objects of active enquiry, both in the theoretical and the artistic mode.[10]

The territory of the written has not only been subdivided—its very identity has become problematic: Does "written" refer to the visual manifestations of language, or to its durable inscription? The sign language of deaf communities is visual but not permanent, while audio recordings are permanent but not visual. Electronic textuality is generally considered a form of writing, but some of its genres are as volatile as speech: the written conversations of the MOOs (the system may keep a permanent record, but the users experience the exchange in real time), the never-to-be-repeated displays of animated cyberpoems, the self-destructing text. The relation between print, oral, and electronic textuality is best represented as triangular: depending on the genres and features taken into consideration, the electronic text aligns itself with the oral against print, with print against the oral, or stands alone in opposition to both. Cyberpoems and computer games share with the oral, against the written, a real-time dimension which makes it possible to monitor the temporal flow of the encounter between the text and its destinator. Words and situations are displayed on the screen for a fleeting moment, and the reader or player has to seize opportunities that will never present themselves again. Hypertext shares with the written, against the oral, the fact that the entire text is prerecorded. The time-transcending existence of the signs allows the reader to treat the text as a space to be explored with a relative freedom of movement (a freedom limited by the network of roads). Traditional print texts are not considered interactive because they impose a sequential reading protocol, but the accessibility of all their pages at any given time offers an illicit escape from the prescribed order: it enables the reader to skip text, to reread earlier passages, or to take a forbidden peek at the ending. The vaunted interactivity of hypertext may be a reaction against the linear protocol of print, but it is also the exploitation, systematization, and legitimization of a potential inherent to all forms of permanent inscription. In yet another respect, electronic textuality stands alone against print and oral texts. In most forms of print literature—visual poetry being the exception—the written word is treated as a substitute for the spoken word. Poems are meant to be read aloud and novels can be recorded on tape, but neither hypertext nor animated cybertexts can be subjected to oral performance. Electronic textuality could be the advent of a fully non-logocentric mode of expression.

This leads us back to the other significant feature of electronic textuality: the attempt to expand the limits of language. Through its commitment to new forms of signification, electronic literature represents the latest episode of a poetic quest that spans nearly two centuries of literary history. From Romanticism to Symbolism, from Dadaism to Surrealism, and from Modernism to Postmodernism, the persistent dream of a new language has taken many shapes. If the claims of cybertext theorists sound often wildly hyperbolic, they are certainly no more utopian than the ambitions of their predecessors:

The Dream of the Total Language

Here verbal expression is not the sole focus of attention, but one of the components of an artistic event that mobilizes all media and modes of signification. The nineteenth-century expression of this dream was the opera; in the mid-twentieth century, it inspired the dramaturgies of a Brecht or an Artaud—theatrical performances combining text, music, song, dance, and visual elements to promote a critical stance (Brecht) or a ritualistic, deeply transforming immersion of the mind and body

(Artaud). In the electronic age, the total spectacle is reincarnated as either multimedia CD-ROM artwork, or as VR production.

The Dream of the Multisensory Language

In this case, language does not cooperate with other media, but absorbs their properties. Eric Vos observes that in most instances of verbal communication, including literature, language is codified into patterns that seem to reward us for not paying attention to its non-alphabetic aspects, patterns such as "shape, color, permutation, position in and movement through time and space" (232). Modern poetry has waged a sustained campaign against this loss of potentiality: Rimbaud imagined the color of vowels; Apollinaire dreamed a "pure" poetry talking to the soul through a musical mode of signification; concrete poetry and calligrams explored the expressive resources of the visual interplay between the written signs and the blank space of the page; and James Joyce, in *Finnegans Wake*, attempted to create a syncretic and synaesthesic language involving the entire sensorium and simulating the effects of all the media.[11] More recently, video poetry, film, and TV have added a kinetic dimension to language: think of the dancing letters of *Sesame Street* or of the text that summarizes the story and then disappears into hyperspace at the beginning of the *Star Wars* movies. Electronic technology not only synthesizes these various dimensions, it also introduces one of its own: the tactile pleasure of grabbing words with a click of the mouse (Rosenberg 111). By activating the full semiotic potential of language, the electronic text proposes a space as stimulating and challenging as the physical world: a space in which "we need *all* our sensorial capacities to find our way" (Vos 232).

The Dream of the Democratization of Art and of the Transformative Power of Language

Lautréamont claimed (perhaps ironically) that "[p]oetry must be made by all. Not by one" (279). The movements of Dadaism and Surrealism were animated by the belief that poetry was everywhere, and that everybody should live in a constant state of poetry. In proclaiming the death of the author, Barthes hoped to put the mass of readers in control of meaning. The egalitarian dream of the participation of the reader in the creative process is tied to a belief in the performative force of language, in its almost magical power to cause events of lasting consequences for RR (real reality). The claim of hypertext theorists that the medium turns readers into writers (or "wreaders") is the latest variation on this theme of language-induced transformation.[12] Taken literally it may strike some of us as facile hyperbole (wouldn't it be wonderful if writing were as easy as a clicking) and as self-serving flattery ("read me, and you will become author"), but it appears much less arrogant if we read it as a figural expression of the perennial longing of literary authors for a language capable to change mankind and society through the release of creative energies. The main difference between the past and present forms of the dream is that hypertext theorists are more inclined to conceive these energies in terms of critical thinking than their less politically oriented predecessors.

The Dream of the Text That Reflects Its Reader

What could be more fulfilling for the reader than a text speaking not only to her, but also for her, a text adapting itself to her most personal desires? Electronic textuality offers many features that turn the public text into private language: in hypertext and dynamic cybertexts, nobody else will probably see the same sequence of signs; in a computer game you become the hero of the unfolding story; in the textual world of the MOOs you may reinvent yourself; and when you work with an interactive database, you may create your own customized text by cutting, pasting, linking, and annotating. The dream of the text that reflects the individuality of the reader is epitomized by the poetry machines of John Cayley (for instance *Collocations: Indra's Net II*). These works are computer programs that select strings from an input text, perform certain operations on them, animate them, and project the output on a screen. In some of the installations, the reader is free to chose the input text. If she selects samples of her own writing, she will literally become a co-author, and her copy will be unique ("Potentialities" 180–83).

The Dream of the Physically Multidimensional Language

An oral text is linear: the hearer perceives it one sound at a time. Writing uses the two-dimensional support of the page, but it rarely takes advantage of this spatiality: as already noted, most written texts can be read aloud (cf. the "books on tape"), and most of them could be transcribed on a very long line. With visual poetry, language conquers a second dimension: the text cannot be performed in the temporal flow, because it exploits the semiotic potential of the spatial arrangement of the words on the page. Hypertext has developed yet another way to construct a reading space: the multiplication of parallel linear sequences. Each traversal of the network traces a one-dimensional path, but the sum of the possible paths can be represented only on a two-dimensional map. Let us replace these linear paths with two-dimensional screen images—as is the case in interactive visual poetry—and the text becomes a three-dimensional collection of planes; let us animate each of these planes, and the text becomes a four-dimensional space-time continuum.

The Dream of the Text as Sum, or Every Text in One

Every period has its monument to a totalizing vision: in the Middle Ages it was the Cathedral, complex architecture whose windows and sculptures encompassed all of space and all of history; in the Enlightenment it was the Encyclopedia, immense compendium of knowledge; in Symbolism and Modernism, it was the literary text as cathedral: Mallarmé's imagined but never written Book, and the novels of Proust and Joyce. The cathedral work is the only text that the reader will ever need, because it sums up all human experience, because its exploration is never complete, because its architecture is so fluid that it continually rebuilds itself. As Umberto Eco describes Mallarmé's concept of the Book, it is a "multidimensional, deconstructible" "work in movement" (13). In postmodernism, the ideal of the total work gives way to the idea of universal intertextuality: every individual text is linked to countless other ones, and the whole is reflected in every of its parts, as in fractal images. In the electronic age, thanks to the hyperlink, the text literally becomes a matrix of many texts and a self-renewing entity. We need to look no further than the World Wide Web to find the text that contains all others. For Michael Joyce, hypertext narratives are "virtual storytellers," telling a different story with every traversal (*Of Two Minds* 193), while for Jay Bolter, "an electronic text is all architecture, all reference" (160)—a perpetual invitation to try another link and to explore (or build) another structure.

The Dream of a Language That Captures the Emergence of Thought

This dream originates in a rejection of the rationalist view of language: a view according to which thought precedes language, and the function of words is to translate the pure, stable, fully formed ideas that reside in the mind. The eighteenth-century mystic Swedenborg imagined "the language of the angels" as a mode of communication that lets feelings and thoughts flow directly from one soul to the other, without the mediation of the linear patterns of logic and syntax. Surrealism, through its *écriture automatique*, and Modernism, through the development of stream-of-consciousness techniques, attempted the paradox of a language capturing the life of the mind in a preverbal stage. The poly-semous language of Joyce's *Finnegans Wake*, with its simultaneous emissions of associative trails activating meanings in many directions, is perhaps the closest verbal approximation of the thought processes of the neural level. Electronic textuality has brought a renewal of interest for the idea of a language closer to thought. The propaganda of VR developers comes eerily close to the doctrine of Swedenborg. According to Michael Benedikt, the VR experience will be a "post-symbolic mode of communication"; "language-bound descriptions and semantic games will no longer be required to communicate personal viewpoints"; "we will become again 'as children' but this time with the power of summoning worlds at will" (12). As for hypertext, it has been claimed to be better adapted to the spontaneous movements of thought than traditional writing techniques because it enables ideas to grow in rhizomatous patterns, allows jumps and digressions, and because the user never needs to sacrifice those bursts of inspiration that cannot be bent in the direction of a general argumentative or narrative line. If thought is analogical before it is forced into logical patterns, hypertext highlights the truly creative moment. The electronic poet Jim Rosenberg believes that hypertext could come even closer to the dynamics of thought by operating on elementary linguistic material rather than on sizable lexias containing fully formed ideas. Such a system could become a toolkit for thinking, the user putting ideas together by following the links and trying out various combinations.[13] We can also imagine a cybertext in which isolated words and phrases would float on the screen, gather into patterns, break apart, and regroup. As in neural networks, words would fire each other, competing chains of meaning would race across the screen, the winner would dominate the display until new input came in from the user, and the process would start all over again, ideas and associations emerging right here and right now, in a poetic simulation of brain activity.

About This Book

The literature on recent developments in electronic technology and their impact on textuality has generally gravitated around three poles: prophecies of salvation (we are entering the age of the posthuman, and our mental and physical faculties will be enhanced); prophecies of doom (the advent of the posthuman is inevitable, but it will mean the loss of all that is worth preserving in our cultural heritage); and Luddite calls to resistance (something *can* be done to defend our humanity against the steady advance of the machine). Though some of these voices will be occasionally heard in the following pages, the purpose of the present collection is not to pass judgment on the desirability of the electronization of the word, but to usher in a new phase in cybertext criticism. The first wave of literature on electronic textuality has been enthusiastically promotional: in the early days of the new medium, the most urgent task was to convince the public that there was a need for it. When it was not busy vaunting the advantages of cybertext over the Codex book, most of this literature consisted of detailed explanations of how the system works, and of narrowly descriptive presentations of individual examples. In a second wave, the hyperbolic promises of VR and hypertext developers triggered skeptical counterreactions and passionate elegies to the Codex book. What we need at this stage in the development of cybertext theory and criticism is neither wild promotion nor denigration, but (1) a critical, though not hostile, assessment of the claims of the first-generation developers and theorists; (2) a way to read the individual texts that finds a middle ground between pure description of the works and general considerations about the medium; (3) a poetics tailor-made for electronic textuality; and (4) a thematic approach that relates cybertexts and textual constructions of cyberspace to the major human, aesthetic, and intellectual concerns of contemporary culture.

Rather than trying to map the entire territory of electronic writing, the essays gathered in this book explore the area that presents the greatest potential for literary innovation: the forms of discourse in which the computer functions as theater. Because electronic textuality cannot be separated from its cultural environment, the essays will cover both electronic texts and print texts that deal with the imaginative world of cyberspace. Within this general domain, they focus on three areas: poetics and text theory, the question of identity, and the practice of writing. But most of the texts, as one might suspect, have implications for more than one of these topics. It will be left to the reader to actualize other possible books by discovering or creating other systems of links.

The first section examines how postmodern thought has theorized the textual products of the recent electronic revolution, and how, conversely, these new forms of textuality challenge postmodern thought, invite us to reconsider the concept of text, and call for an expansion of the analytical repertory of literary theory. In the first chapter, "Aporia and Epiphany in *Doom* and *The Speaking Clock*," Espen Aarseth lays the groundwork for a poetics of "ergodic art," i.e., of art based on a cybernetic system that generates a different sequence of signs every time the work is experienced. Besides hypertext, ergodic art includes the abovementioned "poetry machines," as well as computer games. The focus of the essay is on how games and dynamic cybertexts introduce a new variable into the textual experience (I use this term to cover both reading and playing): the manipulation of time as strategic element. Classical written narrative plays with the relation between narrated time and time of narration (i.e., how long it takes for the events to happen versus how long it takes to read their report), but the text has no control over the time granted to the reader to absorb the narration. In cyberpoetry and computer games, the time of reading can be determined by the system, and the performance of the user depends on a wise use of this limited resource. It is in this sense that games and cyberpoems operate "in real time."[14] We do not normally think of computer games as art, but in addition to their creative exploitation of the time variable they highlight two features which play a crucial role in art appreciation. The first, *aporia*, occurs when the player takes a dead-end branch on the game-map or fails to overcome an obstacle. The second, *epiphany*, is the solving of a problem that allows the player to progress in his quest. If the goal of the game is to reach the ultimate epiphany (heaven or total knowledge), it is the dangers on the road, the risk of losing one's life, that make it worth playing. The same could be said of literature in general. What makes literature intellectually stimulating is the resistance of the text, its invitation to exercise problem-solving skills, and the fact that not all paths are worth pursuing in the forest of meaning. This emphasis on the necessity of aporia to the aesthetic experience can be contrasted to Jay Bolter's description of hypertext as a network in which "every path defines an equally convincing and appropriate reading" (2). In hypertext, every electronically marked path may be legitimate, but should every possible itinerary guarantee satisfaction? The dilemma here is between a conception of the text as risk and adventure, or as Garden of Delights.

The next two chapters, by Poster and Nunes, investigate cyberspace technologies in the light of the work of some of the most influential figures on the contemporary literary-theoretical scene. The development of electronic writing and VR technology has been hailed by many as the fulfillment of the ideas of Jacques Derrida and Jean Baudrillard on textuality, representation, and the media. Following up on his earlier book *The Mode of Information*, in which he discusses the affinities of poststructuralist doctrine and electronic writing, Mark Poster details the efforts of Baudrillard and Derrida to catch up with the development of computer culture and their self-appointment as the theorists of the new technologies. Refreshingly critical of two figures widely revered as authorities, especially of their tendencies to flee into the symbolic rather than confronting concrete technological phenomena, Poster's essay emphasizes the limitations of Baudrillard's treatment of VR as another manifestation of the hyperreal (alongside amusement parks and television), and denounces the facility of Derrida's claims of political significance for the theory of "hauntology" into which he develops his analysis of the concept of virtuality.

Developing the imaginative potential of the "space" of cyberspace, Mark Nunes's "Virtual Topographies : Smooth and Striated Cyberspace" renews a tradition initiated in the early fifties by Gaston Bachelard's phenomenological investigation of the poetics of space. The development of information technologies and electronic networks, such as the Internet, has exercised a significant influence on the perception of space by the imagination. Whereas classical phenomenological approaches focus on predominantly meditative themes such as space as habitat and its apprehension/appropriation by consciousness and the body, the cybercultural experience privileges active themes of travel, conquest, expansion, colonization, utilization, and above all mapping. The postmodern mind tends to reject Cartesian conceptions of space as continuous spread of fixed (number of) dimensions in favor of topographies made of discontinuities, parallel worlds, black holes, shrinking and expanding substance, and Moebius strip effects. The concepts of smooth and striated space, borrowed from the work of Deleuze and Guattari, offer two complementary models for the apprehension and administration of cyberspace. The prevalent tendency among cultural critics is to describe cyberspace phenomena (such as navigating the Internet or participating in electronic communities) as the triumph of the smooth model. In a more nuanced approach, Nunes shows how "smooth" administrations tend to seek support in the structures of striated space, and how these structures, in hierarchical organizations, tend to dissolve into fluid relations. In their mutual dependency and periodical infiltration by the other, smooth and striated topographies remind us of the dialectical relations between chaos and order. For the literary theorists, the significance of Nunes's contribution resides primarily in his reading of the World Wide Web as a giant text and in the implications of the two models of space for the phenomenology of reading. Striated space suggests a view of the text as a unified work structured once and for all by the mind of the author, while smooth space models meaning as the unstable, unmappable product of an anarchic field of energies. Striation suggests furthermore a goal-oriented, utilitarian reading, while smoothness opens the mind of the reader to the surprise discoveries of wandering for pleasure in a gigantic fair where all texts are on display.

Have you ever wondered what cyberspace is, why everything that happens there is labeled virtual, and how this virtuality relates to "goggle-and-glove" VR? I tackle these questions in the next chapter, "Cyberspace, Virtuality, and the Text," by tracing the history of the word "cyberspace," from its origin in William Gibson's novel *Neuromancer,* through its adoption as marketing device by VR developers, and finally to its extension to networking phenomena, when the Internet displaced VR as the hottest topic in electronic culture. Returning to the etymological source of the word "virtual," and relying on the work of Pierre Lévy, the distinguished French theorist of electronic culture, I distinguish two meanings, the fake and the potential, which correlate to the two constitutive features of the VR experience: immersion and interactivity. In these two features, we hold the cornerstones of what could become a phenomenology of reading encompassing both classical and cyberage textuality. Through immersion in a fictional world we become in make-believe a member of this world, a situation which enables us to relate emotionally to the situations depicted in the work, while through an active encounter with the text, we actualize its semantic potential into an individuated imaginative experience.

The second section focuses on an issue of compelling existential and ethical relevance: how identity is affected by electronic technology, and how it can be constructed through electronic writing. The predominantly anti-Cartesian mood in contemporary culture seeks identity in gender, race, and sexuality—all attributes anchored in the body. If cyberculture matters for the question of identity, it is because electronic technologies have the power of producing virtual doubles of the human body, such as the enhanced (and to some, diminished) bodies of VR, or the textually created character-descriptions of the MOOs. In a culture that worships the slick surface of things, that equals being to presenting, that replaces the idea of a true self hidden in the depth of interiority with a decentered self acting out its many roles in public performance, identity is tied to the body, and the body is an image molded from the raw material of inherited physical properties. Bodies are now conceived as changeable, disposable commodities, and stepping into a new body means adopting a new identity. Officially classified as a disorder, "multiple personalities" is being touted by the prophets of cyberculture as the hippest of mental conditions. But the relation computer/ body is far from univocal. Lovers of the Codex book complain that electronic textuality robs the reader of any sensuous, body-involving relation to the material support of the text. As an often repeated argument goes, you cannot smell the paper of the electronic book, you cannot feel its texture, you cannot flip the pages, you cannot take the computer to bed. Partisans of electronic textuality reply that through the gesture of clicking, the body is actively involved in the reading experience, and that the cursor on the screen represents an extension of proprioceptive boundaries (it often takes the shape of a grabbing hand). The same dichotomies of opinions nourish the controversies that surround VR. Opponents argue that VR is a disembodying technology because it imprisons the physical body in cumbersome equipment and reconfigures its sensorium according to the system designer's specifications. Compared to walking around town, exploring a virtual world through headset, datagloves, or wired bodysuit is a significant loss of corporeal freedom. Proponents of VR claim on the contrary that compared to sitting at a terminal and typing on a keyboard, VR is a tremendous liberation of physical energy, since it uses the entire body as interface. As Brenda Laurel argues, VR is the only technology that makes it possible to take your body with you into worlds of the imagination ("Art and Activism" 14). These ambiguous relations between electronic technology and the body carry equally ambiguous implications for the issue of identity. In one frame of mind, identity must be conquered in a battle against the disembodying effect of electronic technology, while in the other, electronic technology is a tool for the design of freely chosen identities.[15]

The first of four variations on the theme of what may be called "cyberbodidentity," Barbara Page's "Women Writers and the Restive Text" stresses the liberatory potential of electronic writing. The essay describes some features of recent women's print literature that foretell the adoption, by other women writers, of a hypertextual format. (This does not mean, as Page is careful to warn, that the print texts would have been more successful as hypertexts.) In recent years—especially since the publication of Peter Brooks's influential book *Reading for the Plot*—the Aristotelian description of narrative/dramatic structure as exposition, complication, climax, and resolution has come to be perceived as the expression of a male (and to some, Western) pattern of sexual experience. As the sexual analogy has gained currency in critical discourse, a number of woman writers have rejected the linearity of traditional narrative patterns and explored alternative forms of writing as expression of female subjectivity: stopping what Carol Maso calls the "incessant march forward of the plot" through silence (represented graphically as blank space) and discontinuities; letting discourse radiate in many directions, so that story may "blossom like a flower" (Maso again); incorporating multiple voices so that the text will realize a communion of subjectivities; and renouncing the strategies of persuasion that impose one's image at the expense of the other's. It is easy to see how hypertext favors these tendencies. In the new writing technology, some of the women writers discussed by Page see an unspoiled form that has never been used as an instrument of oppression, not just because it has hardly been used at all, but also because its open structure welcomes dialogue and dissident voices. The dream of a new identity begins with new forms of expression, but language itself is not inimical to woman's interests; if it were, silence would be the only option. What has to be sacrificed for women to articulate their own values is the literary forms inherited from the past, because these forms retain the memory of the symbols and narratives through which women have been forced into a role and an image. But Page resists the temptation of promoting the new writing medium as a panacea for all forms of domination. As it orchestrates multiple voices, does hypertext maintain their individual force and urgency, or does it absorb them all in a harmonious concert that covers up conflict and tames their resistance?

In Thomas Foster's "The Souls of Cyber-Folk," electronic technology comes through both as an instrument of alienation for the self and the body, and as a challenge that leads to the conquest of a new sense of identity. Through the reading of a comic-strip version of the myth of the Cyborg, this modern-day inversion of the myth of the Golem (since here humans become machines rather than machines acquiring human power), Foster examines the problem of racial identity and its problematic relation to, or inscription in, the visible body. In the comic strip in question, *Deathlok*, an African-American scientist's brain is suctioned out of his organic body and placed into the frame of a machine. Foster reads *Deathlok* as an allegory of slavery, as well as a warning against the futility of attempting to recover a lost wholeness lodged in the organic body. But if the protagonist cannot reject his Cyborg body, he can use it as material for self-creation. Relying on Allucquere Rosanne Stone's distinction between physical and virtual attributes of the body (those that are given and those that are chosen), Foster suggests that racial identity is not a mimetic representation (or natural expression) of physical properties, but a performance through which a "virtual body" is projected out of a physical one, as a more or less individual, more or less shared core of biologically given properties is complemented by the enactment of potential features. This approach is consistent with the position currently favored by anthropologists. In the new scientific orthodoxy, race is no longer regarded as a discrete set of biological features inherited through a separate origin, but as a manifestation of human variability grounded in a fuzzy set of physical properties which become stereotyped through cultural interpretation. Foster's essay points toward a better possible world in which cultural stereotyping would be replaced by individual performance.

Once upon a time books were to the text what the body was to the mind: solid objects serving as temporary support for a spiritual entity whose existence was regarded as transcending its particular form of embodiment. Is it a coincidence that just as the Cartesian conception of the duality of mind and body came under attack, the body of the text began to lose its solidity? In "The Disturbing Liveliness of Machines," Christopher Keep reads hypertext and the forms of textuality found in Codex books as metaphors (or arguably as *causes*) of certain experiences of corporeal existence. Keep argues that the material form of the codex book—a self-contained, discrete, solid object extending in space and providing tactile pleasure—configures subjectivity as a unified and intelligible self unproblematically lodged in a spatially bound body. This sense of self and of embodiment is associated with the form of textuality most commonly encountered in the codex book: the realistic novel. Through its immersive quality, the realistic novel offers to the reader's fictional self the cozy refuge of an intelligible surrounding world. In contrast to the codex book, hypertext is not a thing that can be held and fondled, but a volatile entity never apprehended in its totality, and never experienced as habitable environment. Keep relates this quality to Lacan's view of the infantile experience of the body as a dismembered entity (a *corps morcelé*), and to an apprehension of the self as an unstable *assemblage* of parts.

The most pessimistic pronouncement on the impact of electronic technology on our sense of identity is Matthew Causey's "Postorganic Performance: The Appearance of Theater in Virtual Spaces." The chapter investigates the significance of the development of dramatic forms of VR for the concept of performance. Lacking most of the feature traditionally associated with performance (existing in the present, resisting repetition, and above all, involving the physical presence of bodies), what Causey calls "postorganic performance" invites a fundamental revision of performance theory. But if performance theory "fails postorganic performance," the reverse is also true. Taking a somber view of VR, Causey argues that theatrical performance would irremediably lose its force as event if the live presence of the actors were replaced by simulated bodies. Causey looks toward a dramatic work, Jean Genet's *The Balcony*, and its depiction of a character deliberately locking himself up in a world of simulacra, for an allegory of what the theatrical experience would become if deprived of its organic component: not the metaphysical shock advocated by Tadeusz Kantor, nor the therapeutic cruelty to the flesh and the self envisioned by Artaud, but the painless, fleshless experience of an incessant parade of images, in which identity would be reduced to its external signs. In this essay, Causey is looking at postorganic performance from the point of view of organically embodied life. But one wonders what would happen if the late-millennium myth of the Cyborg became reality. Would the hybrid of man and machine toward which we are headed (if we believe the myth) still yearn for an encounter with the Other, for cathartic involvement, for the renewal of the self through violence and the contemplation of Death, all conceivable effects of the "organic" theatrical performance, or would the posthuman subject's idea of aesthetic fulfillment be the smooth run and continuous image production of the VR machine?

The third section moves from the performing body to writing itself as performance. Allucquere Rosanne Stone attributes the current tendency to turn scholarly writing into "performance texts" to the impact of cyberculture, but the conception of writing as a free play with language has been in the air even longer than it has been in cyberspace. The influence of Derrida on contemporary thought led to a general erosion of traditional epistemological, generic, and disciplinary boundaries—fact and imagination, history and myth, science and fiction, philosophy and literature, literary criticism and creative writing—which prepared the ground for a blossoming of monstrous hybrids. It is now (almost) acceptable to blend criticism with autobiography, to make theoretical claims by means of make-believe, or to turn academic writing into a dialogue of many voices. This spirit of anarchy spread across the computer world, where it found new forms of expression: the role-playing of the MOOs, the typographical creativity of the World Wide Web, the rhizomatous and parallel structures of hypertext. Through their flaunting of the norms of academic writing, the three texts of this last section complete a process of cross-fertilization with their subject matter, as they import into print the concern of the practitioners of electronic writing for new forms of encounter between the text and the reader.

Katherine Hayles's "Artificial Life and Literary Culture" continues the project of her earlier books: to track down isomorphisms between various disciplines and reveal the hidden unity of the intellectual landscape, or *episteme*, of contemporary culture. Delineating its two voices with graphic contrasts, her text interweaves the narration of an investigator who takes the reader on a tour of the world of contemporary AI with the reflections of a literary theorist who draws an analogy between the idea of artificial life and the postmodern conception of the text. The main point of the analogy lies in the ability of both the text and the artificial life system to generate new life forms on their own, without intervention by the creator. The description of the text as "self-organizing system" may seem at first sight to exclude the reader, but Hayles keeps her distance from the position of those overly radical disciples of Saussure who regard meaning as exclusively produced by language. If she describes the text, particularly hypertext, as a "self-modifying system," it is because the reader is regarded as an integral part of the system. The reader provides the input that enables the pattern of the text to evolve in ways not foreseen by the creator. There are two types of life: the ability of an organism to duplicate itself as pattern of information, and the ability to evolve into new forms. Texts are alive in the latter sense through the relatively unpredictable element injected by the reader into the pattern encoded by the "programmer." Another lesson to be learned from this metaphor of the text as evolving organism is that not all readings are equally viable: in evolution as in interpretation, some new forms present the capability to reproduce themselves (to be accepted and disseminated in a community), while others are dead ends on the tree of life.

A book devoted to cyberspace textuality would be incomplete without a discussion of the foundational text. In a print imitation of hypertext techniques, Lance Olsen takes apart the matrix of the concept of cyberspace: the thirty-three-word passage in which William Gibson inaugurates the term and exposes the idea of the Matrix. As it lets the critic trace a hermeneutic circle between the passage under scrutiny and the whole of Gibson's work, the hypertextual format reveals itself an outstanding instrument of close reading. Olsen interprets the text in the light of two concepts discussed by Gibson in private conversations with the author (themselves borrowed by the novelist from an essay by the film critic Manny Farber): "white elephant art," which "embraces the idea of a well-crafted, logical arena," and "termite art," which "embraces freedom and multiplicity."[16] Itself an exercise in termite criticism, the essay adds yet another item to the list of dichotomies introduced in this volume: smooth and striated space, immersion and interactivity, aporia and epiphany. All of these pairs are inspired by cyberculture phenomena, but their relevance reaches well beyond the domain of electronic literature.

For all their playful attitude, Hayles's and Olsen's contributions remain on what is for literary theory the "proper" side of the fictional divide. The last essay crosses over. In Jon Thiem's "Myths of the Universal Library: From Alexandria to the Postmodern Age," the author emulates the role-playing of the MOOs, as he vanishes behind a fictional persona. Thiem's evocation of the life and death of the Universal Electronic Library is a didactic *tale-à-clefs*, a spoof, a fiction in the spirit of Borges replete with literary allusions that looks at contemporary phenomena from the perspective of the next millennium. Sparing neither Techies nor Luddites, neither Pomos nor Retros, the satire surveys with amused detachment the various sects born out of the cultural war between the Book and the Electronic Text: Anonymists, Apocryphers, Borgesians, Luddies, Nousers, Refusers, and Users for Alpha. Behind the many masks, however, one senses a Luddite nostalgia for the golden age of print literature. This contrapuntal voice is included in the present volume as the grain of salt that should bring out the flavors gathered in these pages.

Notes to Introduction

1. As Jacques Leslie puts it: "Ambiguity Machines. Precision, hah! Computers are better at poetry than they are at math" (lines 452–53).
2. Internet users can talk to Julia at this telnet address: telnet fuzine.mt.cs.cmu.edu; log in as julia.
3. General resources and links to projects on collaborative literature can be found at this Internet address: http://www.cliq.com/literata/coop.html
4. The Hypertext Hotel can be reached through: telnet duke.cs.brown.edu:8888
5. Internet address: http://www.thespot.com
6. This point is made by Jean Clément (67).
7. As reported by Julian Dibbell in "Net Prophet" (Interview with John Perry Barlow), *Details*, August 8, 1994. Quoted by Slouka, 174.
8. Quoted from Cayley's home page on the World Wide Web: http://www.demon.co.uk/eastfield/in/
9. Gibson collaborated with conceptual artist Dennis Ashbaugh on *Agrippa: A Book for the Dead*, a CD-ROM work that erased itself while being read. Within twenty-four hours of its appearance, however, hackers broke the code and put it on the Web in a non–self-destructive form. The ASCII version is available at: gopher://gopher.well.sf.ca.us/oo/publications/poetry/agrippa
10. On the artistic side, the exploration of the properties of the Codex book is pursued in the rich tradition of "Artists' Books." In Johanna Drucker's characterization, artists' books are not books containing reproductions of works of art, but works of art conceived as books (94). In addition to using text and graphics, these works exploit such features as the discontinuities created by the division into pages; the dynamics of the page-turning mechanism (flip-books creating a cinematic effect); the tactile and olfactory sensations provided by the type of paper; or the resistance of the bound spine to a flat opening.
11. These aspects of Joyce's writing are discussed by Donald Theall in *Beyond the Word, Joyce's Technopoetics*, and "Beyond the Orality/Literary Dichotomy."

12. Here is the latest cyberspatial avatar of the mythical wreader (and newest form of collaborative literature): "Toward the end of June [1997], four novelists will each submit the first paragraph or so of a story to a [Microsoft Network] site, four social commentators will submit the beginning of an essay, and four artists will submit a sketch. The networks' subscribers will vote on which one in each category they prefer, and the professionals will then send in a new contribution or sketch that will be a continuation of the winning choices in their category. The process will be repeated twice a week for thirteen weeks, resulting in three complete works" (Collins 33).

13. Cf. the title of an essay by Jean-Marc Lepers: "Hypertext as a Thought Construction Kit."

14. "The Speaking Clock" is actually a pun on the expression of real time: "This (silent) speaking clock in software composes from a given text according to quasi-aleatory procedures and actually tells the 'real time'" (Quoted from Cayley's home page).

15. See Penny on VR as disembodying technology, Laurel (1993) for opposite arguments, and Hayles (1997) on the involvement of the body in electronic writing/reading. See also Turkle for a general discussion of identity in the electronic age.

16. Quoted from Olsen's abstract for the edition of the essay in *Style* 29.2 (1995), iii.

Works Cited

Aarseth, Espen. "Le texte de l'ordinateur est à moitié construit: problèmes de poétique automatisée." Vuillemin and Lenoble 341–54.

Bachelard, Gaston. *The Poetics of Space*. Trans. Maria Jolas. Boston: Beacon Press, 1994.

Barlow, John Perry. "Net Prophet." Interview with Julian Dibbell. *Details*, August 1994.

Barthes, Roland. "The Death of the Author." *Image, Music, Text*. New York: Hill and Wang, 1977.

Benedikt, Michael. "Introduction." *Cyberspace. First Steps*. Ed. Michael Benedikt. Cambridge: MIT Press, 1991. 1–26.

Bolter, Jay David. *Writing Space: The Computer, Hypertext, and the History of Writing*. Hillsdale, NJ: Lawrence Erlbaum, 1991.

Bootz, Philippe. "Gestion du temps et du lecteur dans un poème dynamique." Vuillemin and Lenoble 233–48.

Brooks, Peter. *Reading for the Plot. Design and Intention in Narrative*. New York: Random House, 1985.

Cayley, John, "Pressing the Reveal Code Key." *EJournal* (*Electronic Journal of Virtual Culture*) 6.1 (1996). http://www.hanover.edu/philos/ejournal/archive/ej-6-1.txt

Clément, Jean. "L'Hypertexte de fiction: naissance d'un nouveau genre." Vuillemin and Lenoble 63–76.

Collins, James. "Nerd File." *The New Yorker*, June 2, 1997, 33.

The Dickens Web. Developer, George P. Landow. Eds., Julie Launhart and Paul D. Kahn. Providence, RI: Institute for Research in Information and Scholarship, 1990.

Drucker, Johanna. "The Self-Conscious Codex: Artists' Books and Electronic Media." *SubStance* 82 (1997): 93–111.

Eco, Umberto. *The Open Work*. Cambridge, MA: Harvard UP, 1989.

Hayles, N. Katherine. "The Materiality of Informatics." *Configurations* 1 (1993): 147–70.

———. "The Condition of Virtuality." *Language Machines: Technologies of Literary and Cultural Production*. Ed. Nancy Vickers and Peter Stallybrass. New York: Routledge, 1997.

Joyce, Michael. *Of Two Minds: Hypertext, Pedagogy and Poetics*. Ann Arbor: U of Michigan P, 1995.

Kelso, Margaret Thomas, Peter Weyhrauch, and Joseph Bates. "Dramatic Presence." *Presence: Teleoperators and Virtual Environments* 2.1 (1993): 1–15.

Lanham, Richard. *The Electronic Word: Democracy, Technology, and the Arts*. Chicago: Chicago UP, 1993.

Laurel, Brenda. *Computers as Theatre*. Menlo Park, CA: Addison-Wesley, 1991.

———. "Art and Activism in VR." *Wide Angle* 15.4 (1993): 13–21.

Lautréamont (Isidore Ducasse). *Maldoror* and *Poems*. Trans. Paul Knight. London: Penguin, 1978 [1870].

Lepers, Jean-Marc. "Hypertext as a Thought Construction Kit." http:// asterix.univ-paris.8.fr/jm/echt93.html

Leslie, Jacques. "Ambiguity Machines." *Ejournal* (*Electronic Journal of Virtual Culture*) 5.2 (1995). http://www.hanover.edu/philos/ejournal/archive/ej-5-2.txt

Lévy, Pierre. "Toward Superlanguage." Trans. Rikka Stewen. http://www.uiah.fi/bookshop/isea__proc/nexgen/01.html

Lovejoy, Margot. "Artists' Books in the Digital Age." *SubStance* 82 (1997): 113–34.

Meehan, James. "Tale-Spin." *Inside Computer Understanding*. Ed. Roger Schank. Hillsdale, NJ: Lawrence Erlbaum, 1981. 197–225.

Miller, Rand, and Robyn Miller, with David Wingrove. *Myst: The Book of Atrus*. New York: Hyperion, 1995.

Penny, Simon. "Virtual Reality as the Completion of the Enlightenment." *The Virtual Reality Casebook*. Ed. Carl Eugene Loeffler and Tim Anderson. New York: Van Nostrand Rheinhold, 1994. 199–213.

Perloff, Marjorie. *Radical Artifice: Writing Poetry in the Age of Media*. Chicago: U of Chicago P, 1991.

Poster, Mark. *The Mode of Information: Poststructuralism and Social Context*. Chicago: U of Chicago P, 1990.

Rees, Gareth. "Tree Fiction on the World Wide Web." http://lucilia.ebc.ee/~enok/tree-fiction.html.1994

Reid, Elizabeth. "Virtual Worlds: Culture and Imagination." *Cybersociety, Computer-Mediated Communication and Community*. Ed. Steven B. Jones. Thousand Oaks: Sage Publications, 1995.164–83.

Rosenberg, Jim. "The Interactive Diagram Sentence: Hypertext As a Medium of Thought." *Visible Language* 30.2 (1996): 102–17.

Slouka, Mark. *War of the Worlds: Cyberspace and the High-Tech Assault on Reality*. New York: Basic Books (HarperCollins), 1995.

Stone, Allucquere Rosanne. "Sex and Death Among the Disembodied: VR, Cyberspace and the Nature of Academic Discourse." *The Cultures of Computing*. Ed. Susan Leigh Star. Oxford: Blackwell, 1995. 243–55.

Theall, Donald. "Beyond the Orality/Literary Dichotomy: James Joyce and the Pre-History of Cyberspace." *Postmodern Culture* 23 (1992): file theall.592. Available at
http://www.2street.com/joyce/pmcultur.asc

———. *Beyond the Word: Reconstructing Sense in the Joyce Era of Technology, Culture, and Communication*. Toronto: U of Toronto P, 1995.

———. *Joyce's Technopoetics*. Toronto: U of Toronto P, 1997.

Turkle, Sherry. *Life on the Screen: Identity in the Age of the Internet*. New York: Simon and Schuster, 1995.

Turner, Scott. *The Creative Process: A Computer Model of Storytelling and Creativity*. Hillsdale, NJ: Lawrence Erlbaum, 1994.

Vos, Eric. "New Media Poetry: Theory and Strategies." *Visible Language* 30.2 (1996), 214–33.

Vuillemin, Alain, and Michel Lenoble, eds. *Littérature et informatique. La littérature générée par ordinateur*. Arras: Artois Press Université, 1995.

PART I:
CYBERTEXT THEORY

1

Aporia and Epiphany
in *Doom* and
The Speaking Clock
The Temporality of Ergodic Art

Espen Aarseth

Introduction

After the development and proliferation of personal computers, the Internet, and the World Wide Web, humanists who use these technologies have begun to theorize about their implications for our concepts of text and textual practices. To all but the most conservative observers, these technologies appear to have an all-important role to play in our culture's future, not only socially and cognitively, but aesthetically and academically as well. Like the analog electronic mass media before them, the digital media seem to demand special attention in the form of new disciplines, and in the interim period that we are witnessing now, a number of more or less successful theoretical endeavors seek to describe, contain, and connect to these new and apparently more intimate communicatory modes.

The fact that we are all entangled in their practical mechanisms on a grand scale (word processing, e-mail, and the Web are now among our most intimate tools) ought to make us very cautious, but so far there is little caution to see. Instead, the race is on to conquer and colonize these new territories for our existing paradigms and theories, often in the form of "the theoretical perspective of <fill in your favorite theory/ theoritician here> is clearly really a prediction/description of <fill in your favorite digital medium here>." This method is being used with permutational efficiency throughout the fields of digital technology and critical theory, two unlikely tango partners indeed. But the combinatorial process shows no signs of exhaustion yet.

There is of course no "proper" way to approach the digital media, and most mistakes we make at this still early stage will probably prove to be useful lessons later on. But the prevailing attempts to rejuvenate and relocate existing theories by insisting on their relevance for the new media and their largely unsuspecting users, is a "colonialist" strategy that is always a demonstration of (unnecessary) power and often a misreading of the theory being used. These theories were not developed with the digital media in mind, and their original objects are still valid as the focus of their perspectives. To ignore this is to disregard the competence of the theory founders, who knew, we must still assume, the objects that they were talking about.

Instead of playing the combinatorial game and applying this or that paradigm to the new phenomena, my assumption is here that new media call for new perspectives and conceptual frameworks; and that we must step back from our theories if we are to see something not already inscribed in them. This may sound hopelessly naive, since there can be no thought ungrounded by any theoretical context, but as a preliminary strategy of investigation it may still yield some insights that a less confrontational approach simply cannot reach. This is a rejection of theoretical templates, but of course far from a rejection of theory.

Ergodic Discourse

At the end of *Time and Narrative*, Paul Ricoeur mentions the possibility of

> another way for time to envelop narrative. This is by giving rise to the formation of discursive modes other than the narrative one, which will speak, in another way, of the profound enigma [of time]. (1988: 272)

In this chapter I will focus on two members of a family of such discursive modes, a type that I elsewhere have named "ergodic discourse."[1] These modes are quite probably not what Ricoeur had in mind, but that does not matter here, since it will suffice to establish that they represent something different from narrative, and, in particular, show how the problem of time manifests itself differently in the ergodic modes.

The word "ergodic" is appropriated from physics, and it is constituted by the two Greek words *Ergos*, "work," and *Hodos*, "path or road," and in this context it is used to describe a type of discourse whose signs emerge as a path produced by a non-trivial element of work. Ergodic phenomena are produced by some kind of cybernetic system, i.e., a machine (or a human) that operates as an information feedback loop, which will generate a different semiotic sequence each time it is engaged. Thus, a film such as *The Sound of Music* or a copy of a novel such as *Finnegans Wake* is not ergodic (or only trivially so), since their concretizations will invoke the same sequence of signifiers every time. The experiences of their audience, though individual in an interpretational sense, are singular as far as the material sign production is concerned. It is therefore also possible and natural to describe them as narratives, for even if they should break with narrative tradition (as is the case with a work such as *FW*), their anti-narrative ambitions are based on the sequential, closed form of narrativity.

Not so with the ergodic work of art, such as a hypertext novel, or a three-dimensional computer game. Here, the experienced sequence of signs does not emerge in a fixed, predetermined order decided by the instigator of the work, but is instead one actualization among many potential routes within what we may call the event space of semio-logical possibility. This event space is determined by the content and the infrastructure of the ergodic system, which means that, for every individual system, we have, to some degree, an individual medium, and not just an individual message. To complicate matters, in its potential for reproducing itself differently every time, the ergodic work is individualized or quasi-individualized on the audience level, in that different audiences at different times may have experienced very few (if any) of the same sign vehicles.

This raises an ontological question: Can we then still talk about the same work? Seemingly similar questions have been evoked by hermeneutical relativists like Stanley Fish, but it is important to note that this time it is not the interpretation and construction of the "text" that is questioned, but rather the stable and continuous identity of the material foundation for the "text": the work. (Or perhaps "document" is a better word.) Is a work in which two actual readers do not encounter a single common word, still recognizable as the same work? If the answer is yes (as I believe it should be), then we must be prepared to accept a type of textuality that is not readily understood and described by the traditional theoretical basis for textual understanding. Instead of anchoring our metaphysical concepts of text in the vague but well-known philological span between oral literature and written documents, we must reconceive the notion as a type of object that can reveal different aspects at different times and places, less like a book and more like a complex building with many entrances/exits and labyrinthine, sometimes changing, innards; but one which is still recognized as occupying the same "site" in cultural history. Narrative texts represent a special instance of this broader field of textuality: a single (but historically privileged) structure among many different actual or yet unrealized discursive modes.

Problems in the Aesthetics of Ergodic Art

So far, I have discussed ergodic art in general terms, as if it were an aesthetic mode with one set of standard features and rules of behavior. This is not the case, and we should be extremely careful not to generalize across the spectrum of ergodics. The various types of ergodic art (hypertexts, adventure games, literature generators, dialogue systems, systems for collective improvisations such as the Multi-User Dungeons of the Internet, etc.) are very different from each other, sometimes much more so than some of them are different from the narrative mode. The worst kind of mistake an aesthetic theory of ergodic art can make is to assume that there is only one type with which to be concerned, e.g., "the electronic text," "electronic literature," etc., with a single set of properties. This is just not the case, and by comparing such different specimens as the computer game *Doom* (1993) and John Cayley's poetry generator *The Speaking Clock,* I hope to convey some of the breadth and variety within this loosely constructed and still poorly understood field.

It is equally unwise to address "the aesthetics" of ergodics, since we would be much safer in addressing the aesthetics of individual works, one by one. When I deliberately attempt to generalize, it is with the acceptance that only very superficial and simple conclusions can be reached at this stage.

The ergodic work is typically, but not necessarily, embedded in a computer system of some sort. That holds for the two works examined here, but it is not a requirement for membership in the category, just as novels typically, but not necessarily, exist as print on paper. (They might also exist as sounds on tape recordings.) There are many different ergodic media and genres, and (probably) the oldest and one of the most successful, the Chinese classic *I Ching,* goes back at least three thousand years.

The relationship between the narrative and the ergodic is dialectic, not dichotomic. Narrative structures and elements can be found in ergodic works, and narrative works may contain ergodic features, to the extent that only a single element from one mode is found in a work belonging to the other. A typical example is a narrative work that contains a single forking path, such as Ayn Rand's *Night of January 16th,* a play with two alternative endings, or an ergodic work (for instance a computerized adventure game) that forces a narrative structure (in the form of a single "correct" sequence of events) on its players. Usually, however, narratives will not employ ergodic structures, although they may pretend to do so (see the beginning of Calvino's *If on a winter's night a traveler*). Also, some ergodic works may contain event spaces that are little more than closed event sequences in disguise, such as an animated but static beginning of a graphical adventure game where the player is not yet in control of the character's actions. But there seems to be a limit to the usefulness of these kinds of modal crossovers, in that an audience will want the work to perform as either one or the other, and their own role to be either that of player or observer. Perhaps more complex works yet to come will have solved the aesthetic problems of games trying to be narratives and narratives trying to be games, by implementing a "model user" position in balance between the two. If we look at the current "interactive movie" productions, however, such as Sierra's *Phantasmagoria*, there is not much evidence that this will happen.

To sum up the difference between narrative and ergodic modes, I have found Gerard Genette's distinction between description and narration very useful. For Genette, description ("the house was white, with a red door") and narration ("the student pulled a knife and stabbed the professor") are two different levels of discourse, with the latter dominant but relying on the former. This model may be expanded to describe ergodic discourse levels as well. Compared to a non-textual game such as football, which has only action (i.e., ergodic elements), the computer game has both ergodics (action) and description (graphics, sounds), but not narration, since the event space is not fixed before the time of play. Thus, a computer game is textual (it has description, unlike football) but it is not narrated, since there is no such thing as the unfolding of a predetermined story. The ergodic level usually dominates the descriptive (but not always; cf. the visually beautiful but otherwise uneventful graphical adventure game *Myst*), while depending on the descriptive elements to concretize the path through the event space. Once realized, the ergodically produced sequence may be regarded and narratively reproduced as a story, but not one told for the player's benefit at the time of playing. (And many games do include narrative playback of the user's events, but not as a necessary part of the game play. Recent games, such as *Doom*, *Duke Nukem 3-D*, and *Marathon*, will let the player record films of their play, which they can share with other players, thus staging their own skills for the gaming community.) The production and reproduction of such a sequence are two very different things, just like the difference between the video-record of an event and the event itself. A video of a game is not the game itself, any more than a photograph of a cake is the cake itself. The problem of confusing these two types of phenomena comes, however, when we make the mistake of comparing only the (identical) semiotic sequences, with no concern for what goes on beneath the surface. This is why purely semiotic theories of computer-mediated phenomena generally fail: they are not concerned with the sign-producing mechanisms, without which the cybernetic sign processes cannot be properly understood. Semiotic theory is not well-equipped to describe ergodic modes of discourse.

These simple epistemological lessons ought not to come as a surprise to anyone trained in interpreting cultural objects, but the hermeneutic short-sightedness produced by the theoretically hegemonic paradigms of narrative discourse can be very hard to overcome for the aesthetic scholar who encounters ergodic art forms for the first time.

Doom and the Architecture of Ergodic Desire

When the three-dimensional action game *Doom* was released on the Internet and on various bulletin board systems on December 10, 1993, it had already developed a large, impatiently waiting audience, who quickly downloaded the game and spread it over most of the industrialized world in less than a day. Reports of the game had been discussed for at least half a year on several Internet discussion groups, and Id Software, a small, independent production company that had previously been responsible for the innovative and violent success of the game *Wolfenstein*, used the informal structures of the BBSs and the Internet to promote and distribute the game at almost no cost to itself, as its users paid for the storage space and the transfer costs. (BBSs—Bulletin Board Systems—are local, modem-based computer communities that were quite popular just before the Internet became a mass phenomenon in the early nineties.) In this cheap and efficient way that distinguishes the postindustrial digital culture of immaterial (or better, transmaterial) artifacts and information networks, a working version with the first levels was allowed to spread freely, and the rest of the game could be ordered directly from the company. This, and the notoriously violent content of the game quickly made it a cult classic. (Perhaps "classic" seems inappropriate for a work less than five years old, but the computer game culture evolves so fast that I think it is justifiable.)

Other games, such as the role-playing action adventure *Ultima Underworld* (Origin 1992), had pioneered the same 3-D technology (and a rather more intricate and complex event space), but *Doom*, where the player must combat an endless stream of monsters, demons, and "former humans" on his way into the inner circles of Hell, demonstrated a superb combination of creepiness, eeriness, fun, and increasingly hard challenges, which made it a major step in the evolution of computer games. *Doom* also had two social aspects that made it stand out compared to similar games: up to four concurrent users could play together in the same event space over a network; and the users could easily make their own versions of the game, by designing their own event spaces or modifying existing ones. In the postindustrial culture industry that *Doom* represents, game design becomes part of the game play, and the distance between makers and users becomes less.

It is *Doom*'s raw, minimalist event space that makes it particularly relevant as an illustration in the analysis of ergodic time. The choice of actions is simple: explore, destroy, and protect yourself. The player must wander a series of labyrinths, shooting or avoiding the deadly monsters as best he can. Graphically the game is crude, but effective (the players often duck as missiles fly toward them on the screen), and the use of sound is especially dramatic, with the rasping breath of the protagonist and the horrible grunts of nearby, but yet unseen monsters. The sheer intensity of the game play is far more striking than the blood effects and the violence, which are repetitive and subrealistic.

In ergodic art, the time of the audience matters, as an intrinsic part of the realization of the work. Where narrative time can be divided into the time of the tale and the time of the teller/telling, and the reader's time is of little consequence, ergodic time, e.g., in the case of *Doom*, depends on the user and his actions to realize itself. There is no action without a participating observer. At the same time it determines the user's sense of experienced time within the event space. In the clockwork world of the game, events occur when the controlling program enacts them, and when the user acts on the same level. The event time is the basic level of ergodic time. As in the movie *Groundhog Day*, where the protagonist experiences the same day over and over, but with variations caused by his own choice of actions, the event time is a result of the user's growing knowledge of the event space, as laid down by the designer of the game.

This knowledge process takes place on a level outside the game's event time, which may be seen as a level of negotiation, where the possible event times are tested and varied, until a sufficiently satisfying sequence is reached, or not reached. If it is reached, a third level of time has been affected: that of the progression of the game from beginning to end. Some games explicitly acknowledge the need for a "negotiation time" level, by letting the user "save" their progress (i.e., start over from a certain state of events, instead of at the beginning), in order to repeat difficult actions. Other games must be played repeatedly to gain the necessary experience that will allow a successful progression. The negotiation level may thus be structurally different from game to game, but the user's strategy of gaining experience by varying a difficult maneuver until a useful technique is reached, is the same for every game.

These three temporal levels may be regarded as aspects of a single dynamic: the basic structure of any game, which is the dialectic between aporia and epiphany. In narratives, aporias are usually informal structures, semantic gaps that hinder the interpretation of the work. In ergodic works such as *Doom*, the aporias are formal figures, localizable "roadblocks" that must be overcome by some unknown combination of actions.

When an aporia is overcome, it is replaced by an epiphany: a sudden, often unexpected solution to the impasse in the event space. Compared to the epiphanies of narrative texts, the ergodic epiphanies are not optional, something to enhance the aesthetic experience, but essential to the exploration of the event space. Without them, the rest of the work cannot be realized.

There are of course various types and degrees of aporia and epiphany in ergodic discourse. Some are carefully planned, others are determined by the basic parameters of the event space, and some are completely unintentional, e.g., when a programming "bug" or simply the complexity of the system causes an unplanned event to happen. The last type is especially interesting, as it opens up the possibility of event times that are not controlled by the originator of the event space, and must be seen as uncontrollable: a zone of free play within the usually cybernetically controlled space of the ergodic work. In *Doom*, this type of epiphany is very rare, if it exists there at all.

A typical aporia/epiphany pair in *Doom* is the following: At a certain place in the game, the player emerges from a door at the top of a slope, looking out over a lower area filled with gnawing, slashing, lethal pink monsters. They have not yet seen the player, but at any time they may come running. The player may attempt to run around the monsters, or to gun them down, but the monsters are too many, so it will not work either way. Perhaps, the player thinks, I am simply not fast enough, or lucky enough; and he will try and retry until he runs out of patience. This is a typical aporia, even if it is just an apparent one, and may lead the player to abandon the game. But there is a solution, which demands a totally different approach: Near the monsters there is a series of barrels with toxic waste, any one of which, as every seasoned *Doom* player knows, will explode if fired at. One shotgun round will set off a chain reaction, exploding all the barrels and killing all the monsters. Now the player is free to continue uneaten to the next apparent aporia.

By telling you this, I commit an act of narration, based on an experience from the game. I do not, however, narrate the game, only my experience of it. I base my narrative on a more fundamental structure, the event space of aporias and epiphanies, which are the prenarrative master-figures of experience, from which narratives are spun.

Cyborg Poetry: "The murmur of indifference"?

If games such as *Doom* demand ergodic closure, the reduction of an event space into a single, successful event time, poetry generators such as John Cayley's *The Speaking Clock* challenge our sense of temporal, aesthetic experience in a totally different and open way. Where *Doom*'s event space is controlled and reductive, *Clock*'s excessive combinatorics, which produces a different verbal sequence for every moment the program runs, is based on the internal clock in the computer. This is done by an intricate algorithm, which will not be described in detail here. By the bold letter in the words in the middle, each of which corresponds to the numerical value associated with the position of the same letter on the rim, the actual time at the moment of production can be read, in the case below, "April 24th, 16:05:55" ("n" = 4 = April, "t" & "n" = 24, etc.).

```
                  The Speaking Clock
        IV  each moment appears to be given  a unique name
     the city ran on local      ↖ II         not mean time
     town hall clock   III              I   with a second
  minute hand ahead                       east of its capital
        V  what if  E..                  T  every clock
        was like           under  sun        the speaking clock
     she'd never           this  season      known
  this season here  R                     A  wild flower
        briefly           here on            painted trillium
     high bush            her  time          cranberry
     each bird   L                       N  each animal
     indignant                              at this presence
     VI  day lengthens                      under sun
     if it was impossible  S           I    to apply a single name
        from a finite set       D        to a moment
     which seems to recur   in an acknowledged  cycle of time
```

The words change letter for letter, replaced by others containing the correct letter in the correct time-slot. One by one, each word is replaced in a slow but continous cycle, and every letter position in the word flips through the alphabet until the correct letter is reached. The words are chosen from the rim text composed by John Cayley, of which there are four cards or faces, also divided into twelve parts or "months" (I–XII), with 365 words altogether, one for each day of the year. The algorithm prefers to use original word sequences from the rim text when possible, but is bound by the mesostic selection process of choosing words which contain the letter(s) representing the time.

In more than one sense, the clock is speaking of time: the time of the machine (which may be incorrect), the time of the observer (who has little time to make sense of the oracular clock), and of the reading of time, which is not time itself. Here, ergodics speaks of the "profound enigma" (to quote Ricoeur, 272) in a way denied narrative, but also with an aporetics of its own.

For what is being said? Who (what) says it? And who will read it? As I write this, *The Speaking Clock* is running in another window on my screen, but this is covered by my word processing program in such a way that I am not able to see it. All those verbal moments are lost as they disappear, in a conversation from no one to no one; in other words, a nihilogue. Yet something has been said, words have been produced, and the fact that we are not there to listen seems to be our aporia, not the Clock's. In this case, the time of the work is the only time, since there are no outside positions to contest it.

Once we are watching, the work is changed by our change in position, our intrusion. The conversation becomes between no one and someone, as the time of the intruder confronts the time of the work. But what is being said? As I try to explain the unexplainable, I again turn to listen to the Clock, which simply informs me, "the awareness/ironic capital."

Is some ghost or god in the machine trying to tell me something? This oracular answer is certainly open to interpretation, but I will not insult the non-entity of the Clock by trying to explain what "ironic capital" really means. It is hard enough to convince myself that it means nothing, that no one has spoken.

The aporias of *The Speaking Clock* are easy to see. Its epiphanies are harder, both to discover, and to deal with. The rhetorical question "what matter who is speaking?" that Michel Foucault (210; paraphrase) formulated at the end of his famous essay on the author, is perhaps more relevant in this age of ergodic aesthetics and cyborg authorship than ever before, but the final irony is that our awareness of these meaning-producing machines has not advanced since the seventies, while the machines certainly have, from the simple but effective experiments of the French avant-garde group OuLiPo (for Ouvroir de Littérature Potentielle) to today's complex computer programs.

Conclusion

The ergodic modes of discourse provide a rich laboratory in which to explore the "profound enigma" of time and experience, or at least one in which to discover new aporias connected with it. The traditional hegemony of narrative in aesthetic theory might be over soon (though I doubt it); it is certainly challenged by the slowly rising awareness of ergodic art, just as ergodic discourse modes challenge narrative modes in contemporary culture, both popular and avant-garde. There are many interesting aspects of ergodic art forms that are left unexplored, but the master figures of aporia and epiphany seem to be key terms with which to investigate some of the problems of ergodic aesthetics.

Notes

1. See Aarseth. The key issues of ergodic textuality are discussed there at much greater length.

Works Cited

Aarseth, Espen. *Cybertext: Perspectives on Ergodic Literature*. Baltimore and London: Johns Hopkins UP, 1997.

Cayley, John. *The Speaking Clock*. For Macintosh computers. London: Wellsweep, 1995.
http://www.demon.co.uk/eastfield/in/incat.html#CLOCK

Foucault, Michel. "What Is an Author?" *Modern Criticism and Theory*. Ed. David Lodge. London and New York: Longman, 1988. 196–210.

Genette, Gerard. *Narrative Discourse: An Essay in Method*. Trans. Jane E. Levin. Ithaca: Cornell UP, 1980 [1972].

Rand, Ayn. *Night of January 16th*. New York: Longmans, Green and Co., 1936.

Ricoeur, Paul. *Time and Narrative*, Vol. III. Chicago and London: U of Chicago P, 1988.

2

Theorizing Virtual Reality

Baudrillard and Derrida

Mark Poster

Information was free once. Then the telephone company
began charging for it.

The Limits of the Virtual

Virtual reality systems continue the Western trend of duplicating
the real by means of technology. They provide the participant with a
second-order reality in which to play with or practice upon the first
order. Flight simulators in their military and game varieties, architects'
"model" houses, and medicine's computer bodies—to mention only the
most prominent virtual reality applications—provide substitutes for the
real which are close enough to the real that its conditions may be tested
without the normal risks. In these cases technology provides prostheses
for the real in order to better control it, continuing the Enlightenment
project of modernity. Yet this doubling, as many have noted, puts the
original into question: the virtual upsets the stability of the real in ways
that were perhaps unintended but certainly unwanted by proponents of
the modern.[1]

A careful examination of the technology makes this clear. Virtual reality extends the line of technologies of the sensorium, as Jonathan
Crary has shown. Like the stereoscope, the panorama, and other nineteenth-century visual apparatuses, virtual reality addresses the peculiar
traits of human perception, for example, the way binocular vision constructs a field of depth. It does not assume that sensation provides a
basis for objective truth about the world, as in the model of the camera
obscura. It does not assume the neutrality of the technologies of the
human senses, as in Lockean epistemology. Instead virtual reality technology provides sensations for the eyes in line with the manner in which

they process this information. But virtual reality goes one step beyond the stereoscope: it bypasses the system of light reflecting off objects to bring directly to the eye patterns of light generated by the computer, an alteration in the process of perception in which the machine has been integrated within the body at a new level of symbiosis (Holmes, "Breaking"). Beginning then with the late modernist acceptance of senses as constructing the real for the human body, virtual reality engenders a new combination of a human-machine which places in question the fixity and naturalness of the human perceptual apparatus.

Reactions to virtual reality technologies are, as one might expect, extreme. Jaron Lanier, one of the founders of the apparatus as head of Virtual Programming Language, Inc., celebrates it: "Virtual Reality exists so that people can make up their reality as fast as they might otherwise talk about it. The whole thing with Virtual Reality is that you're breeding reality with other people. You're making shared cooperative dreams all the time. You're changing the whole reality as fast as we go through sentences now. Eventually, you make your imagination external and it blends with other people's. Then you make the world together as a form of communication. And that will happen" (Lanier 46). With almost the same level of expectation Michael Heim affirms: "Cyberspace is more than a breakthrough in electronic media or in computer interface design. With its virtual environments and simulated worlds, cyberspace is a metaphysical laboratory, a tool for examining our very sense of reality" (Heim 83). Observers more attached to modern perspectives are skeptical of these claims. One Marxist critic notes that virtual reality was extended beyond the narrow confines of the military and science fiction only through the discursive effect of advertising. Chris Chesher writes, "VR's appeal has largely been due to its marketing. It proposed a paradigm shift: that computers can be 'reality generators,' not just symbol processors. This shift allowed VR to become associated with a far broader range of cultural tropes than computers had been before." And in the end, as Stallabrass argues, this simply reproduces and extends the baleful imperatives of Capital in the age of global commodification. Others find in VR not simply a marketing success but dangerous and threatening possibilities. Opponents of VR, from presidential contender Pat Robertson to the Pope, discern effects such as ontological insecurity, moral confusion, sexual impotence, political apathy, irrationality, dehumanization, and narcissism.[2]

The term "virtual reality" quickly spread beyond "computer generated immersive environments" (the helmet-glove-computer assemblage) to include first certain communications facilities on the Internet—bulletin boards, MUDs, MOOs, Internet Relay Chat—and then to the Internet more broadly—including e-mail, databases, newsgroups, and so forth—also known as "cyberspace." In these cases, as distinct from helmet-and-glove VR, the salient trait of the virtual is community—electronic cafés, cybersalons, in short "places" where conversation takes place either in real time or by message facilities. Those who are critical of helmet-and-glove variety virtuality because of its seeming narcissism, even solipsism, need to note that virtual reality in cyberspace tends to be preeminently social, at least in the sense that many people participate. Yet one must be careful using terms like "social" in regard to virtual reality unless it is kept in mind that the interactions at issue are purely electronic. VR in either case is not disembodied since the messages or signals are composed by human beings, but the VR meeting place does exclude bodily presence. As sound and images are added to the textual communities on the Internet, skeptics may be forced to reconsider the nature of these exchanges. Those who dismiss them today as "disembodied" need to ask themselves if full video/audio will make a difference, and if so, why?

More generally still, the term "virtual reality" began to expand its associations to all electronically mediated exchanges of symbols, images, and sound so that a second world is constituted over against the "real" world of sensory proximity. The mode of information, as I have termed this virtual world, is one way of conceptualizing the cultural significance of the new phenomenon. In some discussions of virtual reality, especially among some literary critics, the term refers not simply to electronically mediated communication but to all reality. The term "virtual reality," in many of these discussions, so destabilizes the real that the real itself is understood as "virtual," as provisional, constructed, and mediated by processes of signification or interpretation. Hence for these literary interpreters, virtual reality is not a new technology that has general cultural significance that would put reality into question. Here reality is "always already" virtual, while the helmet-glove technology is a mere machine. In the hands of certain literary theorists the virtual becomes transcendental and founds the real in its own image. Thus novels are just as much virtual realities as computer-generated immersive environments. And since novels are more "real" than experience, fiction more true than facts, a new disciplinary foundation for Literature is constructed. In discussions of virtual reality it is imperative to guard against the "transcendentalist gesture," as I would like to call these discursive maneuvers, by keeping in mind the material basis of the term, the machinic assemblages of cyberspace and helmet-glove apparatuses.

Baudrillard's Crime against Reality

Baudrillard's work has proven enormously suggestive in the interpretation of the media and of cultural phenomena generally, like Disneyland, which seem in some ways to share its principles.[3] His notion of simulational culture, later termed "the hyperreal," captures as no social theorist before him the linguistic gestures and the unique configurations of electronic media as they course through the wired capillaries of the postmodern body social. Beginning with *Simulacra and Simulation* of 1981 and continuing at least through *The Illusion of the End* in 1992, Baudrillard interrogates the cultural forms of media communications from a consistent if ambivalent standpoint. For Baudrillard of the 1980s our culture is simulational. Driven by the media, especially television, popular culture preempts the exchange of symbols between individuals, introducing another layer of experience that undermines the subject's ability to define and to grasp the truth. Electronic mediation cripples the modern system of representation, folding it into a new mode of signification in which signs are divorced from their referents in the object world, becoming reorganized into a "hyperreal" of screen surfaces.

It might appear that the terms "simulation" and "virtual reality" are equivalent, each suggesting a sign system in which cultural objects are divorced from their referents, in which words and images appear in their electronic reproduction without firm connection to a prior real world, thus functioning not as representations but as objects themselves, as entities whose meaning resides within. For Baudrillard in 1981, " . . . the age of simulation begins with a liquidation of all referentials—worse: by their artificial resurrection in systems of signs . . . " (Poster, *Jean Baudrillard*, 167). This revolution in the structure of language unsettles thought systems of an earlier epoch. Simulation, Baudrillard contends, threatens the distinction true/false: " . . . truth, reference and objective causes have ceased to exist" (ibid. 168). In dramatic, totalizing prose, Baudrillard discounts the multiplicity of language games at play in the seeming infinite complexity of the social in favor of a one-dimensional theory of the hyperreal. In any case, simulation denotes a major cultural change.

Baudrillard's writing begins to be sprinkled with the terms "virtual" and "virtual reality" as early as 1991. But he uses these terms interchangeably with "simulation," and without designating anything different from the earlier usage. Concerning the Gulf War of 1991, for example, he writes: "In our fear of the real, of anything that is too real,

we have created a gigantic simulator. We prefer the virtual to the catastrophe of the real, of which television is the universal mirror."[4] The
virtual is equivalent to the hyperreal or to simulation. In all cases the
electronically mediated communication stands in a double relation to
reality. Mediated communication both reflects reality by delivering signals from a sender to a receiver that are somehow about it; and it substitutes for reality in the sense that it never simply represents reality but
puts forth its own reality. Simulations and the virtual, for Baudrillard,
are different from reality but always stand in a certain relation to it.

With *Le Crime parfait* (1995), however, things have changed. To paraphrase Marx speaking of communism as the solution to the riddle
of history, Baudrillard has become virtual and knows himself to be
such: he argues that his critical theory of simulation has become nothing less than the principle of reality.[5] The world has become virtual;
Baudrillard's theory is no longer true, but real. What use then for
Baudrillard's writings in the age of virtual reality machines?

> The idea of simulacrum was a conceptual weapon against reality,
> but it has been stolen. Not that it has been pillaged, vulgarized, or
> has become commonplace (which is true but has no consequence),
> but because simulacra have been absorbed by reality which has
> swallowed them and which, from now on, is clad with all the rheto-
> ric of simulation. And to cap it all, simulacra have become reality!
> Today, simulacra guarantee the continuation of the real. The simu-
> lacrum now hides, not the truth, but the fact that there is none,
> that is to say, the continuation of Nothingness. (*Le Crime parfait*
> 146)[6]

Since simulation is now the dominant form of culture, Baudrillard's
concept of simulation, he thinks, no longer functions as a concept.
Somewhat immodestly he suggests that theory (his own) that realizes
itself is no longer a theory ("Radical Thought" 19). Unsympathetic
critics may find lurking in this revisiting of the Hegelian dialectic
synthesizing itself in and for itself a whiff of Marx's comment about
Napoleon III: repetition as farce.

Baudrillard is too competent a social theorist not to see the problem
he is raising in its general significance. If the concept of simulation is
now reduced to mimetic description, critical theory (and Enlightenment
discourse more generally) is nullified:

> We have lost the advance that ideas had on the world, that distance
> that makes an idea stay an idea. What to do then? What is there
> to do when suddenly everything fits the ironic, critical, alternative,

and catastrophic model that you suggested (everything fits the model you gave beyond any hopes you had because, in a sense, you never believed it could go that far, otherwise you would never have been able to create it)?

Baudrillard argues that a crime is responsible for the current predicament, the perfect crime alluded to in the title of the book. This crime is the theft of reality by virtual reality. Much of *Le Crime parfait* is a demonstration of the new circumstances through analyses of cultural figures (the usual suspects) such as Madonna and Andy Warhol and a playing with the concept of perfect crime in the context of the virtual. What can a perfect crime be if the image is the real and the real is virtual reality? What sort of jurisprudence fits with this brave new world? You can imagine the fun Baudrillard has with his illicited world.

Baudrillard understands the passage from the hyperreal to virtual reality as an intensification in kind rather than a new direction. Virtual reality equals simulation as cultural dominant, to use Fredric Jameson's term. Here is Baudrillard's compelling description of the culture of virtual reality: "It is as if things swallowed their mirrors, and became transparent to themselves, entirely present to themselves, in the light of day, in real time, in a pitiless transcription. Instead of being absent from themselves in illusion, they are forced to inscribe themselves on millions of monitors at the horizon of which not only the real but the image has disappeared" (*Le Crime parfait* 17). The culture of the screen has now become the norm of culture itself, according to Baudrillard. The consequence is that reality is lost, and along with it go critical thought and the concepts that defined an emergent screen culture, such as simulation and the hyperreal.[7]

What then is the difference between Baudrillard's theory of simulation and virtual reality? For one critic, C. J. Keep, the difference between Baudrillard's concept of the hyperreal and virtual reality is this: Where the "hyperreal" is constituted by the play of surfaces, by a paralytic fascination with exteriority, the "virtual" offers images with depth, images which one can enter, explore, and, perhaps most importantly, with which one can interact (Keep 1993). The difference enunciated by Keep is one between a passive or specular hyperreal (television technology) and an active or interactive and immersive virtual reality (headset-glove-computer technology). There is much to this argument because Baudrillard does not define virtual reality in relation to any particular technology but to a certain stage of technology in general. In fact the one place where he actually describes helmet-glove VR using the English phrase "body simulation," he does not mention the term "virtual reality" (*Le Crime parfait* 174). Instead we have a Heideggerian lament: "With Virtual Reality, and all of its consequences, we are delivered over to the extreme of technology, to technology as an extreme phenomenon . . . " (ibid. 56). Or again in an allusion to McLuhan, Baudrillard warns that the logic of technology as extension of man is carried to the point where it goes beyond itself and becomes "virtuality without limit." All of this sounds surprisingly like an old-fashioned humanist's jeremiad against the evils of technology. Indeed the great weakness of Baudrillard's effort to theorize VR is his inability to recognize assemblages of human and machine practices and account for their differential realizations. Instead Baudrillard is the unconscious ideologist/theorist of the television screen, imposing that vision upon cybernetic technologies.[8] It may be that the conservative overtones in the political implications he draws from the new order of virtual reality in Part Two of *Le Crime parfait* derive from his failure to come to grips with the new level of human-machine imbrication represented especially by the "virtual communities" of the Internet and VR technology.

Critical reflection upon new technologies requires some exploration of the domain of the computer and some experience with the communications patterns it affords. One needs to do more than expatiate upon VR as a metaphor; one must look closely at its forms. One needs to differentiate between the TV screen and the computer screen. Such research often yields suggestive models that begin to come to grips with the true novelties we are confronted with. For instance, Kate Hayles argues compellingly that virtual reality technologies require and put forth new epistemologies: "The new technologies of virtual reality illustrate the kind of phenomena that foreground pattern and randomness and make presence and absence seem irrelevant" (Hayles 72). The shift in the location of the body in cybernetic technologies, Hayles suggests, reorganizes the field of analysis and the categories one may deploy to render it intelligible. Another example of a discourse on VR that speaks to its peculiar features is Marie-Laure Ryan's analysis of the relation of fiction and new technologies. If VR is distinguished by the immersion of the individual into computer-generated space, does not the novel also bring the reader into another world, a virtual world? Ryan sorts through this issue in relation to technologies of both immersion and interactivity, not simply being within a world but also acting upon it to change it. Though she is quite cautious of certain features of the new technologies, such as the limits imposed by the computer code upon the VR experience, in the end she recognizes important differences between literature and VR as well as between different applications of VR itself. She concludes, "The most immersive forms of textual interactivity are

therefore those in which the user's contributions, rather than performing a creation through a diegetic (i.e., descriptive) use of language,
count as a dialogic and live interaction with other members of the fictional world." VR enables, indeed requires, the individual to participate
in constructing the world as s/he experiences it, rendering it distinct
from reading a fixed text. As with Hayles, Ryan's analysis of VR begins
to locate the specificity of the experience in terms that are not beholden
to face-to-face or print modes of cultural practice.

Baudrillard's response to VR, by contrast, is to invent a new kind
of discourse, dubbed radical thought, in order to maintain his distance
from it, to preserve his place in front and ahead of VR, in short, to
repeat the gesture of the avant-garde. The problem he sees with "critical thought" is that it takes a stance in opposition to the real, setting
up a dialectic of negation. But the real itself is structured in that way
so that the gesture of opposition is already nullified. As an alternative
Baudrillard offers radical thought as "the putting into play of this
world, the material and immanent illusion of this so-called 'real'
world—it is a non-critical, non-dialectical thought" ("Radical Thought,"
not paginated). Thinking for him would be a non-oppositional alterity
to the real, one that, through its difference from the real, exposes it,
mocks it, destabilizes it.

Baudrillard takes language as his model for radical thought: " . . .
language," he writes, sounding very much the poststructuralist or even
Derridean, "is an illusion in its very movement, . . . it carries this continuation of emptiness or nothingness at the very core of what it says,
and . . . it is in all its materiality a deconstruction of what it signifies"
(ibid.). The insubstantiality of language allows it to escape the "evil
transparency" of the real, its logic of identity, fullness, and performativity.[9] Such a position would restore the world as illusion rather than as
real. As illusion, the world takes many forms, among them the virtual
reality of today, the "apocalypse of simulation."

Against his critics, Baudrillard denies that radical thought is nihilist.
Refusing to defend himself, he still insists that " . . . we have to fight
against charges of unreality, lack of responsibility, nihilism, and despair. Radical thought is never depressing" (*Le Crime parfait* 148). His
apparently outrageous pronouncements such as "What are you doing after the orgy" or "The Gulf War did not take place"[10] are not examples
of cynical reason but a sort of desperate playfulness in the face of extreme phenomena. Radical thought is not a failure to decipher or decode
the world but to stand as witness in poetic and ironic enunciations of
language. But is not language itself taking on new forms in the era of
virtual reality and cyberspace? Can one rest with a self-styled decon-

structive stance when the material infrastructure of the sign is being so drastically reconfigured? Baudrillard's virtual reality has not taken into account, with enough rigor and seriousness, the condition of the body, the material, the trace. Though he calls for a "fatal strategy" of the object, this object is without substance, depth, resistance so that the reconfigured cultural world of the mode of information remains, to him, a distant, threatening horizon of America, the desert.

In the end his world of totalized simulation remains limited by the model of simulation. Simulations rely upon their difference from representations. If simulations refute the logic of representation—its dualism of active subject, passive object—they maintain the linguistic stability of representations. Simulations are coherent sets of meanings, even if they are detached from referents and precede their objects. From first-level simulations like maps to third-level simulations like the televised Gulf War, this cultural form retains its fixed matrix of meanings. TV shows and theme parks organize a cultural world that the individual consumes. What distinguishes VR from simulation is its transformational structure: subjects and objects interactively/immersively construct cultural spaces and events. They do so not in the present/absent logic of the first media age but in the informational logic of pattern/ noise of the second media age. The cultural space of VR is not preceded by the model as in simulations but is continuously invented and reinvented through the material parameters of the media apparatus. As cybervillage and helmet-glove construct, VR discombobulates earlier cultural and social forms in order to recombine them in a new constellation, one not without its own constraints but with constraints that are peculiar to it and immune from complaints by modernist viewpoints.

Derrida's Ghosts

In *Specters of Marx* Derrida engages the issue of virtual reality, connecting it with the general question of politics, the media, and their interpretation. He first shows how the virtual is the supplement to the real: "*What is* a ghost? What is the *effectivity* or the *presence* of a specter, that is, of what seems to remain as ineffective, virtual, insubstantial as a simulacrum?" (*Specters of Marx* 10). Deconstructive analysis will show that the virtual is essential to the real, that "ghosts" haunt the full presence of the real in the forms of the debt to the past and the promise of justice in the future. Derrida announces a theory of "hauntology" to indicate the imbrication of the virtual in the real and declares the foundation of a "new international" to promote the aims of this promise, to sustain the alterity of justice against those who proclaim the "good news" of an uncontested liberalism, to foster the secular messianism of the virtual against the claim of the full presence of democracy.

If virtual reality is always already inscribed in the event, rendering history forever a "time out of joint," resisting the transparency of the real, it is also, for Derrida, a particular exigency of our age. Today virtual reality takes the form of the media and technology more generally. Derrida praises Marx's *Communist Manifesto* for its acumen on this score: "No text in the tradition seems as lucid concerning the way in which the political is becoming worldwide, concerning the irreducibility of the technical and the media in the current of the most thinking thought . . . " (13). *Specters of Marx* consistently affirms the centrality of new media to a comprehension of the present age. "The analysis of public space today," he writes, "must take into account so many *spectral* effects, the new speed of *apparition* . . . of the simulacrum, the synthetic or prosthetic image, and the virtual event, cyberspace and surveillance, the control, appropriation, and speculations that today deploy unheard-of-powers" (54). Or again, "the logic of the ghost" "points toward a thinking of the event" and is "demonstrated today better than ever by the fantastic, ghostly, 'synthetic,' 'prosthetic,' virtual happenings in the scientific domain and therefore the domain of the techno-media and therefore the public or political domain" (63). And again, Western democracy "is exercised with more and more difficulty in a public space profoundly upset by techno-tele-media apparatuses and by new rhythms of information and communication, by the devices and the speed of forces represented by the latter, but also and consequently by the new modes of appropriation they put to work, by the new structure of the event and of its spectrality that they *produce*" (79). The speed of the media, their pervasiveness, produces, Derrida contends, a condition of virtual reality which undermines modern institutions and evokes the need of a "new international" to assert the claims of justice.

The term "virtual reality" oscillates in Derrida's text between a general, transcendental aspect of the event and a particular configuration of the present associated with a specific set of technological apparatuses. On the one side, Derrida insists that his "hauntology" is "not an empirical hypothesis," relevant only to an age of computers for example (161). As the term "iteration" suggests, a given technology may be redeployed elsewhere, by an other and therefore "projects it *a priori* onto" all scenes of technique, media, and so forth. On the other side, Derrida, with equal vehemence, insists that he is not advocating an undifferentiated virtuality, "a general phantasmagorization" in which all technological cows are grey (163), in which immersive virtual realities are the same as fictional worlds of novels. Rather he calls for new concepts that are more refined than those we presently have, concepts that would specify the different structures of virtual reality, the different forms of haunting in each technological apparatus. He writes, "the differential deployment of *tekhn*, of techno-science or tele-technology . . . obliges us more than ever to think the virtualization of space and time, the possibility of virtual events whose movement and speed prohibit us more than ever (more and otherwise than ever, for this is not absolutely and thoroughly new) from opposing presence to its representation, 'real time' to 'deferred time,' effectivity to its simulacrum, the living to the non-living, in short, the living to the living-dead of its ghosts. It obliges us to think, from there, another space for democracy" (167). Unlike Baudrillard, Derrida senses the need to account for differential materialities of the media, for the ways in which the ghosts of television structure subjects differently from the virtualities of computer screens, for the ways in which Internet communities are different from helmet-and-glove computer-generated worlds. As in his earlier works, Derrida is attentive to the trace and to its material manifestations.

But Derrida does not provide the concepts needed for the analysis of the new technologies, and his discussion of "the virtualization of space and time" tends to preserve the philosopher's taste for the general over the cultural analyst's penchant for the particular. For instance, just after insisting upon deconstruction's actuality, that it is no mere "critique of a critique" but a positive intervention, establishing new institutions (an international) and new categories (for the analysis of the spectrality of the media), Derrida warns that this is all nothing new, that there will always be the need for new concepts, for "constant restructuration" (162). The questions that remain then are these: Can hauntology take the next step and begin to specify the criteria by which these new concepts would be evaluated? And even further: Can it specify which are the pertinent domains of materiality that can be differentiated and analyzed in their effectivity? Instead of this initiative Derrida provides strings of hyphenated terms: "tele-technology" or "techno-scientifico-economico-media" (70) that vaguely point in a direction without guiding the virtual traveler in any particular direction.

There is at least one place, however, where Derrida has begun an analysis of the "tele-technological": his recent essay "Archive Fever: A Freudian Impression" (1995). Here Derrida does more than name the phenomenon or point to it. He specifies its characteristics and determining features. If an archive is a necessary supplement of discourse, as Derrida argues, its specific form, its technical level, determines its effectivity as archive, its ability to preserve information both in time and in extent. Electronic databases, he surmises, would have changed the

Freudian movement by their abilities in this regard alone. Secondly, the electronic archive also determines *what* can be preserved: the technical structure of "the *archiving* archive also determines the structure of the *archivable* contents . . . " ("Archive Fever" 17). Whatever can be digitized can be stored. For example, audio- or even videotapes of meetings of the Psychoanalytic Society and of sessions with clients might be archived. In particular Derrida muses that electronic mail, with its automatic archiving function, changes stored memory in particular for a group such as psychoanalysts because of their extensive correspondence. But more than any of these features, the impact of teletechnology is most exigent in its transformation of what Derrida calls the public and the private. In his words, "electronic mail today, and even more than the fax, is on the way to transforming the entire public and private space of humanity, and first of all the limit between the private, the secret (private or public), and the public or phenomenal" (17). Derrida does not elaborate on this suggestive claim. Still many have observed this phenomenon and commented extensively upon it. Electronic surveillance and computer databases reduce if not erase the domain of the private. Computers are not alone in working to erode the privacy of the modern era. Television also, as Joshua Meyrowitz argues, by its framing structure and its location in the family living room, transforms public, formal occasions and spaces into intimate, private ones. The modern subject's sense of its exclusive awareness of its own thoughts and inclinations, however much a historical construction as Francis Barker shows, is restructured by electronic communication systems so as to render nugatory its private, interior space.

In these ways Derrida enumerates specific features of one teletechnology, e-mail, as it profoundly affects the question of the archive. Yet does so in relation to a discussion of Freud and the early psychoanalytic movement, when there was no e-mail. Derrida takes a current topic of great urgency and controversy and reviews its character not in the present but in a hypothetical time, even an anachronistic time. For him, in a discursive act which he labels "retrospective science-fiction," e-mail *would have* changed psychoanalysis. But why transform e-mail first into science fiction in order to set it up as a topic of analysis when it is in full use today? Perhaps Derrida requires this rhetorical move in order to energize his hauntology, in order to animate the ghost in Freud's archive with an anachronistic teletechnology? Or perhaps teletechnology may enter deconstruction only indirectly, through the temporal distance inserted by Derrida's discourse, the temporal distance of a retrospective science fiction? This making absent of e-mail and of the teletechnological, displacing it from its moment of inception and dissemination, occurs while the librarians at the University of California, Irvine are accumulating the manuscript corpus of deconstruction for future scanning into an electronic archive.

In *Specters of Marx* Derrida discusses an example of a "tele-technology": the "viser-effect" or "helmet-effect" of the ghost in Shakespeare's *Hamlet*. Derrida is concerned to portray the materiality of the ghost through its partial or evanescent visibility. Ghosts refute the transparency of the "real" body, resist the perception of objectivity of the everyday. In Derrida's words, the ghost presents " . . . the furtive and ungraspable visibility of the invisible . . . the tangible intangibility of a proper body without flesh . . . " (7). If an ordinary ghost evinced such chaos in the visible, then the helmeted ghost of Hamlet's father, with his visor preventing certain identification, plays worse havoc with the real and does so in another material region: the ghost with helmet. This "the helmet effect" offers "incomparable power" to its bearer, "the power to see without being seen" of hiding "his identity" (8). But is the Danish king's helmet a "real" helmet? Do ghosts wear metal on their heads or only simulations of metal? In Shakespeare's play, no doubt this distinction makes no difference, at least when it is performed in the seventeenth century. But at the close of the twentieth, when we possess "tele-technologies," would a film of Hamlet be required to make a visible distinction, since it is technically possible, between the ghost's helmet and a non-ghost's helmet?

The materiality of the helmet emerges when we consider another user from the canon: Wagner's Alberich from *The Ring of the Nibelungen* in which gold is fashioned into a magical helmet (the tarnhelm) which makes its wearer invisible. In this case the material for the helmet, gold, is itself a specular material, containing fantastic powers not visible on its surface but inscribed in the social imaginary of Western (and other) society. The gold is reshaped by a master craftsman (Mime, who is Alberich's brother), evoking the society of guilds and the power of human labor to infuse matter with special, even unimaginable, qualities. Finally, Alberich uses the tarnhelm to control his laborers, his invisibility providing an extra amount of power. This capitalist imaginary, with panoptic surveillance capacities, refunctions yet again the material of the helmet effect, introducing into Wagner's music-drama the contest between patriarchs of the feudal and capitalist variety. Ghostliness and materiality again combine in unanticipated ways.

The problems left by deconstruction's hauntology are particularly acute when the issue of political analysis is raised. Derrida provides a reasonable tablet of the ten major ills of present-day capitalist democracy: from unemployment and homelessness to market irrationalities, arms dealing, ethnic wars, and international law. Yet this analysis requires no hauntology or even deconstruction. Basic Marxism, or even left-liberalism would do just fine in enumerating the political and economic plagues of the waning years of the millennium. Derrida admits as much, presenting this analysis with explicit debts to Marx. He writes, " . . . without necessarily subscribing to the whole Marxist discourse . . . one may still find inspiration in the Marxist 'spirit' to criticize the presumed autonomy of the juridical and to denounce endlessly the *de facto* take-over of international authorities by powerful Nation-States, by concentrations of techno-scientific capital, symbolic capital, and financial capital, of State capital and private capital" (85). But if Marxist categories suffice for such a discourse, is not hauntology little more than a critique of a critique, a reminder of the ghost, an insistence on alterity, and a vigilance against ontologizing presence? In Sue Golding's words, " . . . when Derrida speaks of a virtual limit, he replaces the politics of virtual being-there with 'the logic of the ghost.' . . . " If he does not "replace" the one by the other, he certainly opens his analysis to that danger.

The question remains of deconstruction's purchase of justice when Marxist analysis depicts injustice so well. Why does justice require Derrida? What is it about deconstruction that gives it a claim to witness justice? If the ghostly promise of justice to come is to haunt the present world, why must it appear in a specifically Derridean guise? Or should its identity even be known? Ought not Derrida, when announcing the New International and avowing its dedication to justice, hide himself in a visor or present himself in a virtual form? What necessary connection exists between the critique of the logocentric tradition, for which deconstruction is as fine an instrument as exits, and justice? Is Derrida's commitment to justice consonant with deconstruction or a departure from it?

In his review of *Specters of Marx*, Fredric Jameson raises this question in a particularly acute manner: "whether the new figurality, the figured concept of the ghost or specter, is not of a somewhat different type than those that began to proliferate in Derrida's earlier work, beginning most famously with 'writing' itself and moving through . . . terms like dissemination, hymen . . . " (79). Does the introduction of the ghost in the *mise-en-scène* of deconstruction cause an alteration in its theoretical composition? Jameson reasons that it does because Derrida's messianism harkens to the "postmodern virtuality" of new communications technology, in other words to a reconfiguration of materiality (108). And I agree. To the extent that the mode of information restructures language and symbols generally into a configuration that is aptly termed "virtual reality," the particular form of the messianic, of our hope for justice, must go through this technological circuit and must account for the difference between writing and e-mail, dissemination and the Internet, the parergon and the World Wide Web. Unless such an account is provided, deconstruction may return to its minimalist position as critique of critique, as disavowal of ontology, forever incapable of an affirmative sentence.

Specters of Marx instantiates an equivalence between the defense of the virtual, deconstruction, and justice. Evoking Nietzsche's prophetic yea-saying, Derrida writes, "A deconstructive thinking, the one that matters to me here, has always pointed out the irreducibility of affirmation and therefore of the promise, as well as the undeconstructibility of a certain idea of justice . . . " (90). Very much like Foucault in "What Is Enlightenment?" who affirms "a permanent critique of our historical era" (36), Derrida posits "a new Enlightenment for the century to come," animated by "an ideal of democracy and emancipation" (90). The poststructuralists link themselves tightly with a Nietzschean spirit of critique, Nietzsche as an affirmative philosopher of the will to power, the transvaluation of values, the creative soul who celebrates giving birth to a "dancing star." Yet this side of Nietzsche's thought had been noticeably absent from the poststructuralist appropriation beginning with Gilles Deleuze's *Philosophy of Nietzsche* (1962), and continuing with Foucault's "Nietzsche, Genealogy, History" (1971), and finally Derrida's *Spurs: Nietzsche's Styles* (1978).

The danger of Derrida's association of democracy, Enlightenment, emancipation, and justice with deconstruction, all in a New International, is pointed out by Ernesto Laclau in his review of *Specters of Marx*. The danger is an automatic association of deconstruction with justice. Deconstruction becomes an ethical practice equivalent to emancipatory politics. Laclau writes, "The illegitimate transition is to think that from the impossibility of a presence closed in itself, from an 'ontological' condition in which the openness to the event, to the heterogeneous, to the radically other is constitutive, some kind of ethical injunction to be responsible and to keep oneself open to the heterogeneity of the other necessarily follows" (92–93). In this case, the ontological moment that Derrida would avoid returns through the back door of hauntology. The ghost loses his/her partial invisibility and becomes a witness of justice and bearer of the messianic promise. This strategy may stave off those critics of deconstruction, and poststructuralism more generally, who find in it an opening to neoconservatism or even neofascism, but it risks a theoretical step backward into the very ontological security these positions at their best have always sought to avoid. A commitment to justice and democracy is not in question. What is at issue is the way these are linked to theoretical strategies. If there is to be a New International, who will be part of it? What will be its aims? And what will be its strategies and methods? None of these questions is confronted in *Specters of Marx*, and until they are, it is difficult to see in what sense a New International exists.

Derrida's work, from *Writing and Difference* to *The Postcard*, is informed by a sense of being in a new context, a transitional period in which what is emerging cannot be clearly discerned, but dimly appears in the form of a monster. Writing in the late 1960s, Derrida positions himself clearly at a point of historical uncertainty:

> For my part, although these two interpretations [of interpretation] must acknowledge and accentuate their difference and define their irreducibility, I do not believe that today there is any question of *choosing*—in the first place because here we are in a region (let us say, provisionally, a region of historicity) where the category of choice seems particularly trivial; and in the second, because we must first try to conceive of a common ground, and the *différance* of this irreducible difference. Here there is a kind of question, let us still call it historical, whose *conception, formation, gestation,* and *labor* we are only catching a glimpse of today. I employ these words, I admit, with a glance toward the operations of childbearing—but also with a glance toward those who, in a society from which I do not exclude myself, turn their eyes away when faced by the as yet unnameable which is proclaiming itself and which can do so, as is necessary whenever a birth is in the offing, only under the species of the nonspecies, in the formless, mute, infant, and terrifying form of monstrosity. ("Structure, Sign and Play" 93)

The historical question for Derrida is the naming of the "unnameable," the "nonspecies" which is emerging. And it cannot be done and ought not be done. In 1967 Derrida thinks within the process of the birth of a world, and deconstruction bears the marks of its term of gestation as the philosophy of the undecidable. In this context the old metanarratives and totalizations are no longer credible, but neither are new general political stances perceptible. In such a condition the deconstruction of Western culture labors in the horizon of the undecidable. With the avowal of emancipation and the declaration of a New International, Derrida, it would seem, collapses the critical ambivalence of the 1970s and 1980s into a positivity that is well-meaning, to be sure, but without much force of conviction.

The question of politics in the age of virtual reality must depart from a new materialism, a new theory of the imbrication of technology and culture, one that comes to terms with the transformation of mechanical machines into smart machines, into "artificial intelligence," self-regulating systems, digitizers of images, sounds, and text; it must commence from an appreciation of the dissemination of these software-hardware systems throughout social space and the installation of interfaces that unite humans and machines in new configurations of agency.[11] This gigantic task of conceptual/empirical development no doubt relies in part on deconstruction, especially in its hauntology phase. But it does not guarantee a politics of emancipation, however much one would wish it were so. While Marxist and liberal critiques continue to have important but limited effectivity, a general new politics of radical democracy must await the substantial analysis of an emerging global mode of information. The reconfiguration of time and space, body and mind, human and machine, imagination and reason, gender and ethnicity, the virtual and the real must congeal into a postmodern relation of force before critical theory's owl of Minerva takes flight.

Notes

1. For some treatments of this theme that may be found on the Internet see Diana Saco, "Cybercitizens: Reflections on Democracy and Communication in the Electronic Frontier," Morten Soby, "Possessed by Virtual Reality," and Michael S. Rosenberg, "Virtual Reality: Reflections of Life, Dreams, and Technology: An Ethnography of a Computer Society."

2. See the article "Cybersex Threatens Plain Old Kind: Church, Lay Experts," distributed on the Internet by Agence France Presse (May 13, 1995).

3. For an interesting work on this topic see Mark Nunes, "Baudrillard in Cyberspace: Internet, Virtuality, and Postmodernity," *Style* 29 (1995): 314–27.

4. Jean Baudrillard, "The Reality Gulf," 25. See also the discussion of Baudrillard's political analysis in Der Derian.

5. This Hegelian gesture of identifying one's thought with reality is also made by Derrida, albeit more modestly, when he reports that, on a trip to Moscow, his then Soviet hosts defined Perestroika as deconstruction: " . . . a Soviet colleague said to me, scarcely laughing, 'But deconstruction, that's the USSR today' " ("Back from Moscow" 222). Derrida relates this incident anew in *Specters of Marx* 89. One is tempted to make a comment about the role of intellectuals in the age of mass media as a condition for this new insistence on the inscription of theory in history.

6. This translation by François Debrix appeared in "Radical Thought," and is taken from a pamphlet Baudrillard published as *La Pensée Radicale* which appears in revised form in *Le Crime parfait*. The same text has been published in another translation in *Parallax*.

7. Baudrillard is not wholly consistent in this regard. *Le Crime parfait* contains many passages that read like the Baudrillard of the 1980s, as for example: "That thought disappeared under the pressure of a gigantic simulation, a technical and mental one, under the pressure of a precession of models to the benefit of an autonomy of the virtual, from now on liberated from the real, and of a simultaneous autonomy of the real that today functions for and by itself—~motu propio~—in a delirious perspective, infinitely self-referential" (141).

8. For a suggestive genealogy of the screen with a differential analysis of screens see Manovich.

9. See *La Transparence du mal*.

10. "What Are You Doing after the Orgy" and *La Guerre du golfe n'a pas eu lieu*. Baudrillard responds to such critics as follows: "Because of the media, our scientific means, our knowhow progress all take an uncontrollable, inhuman dimension. Evil, for me is just that form" ("Vivisecting the 90's.")

11. For an important deconstructionist analysis of the screen as a technology of reorganization of space and time see Samuel Weber, *Mass Mediauras: Essays on Form, Technics and Media* and "Humanitarian Interventions in the Age of the Media."

Works Cited

Barker, Francis. *The Tremulous Private Body: Essays on Subjection.* Ann Arbor: U of Michgan P, 1995.

Baudrillard, Jean. "What Are You Doing after the Orgy ?" *Artforum* (October 1983): 42–46.

———. *La Transparence du Mal: essai sur les phénomènes extrêmes.* Paris: Galilée, 1990.

———. *La Guerre du golfe n'a pas eu lieu.* Paris: Galilée, 1991.

———. *La Pensée Radicale.* Paris: Sens & Tonka, 1994.

———. "Vivisecting the 90's." Interview with Carolyn Bayard and Graham Knight. *CTHEORY* 18 (August 3, 1995): 1–2.

———. "Radical Thought." Trans. David Macey and Mike Gane. *Parallax* 1 (1995).

———. *Le Crime parfait.* Paris: Galilée, 1995.

Chesher, Chris. "Colonizing Virtual Reality." *Cultronix* 1.1 (1995).

Crary, Jonathan. *Techniques of the Observer: On Vision and Modernity in the Nineteenth Century.* Cambridge: MIT P, 1992.

Der Derian, James. "Simulation: The Highest Stage of Capitalism?" Kellner 189–208.

Derrida, Jacques. "Structure, Sign and Play in the Discourse of the Human Sciences." *Writing and Differance*. Trans. Alan Bass. Chicago: U of Chicago P, 1978.

———. "Back from Moscow, in the USSR." Poster 1993, 197–236.

———. *Specters of Marx*. Trans. Peggy Kamuf. New York: Routledge, 1994.

———. "Archive Fever: A Freudian Impression." *Diacritics* 25.2 (1995): 9–63.

Foucault, Michel. "What Is Enlightenment?" *The Foucault Reader*. Ed. Paul Rabinow. New York: Pantheon, 1984. 32–50.

Golding, Sue. "Virtual Derrida." *Philosophic Fictions*. Ed. Jelica Sumic-Riha. Slovenia: Academy of Philosophy, 1994. 61–66.

Hayles, N. Katherine. "Virtual Bodies and Flickering Signifiers." *October* 66 (Fall 1993): 69–92.

Heim, Michael. *The Metaphysics of Virtual Reality*. New York: Oxford UP, 1993.

Holmes, David. "The Breaking Down of the Senses: Virtual Reality and Technological Extension." Unpublished essay, 1994.

Jameson, Fredric. "Marx's Purloined Letter." *New Left Review* 209 (January–February 1995): 75–109.

Keep, Christopher J. "Knocking in Heaven's Door: Leibniz, Baudrillard and Virtual Reality." *EJournal* 3:2 (1993). http://www.hanover.edu/philos/ejournal/archive/e-j-3-2.txt

Kellner, Douglas, ed. *Baudrillard: A Critical Reader*. London: Blackwell, 1994.

Laclau, Ernesto. "The Time Is Out of Joint." *Diacritics* 25.2 (1995): 92–93.

Lanier, Jaron. "Life in the Data-Cloud" (Interview). *Mondo 2000* 2 (summer 1992).

Manovich, Lev. "An Anthology of a Computer Screen." *Telepolis* at http://www.irz-muenchen.de/mlm/telepolis/english/tpj.htm

Meyrowitz, Joshua. *No Sense of Place: The Impact of Electronic Media on Social Behavior*. New York: Oxford UP, 1985.

Nunes, Mark. "Baudrillard in Cyberspace: Internet, Virtuality, and Postmodernity." *Style* 29.2 (1995): 314–27.

Poster, Mark, ed. and intro. *Jean Baudrillard: Selected Writings*. Stanford: Stanford UP, 1988.

———, ed. *Politics, Theory, and Contemporary Culture*. New York: Columbia UP, 1993.

Ryan, Marie-Laure. "Immersion vs. Interactivity: Virtual Reality and Literary Theory." *Postmodern Culture* 5.1 (1994). http://muse.jhu.edu/journals/postmodern_culture/v005/5.1ryan.html/.

Stallabrass, Julian. "Empowering Technology: The Exploration of Cyberspace." *New Left Review* 211 (May–June 1995): 3–32.

Weber, Samuel. *Mass Mediauras: Essays on Form, Technics and Media*. Stanford: Stanford UP, 1995.

———. "Humanitarian Interventions in the Age of the Media." Forthcoming.

3

Virtual Topographies
Smooth and Striated Cyberspace

Mark Nunes

With increasing frequency, cultural representations of Internet call on us to conceive of computer-mediated communication in terms of space: more precisely, "cyberspace." This spatiality writes place and distance onto the medium, creating, as it were, a topography that becomes more salient to the user than the underlying configuration of technology. "Topography" serves as a highly appropriate word within a discussion of how these metaphors "write" space. As J. Hillis Miller uses the term, topographies are performative speech acts that simultaneously map and create a territory (4–5). With Internet, this performative function is even more marked, since no reassuring "ground" rests beneath the writing of place. Miller goes on to note that

> "Topography" originally meant the creation of a metaphorical equivalent in words of a landscape. Then, by another transfer, it came to mean representation of a landscape according to the conventional signs of some system of mapping. Finally, by a third transfer, the name of the map was carried over to name what is mapped. (3)

This blurring of metaphor and metonym describes the current process by which "cyberspace" comes into being. Naming cyberspace reveals and creates a virtual location for actual experiences. This popular acceptance of cyberspace as a space has not needed to wait for the arrival of bodysuit-and-goggle "virtual reality"; for literally millions of users, cyberspace already "exists" as a *place*, as real as the work and play conducted "in" it.

That is not to say that only *one* virtual topography exists. Rather, we see in government documents, in the media, in scholarly journals, and in popular reports signs of cyber*spaces*: multiple and competing spatial figurations. Two metaphors, I would argue, have received considerable amount of currency and describe two very different topographies, found even in the banal expressions "Surf the 'Net" and "Cruise the Information Superhighway." These terms reveal two very different figurations of virtual topography: one that is fluid, plane-oriented, and unbounded; the other that is linear, point-oriented, and Cartesian.[1] These two figurations of space correspond to Gilles Deleuze and Felix Guattari's description of smooth and striated space. The highway metaphor calls to mind a system that facilitates and regulates the flow of traffic from destination to destination. In other words, it striates space by setting up a system where "lines and trajectories tend to be subordinated to points: one goes from one point to another" (Deleuze and Guattari 478). In "surfing" smooth space, however, "the points are subordinated to the trajectory" (Deleuze and Guattari 478). According to Deleuze and Guattari:

> In striated space, one closes off a surface and "allocates" it according to determinate intervals, assigned breaks; in the smooth, one "distributes" oneself in an open space, according to frequencies and in the course of one's crossings. (481)

Those two functions, allocation and distribution, serve as the dominant organizational principle that differentiates smooth and striated space.

On Internet, however, these metaphors do not just organize space; they *create* a space, or more accurately, they *substantiate* cyberspace as a virtual topography. A striated "highway" topography determines cyberspace as a system of regulated connections between determined points on dedicated lines; conversely, a smooth "plane" topography "writes" a cyberspace of fluid transit and continual passage. The 1995 Microsoft "Where do you want to go today?" campaign, for example, makes use of both topographies, creating two very different images of "cyberspace." In a Microsoft Office and Mail commercial, a female executive in mid-flight calls upon the services of people in Spokane, Washington, who work with her once she arrives in Spain. "Jane on the plane" *cruises* from site to site via global information networks in the same way that her plane travels from point A to point B. In contrast, the Microsoft Encarta commercial shows a man researching hang-gliding who soon finds himself gathering information on birds and other "wingéd things," then drifting off on the winds of a monsoon to India, and finally to the Himalayas. Both commercials ask the viewer to conceive of a virtual topography by presenting an image of navigation (asking, "Where do you want to go today?" at the end of the spot), but the space that the Encarta user traverses is significantly different from the space portrayed in the Office ad. The Encarta commercial writes a space that is planar and fluid, whereas in the Office commercial, cyberspace is a highway of sorts connecting terminal points in a simulated world.

In their general discussion of smooth and striated space, Deleuze and Guattari associate these two spatial arrangements with two systems: one that is State-oriented and static, the other nomadic and fluid. Striation allows for State functioning by creating what Michael Menser calls a "gravitational space," which sets up the State as "the central organizational organism" or regulatory body (298). That does not mean that striation attempts to *shut down* the medium; rather, it allocates and organizes functionalities into productive modes. Striated cyberspace sets out to function as a simulated world that overcomes real space by providing more direct (point to point) contact and therefore greater efficiency. This image forms the core assumption of the White House's National Information Infrastructure (NII) "Agenda for Action," which presents the NII (and for now, Internet) as a surrogate space that replaces the real world by overcoming the real world's limits. In cyberspace "the best schools, teachers, and courses [are] available without regard to geography, distances, resources, or disability. . . . The vast resources of art, literature, and science [are] available everywhere" ("Agenda"). But these resources can only become "available everywhere" once "everywhere" is connected through this striated topography of point-to-point contact. Furthermore, in a striated space, if you are *not* connected, you are *nowhere*. By this gravitational principle, then, terminal points can only "signify" once they are allocated to definite positions within a given system.

As Deleuze and Guattari note, striated spaces of grids, contact, and control are a function of all States, not merely overtly totalitarian structures. In fact, one might argue that much of the desire for a striated virtual topography has its origins in the Enlightenment desire to define natural, political, and ethical laws that would render "the world" comprehensible and controllable. Following this utopian telos brings us, in Baudrillard's words, to a hyperreal moment beyond its own ends: when the ideal model for the world *becomes* the world itself (3–4). Striated cyberspace promises to outdo the real world by freeing action from the limit(ation)s of real space. Discussions of Internet that assume a striated topography see the medium as not only providing for more efficient commerce, but also "develop[ing] new 'electronic communities' [for sharing] knowledge and experience that can improve the way that [citizens] learn, work, play, and participate in the American Democracy" ("Agenda"). Other utopian conceptions of cyberspace make use of the metaphor of the city or "electronic agorae": points of community stockpile or "collective goods," with an implicit or explicit call for citizenship in a collective (state) body (Rheingold 13). At a further extreme, Internet-as-cyberspace provides the site for virtual realities that can create "societies more decent and free than those mapped onto dirt and concrete and capital" (Dibbell 37). Implicit in each description of a utopic cyberspace is a topography of "lines and trajectories . . . subordinated to points" (Deleuze and Guattari 478). Cyberspace figures as a multitude of interconnected "sites"; thus, the "highway," however poor a metaphor it may be for the *technical* functioning of Internet communication, accurately captures the topography of *user interface*: a striated space in which lines connect terminal points.

In representations of smooth cyberspace, however, as in the Encarta ad, "lines of flight" replace points of contact. For Deleuze and Guattari, smooth space sets up a nomadic system of movement (480). Lines become vectors, rather than units of measurement: "a direction and not a dimension or metric determination" (Deleuze and Guattari 478). As opposed to the gravitational space of a striated topography, a smooth topography provides a space of "deterritorialization" in which points "are strictly subordinated to the paths they determine. . . . Every point is a relay and exists only as a relay" (Deleuze and Guattari 380). The most frequent references to a smooth cyberspace concern hypertext applications like Encarta, or more significantly, the World Wide Web (WWW). As Netscape's ship-wheel logo implies, the smooth topography of the WWW more closely resembles the sea than the highway, giving users "infinite" degrees of freedom. Here we need to rethink "topography" as an opening of terrain to multiple passages, rather than as the mapping of a specific *topos*.[2] Jay Bolter uses similar language to describe the topographic "writing space" of hypertext: "not the writing of a place, but rather the writing with places, spatially realized topics" (25). Instead of allocating virtual space, the WWW distributes and displaces it; it presents a "rhizomatic" 'Net-scape' in which "webpages" serve as pointers rather than terminal points. This topography, of course, provides no more accurate a portrayal of the technical functioning of networked communication than striating metaphors, but at the level of user interface, "surfing" accurately depicts this process of distributing oneself across smooth cyberspace.

While "surfing" has been the predominant media image associated with smooth topography, in some circles, this image of a smooth cyberspace draws explicitly on the language of Deleuze and Guattari and the rhizome. As Douglas Stanley notes on the Deleuze-Guattari listserv: "Rhizome has become a kind of catchword in 'cyberspace': almost as if Gibson and McLuhan were a little old-hat and hipsters had to find other *dinosaurs*" ("More").[3] Likewise, Steve Shaviro quite explicitly claims:

> World Wide Web browsers turn the Internet into what Deleuze and Guattari call smooth or *rhizomatic* space: a space of "acentered systems, finite networks of automata in which communication runs from any neighbor to any other, the stems or channels do not preexist, and all individuals are interchangeable, defined only by their state at a given moment." ("12.Bill")

Shaviro describes Internet, and in particular, networked virtual realities, as a realization of Foucault's heterotopias: metastable and dynamic "otherspaces, or spaces of otherness," formed by "shifting subjectivities" and "nomadic displacements" ("13.Pavel"). The result of this embrace of Deleuzean language, particularly among various hypertext theorists, has been an attempt to create from these smooth figurations a space in which "theory" becomes an actuality. George Landow, for example, comments that hypertext provides an "almost embarrassingly literal embodiment" of literary theory (34). He writes:

> Critical theory promises to theorize hypertext and hypertext promises to embody and thereby test aspects of theory, particularly those concerning textuality, narrative, and the roles or functions of reader and writer. (3)

Unlike the utopic desire to create a body politic in striated space, this smooth space desire creates an embodiment for openness and flow. In the same manner that striating metaphors substantiate a topography of allocation, this spatial embodiment (a "body without organs") provides a ground that substantiates a topography of distribution.

Given the "distance" between these two spatial figurations, it should be no surprise that they often appear as opposing terms to one another. From "within" a State/striated topography, nomad/smooth space appears as a dangerous zone, in need of containment. References to smooth space within striated topographies refer to it as a wild "beyond," or as a frontier waiting for its settlers and pioneers. Services such as CompuServe and America Online, for example, provide Internet access beyond the confines of their closed, regulated domain, but present this "beyond" as an at-your-own-risk wilderness: that which lies outside of community. Much of the concern over pornography on Internet draws on similar language to associate "uncontrolled" and "unregulated" with "dangerous" and "obscene." Gary Bauer of the Family Research Council, for example, evoked images of a perilously "open" cyberspace when calling for legislation that would "eliminate 'cyberspace' as a safe haven for pornographers . . . by criminalizing 'free' obscenity on the Internet" ("Senate"). Conversely, "within" smooth topographies, striation appears as a resistance to the "natural" openness of smooth space. Robert Adrian, for example, describes the "Information Superhighway" as a restrictive and regulatory construct laid on top of a more open and originative "cyberspace":

> Cyberspace has no highways or interchanges or even direction, it is just a vast universe of connections in a multidimensional data grid. You can get lost in cyberspace. . . . Cyberspace is infinite, chaotic and scary, while Mr. Gore's Superhighway is finite, linear, and very familiar—at least to suburban Americans.

The assumptions of a smooth topography imply that striation violates the "nature" of the medium: that information, to borrow John Perry Barlow's phrase, "wants to be free" (Shaviro, "12.Bill"). As a smooth topography, cyberspace is *"emphatically* non-linear and non-local[;] its preferred modes of narration would *inherently* involve distributedness, multiplicity, emergence, and open-endedness" (emphasis mine, Novak, "Transmitting"). In this fluid topography, computer-mediated communication is about the *flow* of information and ideas; regulation and striation amount to a strangulation of that flow and a death of the medium.

If these two competing topographies were simply conflicting figures of speech, then the problem between them would amount to nothing more than a matter of mixed metaphors. Quite the contrary, however; as topographies, these descriptions of Internet create and reveal a spatiality, much in the way that topographies in general function as performative speech acts (Miller 4–5). By calling a virtual topography a performative speech act, I am distinguishing between, in Austin's phrase, *"doing* something rather than simply *saying* something" with words ("Performative" 235). Deleuze and Guattari carry this point further by describing these performative (or "illocutionary") acts as "order-words": utterances that arrange and order (in both senses) the world (78). These acts are immanent and internal to the expression, yet they have a transformative power (Austin's "illocutionary force") on "bodies"—that which occupies space and time in the world. These acts are therefore "incorporeal transformations" in the sense that the acts are without bodies themselves, yet their transformation occurs on bodies in the world.[4] In working through his definition of performative and illocutionary acts, Austin makes a point of emphasizing the importance of a context that will both acknowledge and provide reference for the "force" of an utterance.[5] In a similar way, Deleuze and Guattari stress the context or "pragmatic implications" of these acts. They define this social aspect (the context that gives these order-words force) as a "collective assemblage of enunciation": "the set of all *incorporeal transformations* current in a given society and *attributed* to the bodies of that society" (80). These variable enunciations, given force by a pragmatic context, order and determine subjectivities and relations; it is thus always a matter of the "pragmatic implications" of these utterances, not merely their "signification" (83). In simplest language, then, these assemblages of enunciation are not merely "figures of speech"; they serve as expressions of possible (and variable) relations within a given pragmatic context.[6]

To transpose this vocabulary onto our discussion of Internet, then, would be to describe these two topographies as competing assemblages of enunciation within the shared context of computer-mediated communication.[7] Although these assemblages are variable, they tend to move from expressions of potential ("conditions of possibility") to "determinable relations," at which point the assemblage functions as a "regime or signs" or a "semiotic machine" (Deleuze and Guattari 83). In terms of virtual topography, the more *substantial* the space, either smooth or striated, the more *determined* the sorts of relations that can occur within that space—and the more limited the conditions of possibility. A determined striated topography, then, is "efficient" in capturing smooth space and transforming it into a mode within its regime. For example, in order to maintain its State-oriented ARPANET, the Department of Defense had to find a means of allocating non-governmental communication (mostly discussions about science fiction and interactive fantasy games) within the function of its Advanced Research Projects Agency (ARPA); rather than shutting down communication, ARPANET administrators permitted (captured) this flow, seeing it as a mode within a larger system of productivity (Rheingold 179–80). France's Minitel system provides a similar example of how a striated topography orders space into determined relations. France's initial plan for "the world's largest information utility" failed to the extent that the French citizens were fairly uninterested in the information services offered by the government (Rheingold 11). In fact, the popularity of the system in France came about only as a result of a "hack" to the system that allowed unauthorized user-to-user communication (Rheingold 227–28). The State moved to capture this smooth flow by "legitimating" this feature on Minitel; usage surged, but again in unseen directions—Minitel became a popular forum for on-line sexual encounters and electronic rendezvous. During this first nationwide swell in popularity, the Minitel system was overwhelmed by the volume of communications—at one point to the level of crashing the system (Rheingold 230). The system was failing not through overrestriction, but through the unregulated (smooth) flow of information that could not be brought into a determinable relation in a striated system. Like the ARPA administrators, however, Minitel succeeded as a system when it learned how to allocate these communications under the function of *messageries roses*, just one sexual part in a larger, profitable, State-run body.[8]

While these "historic" examples provide a compelling account of State-based striation, perhaps the most common and clearest means by which a striated virtual topography functions as a "regime" is by setting up a determinable relation of interconnected sites. This allocation of space (architectural and otherwise) is what Michael Menser describes as the "organ-izing" principle of the State (295). This principle defines cyberspace as an interdependent whole (or body), while at the same time establishing individual sites as organs or terminal points. On Internet, these organs often appear as architectural units, or more generally, "virtual cities," in that points of entry and exit delimit their structure. For Virilio, as well as Deleuze and Guattari, the state system functions by "a transformation of the world into a city" (Deleuze and Guattari 212). Conversely, on Internet striation transforms the (virtual) city into a world. The city appears as "the striated space par excellence" to the extent that it functions as a definite/defined site (Deleuze and Guattari 481). William Mitchell's *City of Bits*, for example, returns repeatedly to the determined relation of "the city" as a metaphor for virtual allocative structures. A good portion of his book describes the various forms this new city can take—from simplistic cartological depictions of information sites to speculations about complex "inhabitable" virtual realities in which physical movements effect the user's environment. On-line, he argues, "the solvent of digital information decomposes traditional building types. . . . Then the residue of recombinant fragments yields up mutants" (47). This "recombinant architecture" promises to overcome real-world (striated) spatial concerns of distance and access by creating virtual structures to replace them: structures, however, that depend upon allocation, containment, and geometric navigation. Although "inhabitation" in the virtual city "has less to do with parking your bones in architecturally defined space and more with connecting your nervous system to nearby electronic organs," striation and allocation still remain its condition of possibility (Mitchell 30). The allocative re-gime of the city, real or virtual, depends on this organ-ization of func-tion into modes or discrete locations.

Striation, Deleuze and Guattari note, transforms territory into "land," which awaits allocation as property/proper place (440). Esther Dyson expresses a similar vision of Internet when describing cyber-space as real estate: "an intellectual, legal, artificial environment con-structed *on top of* land" (26). But when distributive principles replace allocative principles, "land" deterritorializes; the striated city space gives way to the smooth "field," where inside and outside no longer de-termine function. In place of the allocative architecture of the virtual city, one finds in smooth cyberspace interactions determined by dis-tributive relations, such as in Lebbeus Woods's conception of free-spaces: "a series of interior landscapes joined only by the electronic in-strumentation of speed-of-light communications, in ever-changing interactions with one another and with a community of inhabitants cre-ated only through the vagaries of dialogue" (286). Woods's descrip-tion of a network of people, machines, and real-world structures spills out beyond the computer screen. This cyberspace is truly "virtual" in the Deleuzean sense: an indeterminate "heterarchitecture" that changes with the participants who interact with the space:[9]

> In freespace, what is lost is the familiarity of architectural and so-cial norms, the reassurance of control by stable authority, and of predictability, certainty, and the routinization of behavior. What is gained is not an answer to the perpetual question of space, but simply a clear articulation of its potential. From this everything else flows. (Woods 290)

Unlike Mitchell's recombinant architecture, with its metaphors for allocation of function, the smooth space of what Marcos Novak calls "liquid architecture" determines a different condition of possibility: a "transphysical city" quite opposed to the notion of stable inside/outside environments (Novak, "Transmitting").[10]

Woods and Novak on one hand, as well as Mitchell on the other, use architecture to discuss the conditions of possibility made actual by assemblages of enunciation. In their most determined forms, these as-semblages express themselves through user interfaces, which do indeed perform the architectural function of creating (and thus revealing) an "environment." Hypertext applications like Encarta, for example, "re-veal" a nomadic information space by providing an interface that al-lows users to "move" in a non-linear or multilinear fashion. Hypertext interfaces take part in an assemblage governed by the semiotic regime of "the network" or "*docuverse*": an expanding, altering realm of connected information (Landow 24). In a hypertext,

> [e]very path defines an equally convincing and appropriate reading, and in that simple fact the reader's relationship to the text [the "writing space"] changes radically. A text as a network has no univocal sense; it is a multiplicity without the imposition of a principle of domination. (Bolter 25)

When World Wide Web designers began to apply this hypertextual interface to the Internet, the result was a user interface that altered and grew with each person using it: a docuverse of worldwide connections. "The variability, the polyvocality of directions" that Deleuze and Guattari associate with the rhizome and smooth space equally describes the topography of hypertext: a "localized and not delimited" variable cartography (382). In place of the "relative global" of the cybernetic city, the World Wide Web's hypertextual links create a nomadic "local absolute" (Deleuze and Guattari 382). The "unfolding" of each page onto another both creates and reveals a smooth topography. The interface encourages users to navigate this space primarily by way of drift: "browsing" from link to link, rather than moving from destination to destination. "Homepages," in other words, function less as architectural homes than as points of passage in a multiplicity.

While hypertext applications like web browsers are capable of substantiating a smooth space in which each "web page" serves as a relay or passage, striating applications such as e-mail, ftp, and telnet create and reveal a cyberspace of definite sites and point-to-point contact. In each of these applications, an address serves as a destination or a resting place, not a relay; with ftp and telnet in particular, "arriving" is followed by logging "into" the site, calling to mind again Mitchell's notion of inhabitation in a virtual city. Unlike the rhizomatic structure that Shaviro and others find in the hypertextual unfolding of the WWW, these striating applications set up a virtual topography that is noticeably organ-ized; more so, this space tends toward hierarchy (or "arborescence"). On-line service "chatrooms" provide perhaps the most well-known example of the hierarchical organization of space, in which discussion topics become discreet *topoi*.[11] Again, this allocative organization of space tends toward the image of the walled-in city, with "rooms" serving as architectural units within a larger, regulated system.

Perhaps the current extreme of this sort of striating application are the "text-based virtual realities" known as Multi-User Domains

(MUDs) or MOOs (MUD, Object-oriented). Like "chatrooms" on AOL and CompuServe, MOO "community" begins with a password-based logon: a passage through the cybercity gates, so to speak.[12] But MOOs carry this medium a step further toward becoming an inhabitable world by encouraging users to "flesh out" this topography by providing written descriptions of themselves (or rather, their "player-object"), their rooms, and their various possessions. Furthermore, the application simulates space by asking users to interact with each other within explicit references to architectural entrances and exits as well as cartological "ways." In a MOO your presence expresses itself in terms of proximity to other players within this "virtual space." In fact, players *literally inhabit* rooms in the MOO; a player-object stays "inside" the MOO, waiting for its player/user to log on and "awaken" it. All actions occur within this closed, defined system of the MOO "as a whole" (a cybercity), and within the strictures of a hierarchical arrangement of permissions. While the notion of a "text-based virtual reality" may seem bizarre to many, in terms of organization of space, this application substantiates an allocative topography that is no different from the highly legible virtual world described in the White House's "Agenda for Action"; it enacts what Roland Barthes calls "the popular and age old image of the perfect intelligibility of reality" by creating a "model" world in which we can live our virtual lives (24).[13] The goal of the application, then, is not to establish a nomadic flow of users and information; quite the opposite, this striating user interface aims at creating a stable, inhabitable world.

Cyberspace, then, reveals itself quite differently depending on whether one is "in" a MOO or "browsing" through websites. In both instances, user interfaces function as part of a regime of signs which, at the level of the user, determines cyberspace. In the same way that World Wide Web browsers attempt to "overflow" location and make individual pages "subordinated to the paths they determine," the gravitational space of the MOO determines a different sort of space, one in which "going" becomes far less important than "arriving" and coming to a rest (Deleuze and Guattari 380). This gravity captures singularities and turns them into modes or parts of the system's own organizing principle. Since the MOO must maintain its hierarchical structure of builder, programmer, and wizard in order to function, one must suspect the ways in which code-level hierarchies of similar applications will eventually undermine the most utopian dreams for egalitarian cyberspace. Although this image of inhabitable cyberspace provides all sorts of opportunities for exploring ontology, and in particular, the assumptions that lead to our understanding of body, presence, and community, the striating desire behind this topography often leads to erasure of these questions, not exploration. This desire for a duplicate world, or rather a more controllable, more "model" world, calls on its residents to *legitimate* community, make it legible, lawful, and "defined," not challenge or destabilize its assumptions.

In the same way that the gravitational space of the MOO tends to reorganize disruption into its own system, one would expect to find in smooth space a tendency to encourage what Deleuze and Guattari describe as a process of deterritorialization. As George Landow notes, this hypertextual docuverse has no center of gravity; the center "exists only as a matter of evanescence" (70). Instead of atoms or organs, the experience of smooth space is one of "morphing": a motion *through* one point on to the next (Novak, "TransUrban"). Community, therefore, would resemble a nomadic band or pack, in contrast to organ-ized structures like family or citizenry (Deleuze and Guattari 33–36). Kathleen Burnett, for example, sees the current rise in academic on-line communication as the emergence of a "modest-but growing community of electronic scholars" ("Scholar's"). She locates this burgeoning "scholars' rhizome" opposite traditional hierarchical academic structures, claiming that hierarchy is "antithetical to the milieu itself," and sees it as heralding massive change in our understanding of authorship, collaboration, and interaction ("Scholar's"). In this regard, theorists like Shaviro are justified in contrasting the tree hierarchy of topic/*topoi*-based communities to the rhizomatic community of webpages, in which a proliferation of connections can lead to decentered communications, self-publishing, and the breakdown of textual hierarchy. Unlike striated community's call to legitimate itself, the smooth nomadic community defines itself by its fluidity and its metastable structure.

But as Deleuze and Guattari point out at the end of *A Thousand Plateaus*, "never believe that a smooth space will suffice to save us" (500). Burnett's description of a "scholar's rhizome," along with numerous other visions of a liberatory cybernetic space that enacts "open" theory, provide in many ways an equally determinate regime of signs. In the same way that the semiotic machine of a striated topography must continually attempt to bring singularities into the gravitational pull of the State, smooth topographies must continually move to overflow all attempts to make the field "productive." A truly rhizomatic space cannot fall into hierarchical organizations of information such as, to use the "scholars' rhizome" as an example, peer-reviewed journals. At its smoothest, then, one could not even talk of a "signal to noise" ratio of information, since nomadic deterritorialization would level any attempt to extract the "productive" as a mode from the general flow of signals from point to point. A *determined* smoothness, therefore, yields its own sort of "death sentence": an "absolute" flight either away from the real or toward annihilation (Deleuze and Guattari 110). While the gravitational space of a determined striated topography functions as a "black hole," a determined smooth topography presents its own inescapable space: a formless, blank wall upon which nothing can be written (Deleuze and Guattari 166–68).

In either topography, then, a problem emerges to the extent that cyberspace becomes determined as *being* one topography or the other. Instead, one finds these competing assemblages of enunciation creating and revealing mixed topographies.[14] Any account of computer-mediated communication that seriously engages the conception of "cyberspace," then, would have to come to terms with the mixing of these two topographies. This vision of computer-mediated communication occurs in Hakim Bey's account of "the Net" and "the Web," in which piratic, nomadic smooth space constantly erupts from within the striated space of legitimated government and business activities, like Mandelbrot peninsulas "hidden within the map" (112). Likewise, the conditions of possibility determined by a smooth regime are not immune to striating forces. Martin Rosenberg, co-designer of the RHIZOME writing application, notes that even the apparently "smooth" multiple, non-linear linkages of a hypertext cannot escape from the striating "geometric ideological construct" underlying its rhizomatic appearances (287). And as Allucquere Stone notes, even at its literary origins in *Neuromancer*, "cyberspace" involves this mixture between the "grid" of information set out in Cartesian space, and the "smoothing" nomadic effect of the hacker "cowboys" who roam this space (Benedikt 104).[15] Unlike descriptions of cyberspace that take part in determined smooth or striated regimes, each of these approaches foregrounds a crucial aspect in the discussion of virtual topographies: that is, the importance of examining the mixtures of these topographies and the passages that occur between these two limits.

The challenge in understanding virtual topographies, then, involves a recognition of the mixture of these two assemblages, as well as an awareness of the attempt of each to deny this mixture. Either determination of cyberspace as smooth or striated topography involves a system of overcoding and a homogenization of space as either "purely" nomadic or state oriented: what Shawn Wilbur called in one on-line discussion the "will to smooth or striate" ("Smooth"). He notes:

Aren't smooth and striated, as such, limits of a sort, not conditions of being? . . . I guess I'm inclined to understand "the net" or "the

WWW" as both smooth and striated. . . . [Arguments for either one] finally tend to come down on the side of control, since the question continues to be one of being, rather than becoming or creation. ("Smooth")

As either topography moves toward an overcoding of Internet into a regime of signs, the topography becomes actual and the ground—either smooth or striated—begins to emerge. At this point, the conditions of possibility set up by a topography begin to close, thus functioning as a limit on the medium, rather than as a liberation.

Perhaps, then, it would be more accurate to refer to Internet not *as* cyberspace, but rather, as the pragmatic context for both enunciations of cyberspace. Within this on-line context, one will find both productions of space playing for their own substantiation. However, one would also expect to find tendencies of each topography in the other: the smooth irrupting in the striated, the striated capturing the smooth. No matter how "rhizomatic" the WWW becomes, striated features will emerge to capture fields and make them productive. Likewise, MOOs and on-line communities will constantly experience the destabilizing emergence of "pirate utopias" within their virtual city walls. In navigating topographies in which striation determines an organ-ized space, one would have to recognize the enunciation of this gravity and search for that which provides an escape velocity from this closed system. Likewise, in smooth topographies, one would expect to find a nomadic regime at work, as well as an inescapable pull toward striation and production. The attempt at a purity through either systematic approach to virtual topography denies that cyberspace hovers between these two regimes. This mixing provides crossings for both systems that keep cyberspace always "virtual," always in the act of becoming: real, yet never completely determined.

Notes

1. It is worth noting that both metaphors present an image (and a stereotypically male one at that) of freedom in motion: to surf and to cruise. What separates these two metaphors is the space in which these activities can occur. "Cruising" involves a linear motion within a bounded space: one moves directionally. In "surfing," however, the ground itself appears unstable; the freedom involves "catching the wave," rather than mastering the routes.

2. The distinction here parallels Deleuze and Guattari's distinction between a "mapping" and a "tracing"; a map marks a variable terrain of passages,

whereas a trace can only repeat the same path. See *A Thousand Plateaus*, 12–15.

3. The Deleuze-Guattari list is part of the Spoon Collective of theory-related discussion lists, housed at the University of Virginia. To subscribe, send an email message reading "subscribe deleuze-guattari" to majordomo@lists.village.virginia.edu

4. In *A User's Guide to Capitalism and Schizophrenia* (Cambridge: MIT P, 1992), Brian Massumi quite simply defines this somewhat awkward term "incorporeal transformation" as an "event" or encounter in which "nothing touched you, yet you have been transformed" (28). This event is "enveloped" in language, but its "nondiscursive force" creates a felt change in the world (29–30).

5. For a more complete discussion of speech acts and "illocutionary force," see Austin's *How to Do Things with Words* (Cambridge: Harvard UP, 1975), and in particular, Lecture IX, pp. 109–20.

6. For further clarification of Deleuze and Guattari's discussion of performatives and incorporeal transformation, see *A Thousand Plateaus* 75–110. See also Massumi, 10–46.

7. Guattari in later writing has addressed how computer-mediated communication can "not merely convey representational contents, but also contribute to the fabrication of new *assemblages* of enunciation, individual and collective" (19). See "Regimes, Pathways, Subjects" (*Incorporations*, New York: Zone, 1992) for a discussion of machines, assemblages of enunciation, and the production of subjectivities.

8. For a complete history of Minitel, see Rheingold's "*Telematique* and *Messageries Roses*" in *The Virtual Community* (Reading, MA: Addison-Wesley, 1993), 220–40.

9. Although the computer industry uses "virtual" to mean "not real, but real enough," for Deleuze, following Bergson, "virtual" implies real potential, standing in opposition to the "actual," an act of determination. In this regard, the "virtual" is always real, but not yet actual. See Deleuze and Guattari 94–99.

10. In a critique of Mitchell's *City of Bits*, Novak makes specific reference to Mitchell's tendency to envision a striated, closed architecture for cyberspace. He writes: "The Aristotelian logic that inspires *City of Bits* also leaves Mitchell waiting for Hippodamos, looking for a grid logic to contain cyberspace. His taxonomic comprehensives [*sic*] is arborescent, not rhizomatic. The book's extrapolations are frequently quite daring, but all too often see" ("TransUrban"). Novak's comments also demonstrate the often antagonistic relation between smooth and striated enunciations of cyberspace.

11. Internet USENET groups function along similiar lines in that discussion "groups" form by way of heirarchical/topical branchings. As Allucquere Rosanne Stone notes, this "tree-structured conference" arrangement of shared writing space (what I would call a striated topography) served as the

basis for the earliest on-line communities. See Benedikt, *Cyberspace: First Steps* (Cambridge: MIT P, 1991) 89.

12. Many of these communities exist within the walls of standards and protocols. Violation of these standards can result in a form of "shunning" by the community, or worse: true ostracism, in which the player is removed from the database and ceases to exist. See, for example, Dibbell's "A Rape in Cyberspace," *Village Voice* 21 December 1993: 36–42.

13. This striating image of cyberspace as a model or simulatory world occurs in the media, interestingly enough, both as a positive and a negative aspect of Internet. It provides ground for Microsoft's "Where do you want to go today?" campaign, but it also provides the context for Volkswagen's skeptical "Are you *real*-ly free?" spots.

14. Although the "regime of signs" denies this mixture, Deleuze and Guattari assert that neither smooth nor striated space exists as a stable entity. Instead, "smooth space is constantly being translated, traversed into a striated space; striated space is constantly being reversed, returned to a smooth space" (474).

15. Recent on-line developments accentuate both the attempt to determine cyberspace as a given topography, as well as the mixed nature of these enunciations. Apple announced early in 1996 that it would close its on-line community, eWorld, and move its services to the WWW: an apparent victory for smooth space. During the same period, however, Netscape was releasing version 2.0 of its application, calling it a (striating) *navigator* and discouraging all references to it as a (nomadic) browser.

Works Cited

Adrian, Robert. "Infobahn Blues." *CTHEORY* (1995).
  http://www. ctheory.com/a-infobahn__blues.html
"Agenda for Action." 1994.
  http://sunsite.unc.edu/nii/NII-Agenda-for-Action.html
Austin, J. L. *How to Do Things with Words*. Cambridge: Harvard UP, 1975.
———. "Performative Utterances." *Philosophical Papers*. Cambridge: Harvard UP, 1962.
Baudrillard, Jean. *Simulations*. New York: Semiotext(e), 1983.
Benedikt, Michael, ed. *Cyberspace: First Steps*. Cambridge: MIT Press, 1991.
Bey, Hakim. *T. A.Z.* New York: Autonomedia, 1991.
Bolter, Jay David. *Writing Space*. Hillsdale, NJ: Lawrence Erlbaum, 1991.
Burnett, Kathleen. "The Scholar's Rhizome." (1993).
  http://www.uni-koeln.de/themen/cmc/text/burnett.93.txt
Deleuze, Gilles, and Félix Guattari. *A Thousand Plateaus*. Minneapolis: U of Minnesota P, 1984.
Dibbell, Julian. "A Rape in Cyberspace." *Village Voice* 21 December 1993: 36–42.

Dyson, Esther. "If You Don't Love It, Leave It." *New York Times Magazine* 16 July 1995: 26–27.

Guattari, Felix. "Regimes, Pathways, Subjects." *Incorporations*. New York: Zone, 1992. 16–37.

Landow, George. *Hypertext*. Baltimore: Johns Hopkins UP, 1992.

Massumi, Brian. *A User's Guide to Capitalism and Schizophrenia*. Cambridge: MIT P, 1992.

Menser, Michael. "Becoming-Heterarch: On Technocultural Theory, Minor Science, and the Production of Space." *Technoscience and Cyberculture*. New York: Routledge, 1996. 293–316.

Miller, J. Hillis. *Topographies*. Stanford: Stanford UP, 1995.

Mitchell, William. *City of Bits*. Cambridge: MIT P, 1995.

"More on D+G+Internet." Ed. and comp. Mark Nunes. 1995.
  http:// www.dc.peachnet.edu/~mnunes/d2.html

Novak, Marcos. "Transmitting Architecture: The Transphysical City." *CTHEORY* (1995).
  http://www.ctheory.com/ a34-transmitting__arch.html

———. "TransUrban Optimism After the Maul of America." *CTHEORY* (1995).
  http://www.ctheory.com/r41-transurban__optimism.html

Rheingold, Howard. *The Virtual Community*. Reading, MA: Addison-Wesley, 1993.

Rosenberg, Martin E. "Physics and Hypertext: Liberation and Complicity in Art and Pedagogy." *Hyper/Text/Theory*. Ed. George P. Landow. Baltimore: Johns Hopkins UP, 1994. 268–98.

"Senate Debate." *104th Congressional Record*. 14 June, 1995.
  Gopher://gopher.panix.com:70/0/vtw/exon/legislation/senate-debate

Shaviro, Steven. "12.Bill Gates." *Doom Patrols*. 1995.
  http://dhalgren.english.washington.edu/~steve/ch12.html

———. "13.Pavel Curtis." *Doom Patrols*. 1995.
  http://dhalgren. english.washington.edu/~steve/ch13.html

"Smooth/Striated Cyberspace." Ed. and comp. Mark Nunes. 1995.
  http://www.dc.peachnet.edu/~mnunes/smooth.html

Woods, Lebbeus. "The Question of Space." *Technoscience and Cyberculture*. New York: Routledge, 1996. 279–292.

4

Cyberspace, Virtuality, and the Text

Marie-Laure Ryan

As computers took over our lives, two words invaded our vocabulary: "cyberspace" and "virtual." The first is a brash neologism, coined (out of two venerable roots) by a science fiction writer: William Gibson in *Neuromancer*. The second carries the prestige and load of a philosophical tradition dating back to the Middle Ages. Yet despite their strikingly different origins, "cyberspace" and "virtual" have come to be almost interchangeable, especially if "virtual" is appended to "reality." To the popular imagination, computers take us into cyberspace, and cyberspace is a virtual reality. The language fundamentalist may object to the semantic slippage that has led to this convergence of originally distinct signifiers. But the historian of the imagination, of culture, and of ideas should find an intriguing field of investigation in the powerful magnetism of these strange attractors. In the present essay, I propose to explore the nexus of ideas that have been associated with cyberspace and led to its merging with virtual reality. For this purpose, I will distinguish VR (the technology) from virtual realities (creations of the imagination), and from the philosophical concept of virtuality. My purpose in trying to unravel these threads is threefold: to give an overview of the intellectual climate that favored the emergence of the forms of textuality discussed in this volume, to prevent the association of VR and cyberspace from being taken for granted, and to gain a better understanding of the significance of the concept of virtuality for theories of textuality.

The entanglement of cyberspace with virtual reality took place in various forms of discourse: literature, technological speculation, and mass media. After its celebrated debut in William Gibson's *Neuro-*

mancer (1981), cyberspace served as the inspiration for the label of a literary movement (Cyberpunk). A few years later it became a leitmotiv in the prophecies of developers of computer technology and theorists of computer culture. By the mid-nineties, it was solidly established in popular media, advertisement, and common parlance, and "cyber" was on its way to becoming a standard English prefix (cyberculture, cyberchat, cybersex, cyberporn). Through these successive recontextualizations, the connotations of the term have swung from dystopic to wildly utopian to an ambiguous blend of fear and excitement. This is a remarkable career for a word whose referent is neither a palpable thing, nor a scientific or philosophical concept, nor even a technology—a word which seems in fact to have been deliberately created to bring support to the non-referential theories of language favored by the latter-day disciples of Saussure. As William Gibson wrote ten years after coining the word: "Assembled word *cyberspace* from small and readily available components of language. Neologic spasm: the primal act of pop poetics. Preceded any concept whatever. Slick and hollow—awaiting received meaning" ("Academy Leader" 27). Born without meaning, cyberspace is born without essence. Free of cultural tradition, the empty vessel of the neologism is pure potential. From its very beginning, cyberspace embodies the virtual.

When cyberspace enters literature on the third page of *Neuromancer*, however, it designates something reasonably precise: the function of a (computer) deck. This function is to connect the user to a system named the matrix: "He'd [Case] operated on an almost permanent adrenaline high, a byproduct of youth and proficiency, jacked into a custom cyberspace deck that projected his disembodied consciousness into the consensual hallucination that was the matrix" (5). The interdependency of cyberspace and the matrix is confirmed fifty pages later, when cyberspace makes its second (and last) appearance:

> "The matrix has its roots in primitive arcade games," said the voice-over, "in early graphics programs and military experimentation with cranial jacks." . . . "Cyberspace. A consensual hallucination experienced daily by billions of legitimate operators, in every nation, by children being taught mathematical concepts. A graphic representation of data abstracted from the banks of every computer in the human system. Unthinkable complexity. Lines of light ranged in the nonspace of the mind, clusters and constellations of data. Like city lights, receding." (51)

This definition of the matrix ties together two themes: the idea of a world-spanning computer network functioning as meeting place for billions of users separated by physical space; and the idea of being immersed in a graphic display projected by computer data. One idea prefigures the Internet, the other VR technology. A mystical experience highly charged with eroticism (the metaphor of the matrix is used to describe orgasm during real-world love-making), Gibson's cyberspace realizes the Platonic dream of a reality fully accessible to the mind because bodies and their "meat" are recreated by the computer as intelligible patterns of information. The user "jacked" into cyberspace is inside a "sea of information" experienced not as information about something (the real world) but as the very texture of a more-than-real reality. In this hyperreality, the mind reaches fulfillment in a state of total knowledge:

> And there things could be counted, each one. He knew the number of grains of sand in the construct of the beach (a number coded in a mathematical system that existed nowhere outside the mind that was Neuromancer [an AI system]). He knew the number of yellow food packets in the canisters in the bunker (four hundred and seven). He knew the number of brass teeth in the left half of the open zipper of the salt-crusted leather jacket that Linda Lee wore as she trudged along the sunset beach. (258)

Despite its mystical overtones, however, the cyberspace experience of Gibson's fiction remains clouded by dystopic connotations. The matrix is less a space of salvation than an escape from a world made unlivable by technology. When the natural world disappears under the clutter of made-made objects (there is virtually no outdoors in *Neuromancer*), when organic life dies out (horses have long vanished), when physical space is compartmentalized to the point of offering no breathing room (Case lives in a three-meter coffin in the "cheap Hotel"), when individuals are mere pawns in the market wars of ruthless multinational corporations, seeking survival in a flight from a world conquered and plundered by technology into one entirely created by it can only be regarded as a pact with the devil.

Cyberspace as Virtual Reality

The ambiguity of Gibsonian cyberspace vanishes in the early nineties, when the term is appropriated by the speculative discourse of developers, promoters, and other prophets of the nascent VR technology. VR, it will be reminded, is an immersive and interactive experience of a world generated by the computer. It places the user inside data itself, in a three-dimensional space projected by digitally encoded information.

The user's interface to the computer-generated world is her own body, enhanced through such prosthetic equipment as head-mounted displays, datagloves, and bodysuits. In 1988, the creators of a software called Autodesk chose the term "cyberspace" to name their research division (Rheingold 184). The term not only avoided the oxymoron of virtual reality, it also seemed particularly well-suited to designate the "substance" of the three-dimensional space projected by the computer: bits of information, rather than physical territory. The name (or nickname) of "cyberspace technology" gave an identity to the products of the VR industry and facilitated their marketing. [1]

In 1990, the first Conference on Cyberspace was held at the University of Texas at Austin. The text of the papers, together with some other essays written later, were gathered in an influential volume titled *Cyberspace: First Steps*. An interdisciplinary cocktail of lyrical effusion, technical discourse, philosophical reflection, and oracular pronouncements, the collection ratifies the marriage of cyberspace to virtual reality. The following sample of opening sentences—quoted from the papers by Heim, a philosopher, Tomas, an anthropologist, Wexelblatt, an engineer, and Meredith Bricken, an educator—should give the reader an idea of the mandatory, but rather vague character of the association (all italics mine): "With its *virtual* environments and simulated worlds, *cyberspace* is a metaphysical laboratory, a tool for examining our very sense of reality" (Heim, "Erotic" 59). "The computer-generated interactive *virtual* environment of *cyberspace* has recently engaged the creative imagination . . . of researchers from various disciplines" (Tomas 31). "*Cyberspace*, or *virtual realities*, provide us with a number of powerful tools" (Wexelblatt 255). "In a *virtual world*, we are inside an environment of pure information that we can see, hear and touch . . . *Cyberspace* technology couples the functions of the computer with human capabilities" (Bricken 363).

A much more elaborate definition opens the contribution of the architect Marcos Novak:

> Cyberspace is a completely spatialized visualization of all information in global information processing systems, along pathways provided by present and future communication networks, enabling full copresence and interaction of multiple users, allowing input and output from and to the full human sensorium, permitting simulations or real and virtual realities, remote data collection and control through telepresence, and total integration and intercommunication with a full range of intelligent products and environments in real space. (225)

Get it? Novak admits (253) that his definition concatenates six different cyberspaces: Gibsonian, Barlovian (from John Perry Barlow, lyricist for the Grateful Dead, who offers this formula: "cyberspace is where you are when you are on the telephone" [180]), VR, simulation, telepresence, and "making reality a cyberspace," i.e., real-world uses of computer simulation. The definition would be a lot easier to read if the listed components were presented as the diverse applications of computing power and not as the facets of a global experience. Let's replace "cyberspace is" with "computers can do these things," and we will realize that the territory of cyberspace covers nothing less than all recent, future, or merely conceivable applications of electronic technology. Taken apart phrase by phrase, Novak's cyberspace definition offers a comprehensive overview of this territory:

1. *Spatialized visualization of information.* Graphs and tables generated by computer programs; also the three-dimensional visual displays of VR applications.

2. *Global information processing systems.* A universal database, such as the mythical universal electronic library.

3. *Pathways provided by present and future communication networks.* No need for a paraphrase here: the Internet is it.

4. *Co-presence:* What VR developers call telepresence. Users separated in physical space being made present to each other through the encoding and transmission of sensory data emanating from their bodies.

5. *Interaction of multiple users.* The creation of communities through the universal network. MOOs, user-interest groups.

6. *Input and output from and to the full human sensorium.* The ambition of VR technology to provide a multisensory experience. "Output from the full human sensorium" could mean a computer's ability to scan bodies for visual, auditive, olfactory, and tactile data, to digitize this information, and to reconstruct the (illusion of) the body for the user on the other end of the line. The phenomenon is limited so far to science fiction (in *Neuromancer*, Case making love to the reconstructed body of Linda Lee), but Howard Rheingold has a name for its eventual implementation: teledildonics.

7. *Simulations of real and virtual realities.* Notice here the partial dissociation of cyberspace from virtual realities. But this does not necessarily loosen the connection between cyberspace and VR, since VR technology can simulate the real world as well as imaginary ones. Examples: flight simulators (real realities); theme park rides using electronic displays (virtual realities).

8. *Remote data collection and control through telepresence.* VR systems operating on physically remote objects by manipulating their digitized representation. This technological form of voodoo is exemplified by medical uses of VR.

9. *Total integration and intercommunication.* All the threads of life, knowledge, and experience tied together by computers. The dream of a global intelligence synthesizing and linking all information. Examples: Gibson's matrix; Borges's Aleph.

10. *A full range of intelligent products and environments in real space.* The use of AI resources to facilitate access to and manipulation of the data stored in the system. Example: searching algorithms for the Internet; mail scanners, and devices blocking access to censured materials.

For most of the contributors, however, cyberspace is much more than a portmanteau term for applications of electronic technology. It is foremost a catalyzer of dreams. True to Gibson's definition, the cyberspace of *Cyberspace: First Steps* is a collective hallucination of unlimited dimensions, since their number is determined by the imagination. Further down in Novak's text we read: "Cyberspace is poetry inhabited, and to navigate through it is to become a leaf on the wind of a dream" (229). Nicole Stenger, an artist and poet using VR technology, chimes in: "Without exaggeration, cyberspace can be seen as the new bomb, a pacific blaze that will project the imprint of our disembodied selves on the walls of eternity" (51). In the introduction to the volume, Michael Benedikt proposes a poetic meditation on the word that explores its thematic range and imaginative value as fully as Novak's definition covers its technological interpretations. In the net of its two roots, cyberspace captures:

1. A separate reality, reminiscent of the alternate possible words of semantic logic and of the theoretical constructs of speculative physics: "A parallel universe, created and sustained by the world's computers and communication lines" (1).

2. A gigantic archive, constantly updated, serving as the depository of the known and as the incubator of knowledge, "where nothing is forgotten and yet everything changes" (1).

3. An ever expanding territory, whose frontiers are continually pushed back by the forward momentum of the inquiring mind: "Its horizon recedes in every direction; it breathes larger, it complexifies, it embraces and involves" (2).

4. A place of circulation, trading, speculation, and relentless activity—the dynamics of capitalism turned into a spectacle: "money

flowing in rivers and capillaries; obligations, contracts, accumulating" (2).

5. A common market of knowledge where information falls into the public domain, and intellectual property dissolves into an unrestricted exchange of ideas: "everything informational and important to the life of individuals will be found . . . for the taking, in cyberspace" (2). (Benedikt also mentions the alternative "offered for sale," suggesting a new form of intellectual capitalism.)

6. A solution to the degradation of the environment in the real world: "[a] realm of pure information . . . decontaminating the natural and urban landscapes, redeeming them, saving them from the chain-dragging bulldozers of the paper industry, from the diesel smoke of courier and post office trucks, from jet fuel fumes and clogged airports" (3).

7. "An extension of our age-old capacity and need to dwell in fiction" (6), joining so many conscious and subconscious, culturally sanctioned and forbidden activities in the pursuit of another reality: dreams, drug-induced hallucinations, myth, ritual, and the arts.

8. A new art medium, marking the last stage in the development of writing technologies: "the tablet become a page become a screen become a world, a virtual world" (1).

From VR to the Internet

The various interpretations proposed by Benedikt confirm the polarization of the Gibsonian concept of cyberspace into a virtual reality and a networking component. At times cyberspace strikes the imagination as an enveloping space, an immersive substance, a cozy habitat; at other times, it is conceptualized as a dynamic environment, a slick surface, a force to catch in order to be transported elsewhere. The VR theme invites plunging into the depth of cyberspace, the networking theme surfing on top of a wave. In recent years, the emphasis has clearly switched from the VR to the networking theme. When the word began to spread into common language, virtual reality was perceived as the hot new thing in electronic technology, "soon coming to an arcade near you." Compared to AI, formerly the most publicized field in computer science, VR represented an entirely different philosophy of the relations between human and machine: whereas AI sought to replace the human mind, VR placed the human element at the center of the stage. Computers were no longer supposed to run the world for us—their purpose was to help create a world in an interactive relation with a human partner. But for all the publicity that heralded its advent, VR has not (yet) had a significant impact on our daily lives. Few people have ever visited state-of-the-art displays, such as what can be experienced at SIGGRAPH conferences on the West Coast, or at the Computer Museum in Boston. Medical and scientific applications of VR technology are not accessible to the general public. For those interested, teledildonics is still years away (and this is being optimistic). The label "virtual reality" has been attached to some computer games using goggles to improve the life-likeness of the visual display, but these applications are a far cry from the interactive, immersive environment described in the VR literature. In short, VR is not much more accessible to most of us in 1997 than it was in 1991. As VR went into a stall, however, telecommunications through computer networks began to monopolize the headlines. The Internet has made a much greater difference in our lives than the simulated worlds of VR technology. This explains why the media have made cyberspace into a second name (nickname? metaphor?) for the Internet. Subscribers to the network are commonly referred to as "cyberspace users" and time spent on-line is time in cyberspace. In the language of the press, cyberspace has become to the Internet what solons are to senators, gridders to football players, and nimrods to hunters.[2] "Jump into cyberspace, get Internet access," a radio ad urges us (heard on 10/12/1996). But as the Internet became the primary referent of cyberspace, the term maintained the connotations inherited from its VR connection. Through these connotations, the label of "cyberspace" has shaped the public perception of the Internet experience, favoring the global assimilation of the network to a virtual reality.

In a strict sense, of course, there is no reason to regard the Internet as a VR system. It exists for the exchange of information, and this exchange can be a way of doing the business of the real world. Do we flee into some other reality when we use on-line services to check the stock market, buy or sell products, find out the amount of new snow at our favorite ski resort, browse the catalog of some remote library, or retrieve a text we need for research purposes? Are we playing roles, building imaginary bodies, and performing on the stage of a fantasy world when we exchange e-mail for professional reasons? Admittedly, there are other uses of the network than doing the real world's business: cruising around for the fun of it, playing games, conversing with strangers, reading the on-line soaps, visiting the genuinely fictional worlds of the MOOs. If a virtual reality is an imaginary world in which we play a role, there are countless pockets of virtuality on the Internet. To the imagination nourished by the discourse of mass media, these pockets threaten to spill over the entire network.

The metaphor of the Internet as cyberspace replaces the idea of mobile information with the idea of a mobile user: the experience of using the Internet is not one of receiving data through the telephone lines but one of being transported to a site functioning as host, heart, and mother lode of the data. In the old regime of the imagination, telecommunication was conceived on the model of epistolary exchange: in a telephone conversation the voice traveled over the lines, as the letter traveled on mail carriers. In the paradigm created by the cyberspace metaphor, Internet and telephone users meet in a common virtual place. As a "cybernaut" told Mark Dery: "One of the most striking features of the WELL [Whole Earth 'Lectronic Link] . . . is that it actually creates a feeling of 'place.' I'm staring at the computer screen. But the feeling really is that I'm 'in' something; I'm some 'where' " (*Escape Velocity*, 7). On-line services and MOO designers did their best to promote the feeling, by naming their services chatrooms, electronic cafés, and hypertext hotels.

As an imaginary country nowhere to be found on the map (also known as Cyberia or Cyberelia), cyberspace presents several properties not shared by physical space. It is traveled by jumps and seemingly instantaneous transportation (known as teleporting) rather than being traversed point by point like Cartesian space. It is not finite, but infinitely expandable: claiming a territory as one's own (for instance, by creating a home page on the Net) does not diminish the amount of cyberspace available to others. Being non-physical, it is equidistant from all points in the physical world: as Benedikt observes, cyberspace is equally accessible (theoretically at least) "from a basement in Vancouver, a boat in Port-au-Prince, a bar in Kyoto, a laboratory on the Moon" (1). Since it expands and changes continually, it cannot be mapped. The path that took you to that fascinating Internet site one day may be gone the next day (in fact, the site itself may be gone). In cyberspace, objects lose their unity: a message sent through the Internet is broken up into packets, and put back together at the end of the trip, after each packet has traveled through a different route. Rewriting the geography of the real world, cyberspace alters physical distance: a user located on the other side of the planet may be easier to reach than your next-door neighbor. It is not continuous but made of gaps and holes: as Nunes argues in this volume, if you are not connected to the Net, you are not part of it. All in all, the Internet and its metaphorical space are the closest approximation of the mystical circle whose center is everywhere and circumference nowhere: every user regards his home site as the heart of the system, and there is no limit on how far the system can reach.[3]

The sense of the virtual nature of the "reality" made accessible by the Internet is intensified by the wide use of the label of "virtual" technologies to refer to the products of the software industry. This use is due to the importance of the concept of virtuality in computer architecture. A computer, it will be remembered, is a machine able to execute sets of instructions, or programs, designed to solve a variety of problems. The electronic circuits that make up the physical machine can recognize and execute a very limited repertory of instructions, known as machine language. This makes programming a very tedious and difficult affair. The task can be facilitated by using higher-level languages with a wider repertory of more powerful instructions, such as BASIC or C, and translating them into machine language through a program (written in machine language) known as a compiler or interpreter. Since the physical machine is unable to execute the commands of the higher-level language, the C or BASIC programmer interacts with a virtual machine. If the language of level 2 is still too difficult to handle, the process can be repeated by creating a level 3 language and translating it into the level 2 language: there is no limit to the number of virtual machines that can be stacked upon the physical machine. At the top of the stack we may find some day a virtual machine that understands spoken natural languages. The idea of virtuality has also been applied to memory management, time-sharing systems, and the problem of portability (making a program run on different types of hardware). Still another use of the concept of virtuality refers to the versatility of the computer. As a machine, a computer has no intrinsic function. Through its software, however, it can simulate a number of existing devices and human activities, thus becoming a virtual calculator, typewriter, record player, storyteller, baby-sitter, teacher, bookkeeper, or adviser on various matters. Or even, as VR suggests, a virtual world and living space.

In a double metonymic transfer, the term "virtual" has been extended from the technical vocabulary of computer science to the technology developed by this science, and from the technology to any of its uses. A romance conducted on the MOO is commonly described as a virtual romance, a group of people connected by the net is known as a virtual community (though old-fashioned pen pals who never meet in reality would never have been called virtual friends in the pre-networking days), universities offering on-line courses are virtual universities, and a political campaign conducted through a home page on the Internet has been recently labeled a virtual campaign.[4] (Will the candidate be a virtual governor if he gets elected?) The titles of recently founded journals confirm the metonymy: *The Journal of Virtual Relations* (meaning electronically mediated) and *The Electronic Journal of Virtual Culture*. The tendency to regard all products of electronic technology as virtual has also affected the textual domain. According to George

Landow, "[s]ince electronic text processing is a matter of manipulating computer-manipulated codes, all texts that the reader-writer encounters on the screen are virtual texts" (19). In the same vein, Katherine Hayles calls writing with the help of a word processor "virtual writing," in part because the signs are "flickering signifiers," lacking any solid materiality. Richard Lanham does not use the word "virtual," but he comes very close when he ascribes to electronic texts a property of potentiality: "[t]he electronic word has no essence, no quiddity, no substance [of the sort embodied by books]. It exists *in potentia* as what it can become, in the genetic structures it can build" (19). It could further be argued that electronic texts are stored in a virtual location, because their material support is not a volume of space (and a volume in space), but invisible silicon chips virtually (I mean almost) deprived of extension. Taken to its limits, the metonymy could even affect the concepts of the self and the real: if technologies construct subjects, then cyberspace users become virtual selves; if they construct the real world, this world becomes another virtual reality. Virtual technologies thus become virtualizing technologies.

The Two Faces of the Virtual

This metonymic extension of "virtual" to describe all computer-mediated activities and all aspects of electronic culture threatens a weakening, or even loss, of semantic substance. If "virtual" becomes simply synonymous with "computer mediated," it will not tell anything of interest about the phenomena it refers to. For the word to capture significant features of electronic culture, it must retain something of its traditional kernel of meaning. To see what may be virtual about electronic texts and culture, let us therefore go back to pre-technological definitions.

Etymology tells us that "virtual" comes from the Latin *virtus* (strength, manliness, virtue), which gave to scholastic Latin the philosophical concept of virtus as force or power. (This sense survives today in the expression "by virtue of.") In scholastic Latin, *virtualis* designates the potential, "what is in the power (virtus) of the force." The classical example of virtuality, derived from Aristotle's distinction between potential and actual existence (*in potentia* vs. *in actu*), is the presence of the oak in the acorn. In scholastic philosophy "actual" and "virtual" exist in a dialectical relation rather than in one of radical opposition: the virtual is not that which is deprived of existence, but that which possesses the potential, or force of developing into actual existence. Later uses of the term, beginning in the eighteenth and nineteenth centuries, turn this dialectical relation to actual into a binary opposition to real: the virtual becomes the fictive and the non-existent. This sense is activated in the optical use of the term. According to Webster's dictionary, a virtual image (such as a reflection in a mirror) is one made of virtual foci, that is, of points "from which divergent rays of light seem to emanate but do not actually do so." Modern uses of "virtual" exploit the idea of fake and illusion inherent to the mirror image. A virtual dictator is a ruler functioning as dictator, without being officially recognized as such. In this sense, the virtual is perceived as both the equal of the real and as its inferior. Even though it is "as good as" the real thing, it suffers from a lack of legitimacy that prevents it from completely displacing the real.

As we see from these lexical definitions, the term "virtual" encapsulates two distinct concepts: the largely negative idea of the fake, illusionary, non-existent, and the overwhelmingly positive idea of the potential, which connotes productivity, openness, and diversity. These features correlate to the two dimensions of the VR experience, as defined by Pimentel and Texeira: "In general, the term virtual reality refers to an immersive, interactive experience generated by a computer" (11). It is through immersion that the VR user experiences the "fake," immaterial world projected by the computer as a physically present reality to which she can relate through the movements of her own body; it is through interactivity that she actualizes one of the many possible worlds contained *in potentia* in the simulative system.

The Virtual as Fake

If the virtual is the fake, cyberspace is a virtual space because it creates a sense of place, even though it does not exist physically; and the Internet provides the experience of virtuality because it transports the user into the non-existing territory of cyberspace.

In the textual domain, the virtual-as-fake is manifested as fictionality. The fictional text invokes the non-existing in the factual mode, thereby inviting the reader to pretend belief (or suspend disbelief) in its (lack of) reality. This idea of suspension of disbelief is the literary-theoretical equivalent of the VR concept of immersion. It describes the attitude by which the reader brackets out the knowledge that the fictional world is the product of language, in order to imagine it as an autonomous reality populated by solid objects and embodied individuals. The importance of the experience of immersion for the phenomenology of reading for pleasure has been acknowledged under various names: being lost in a story (Nell); transportation into a fictional world

(Gerrig); engaging in a game of make-believe (Walton, *Mimesis*); and mental simulation of the represented events (Walton, "Spelunking").

The assimilation of the virtual to the fake reflects the obsession of postmodernism with simulacra and technologies of reproduction, an obsession forcefully described by theorists of contemporary culture such as Eco and Baudrillard. In contrast to the Décadence movement of the late nineteenth century, which cultivated the artificial out of fear or disgust for the natural, the late twentieth century regards the fakeness of the fake as an inherent source of aesthetic gratification. In this frame of mind, the purpose of art is not to redo the creation to make it more livable, as it was for Décadence writers, but to flaunt its own power of simulation by making the copy more desirable than the original. As Eco has argued, the visitors of Disneyland are more thrilled by automata performing as pirates or animals in the jungle than they would be by real animals or by role-playing humans. The worlds created by VR technology promise to outdo Disneyland in their combination of lifelikeness and artificiality. In the recent work of Baudrillard, VR has indeed displaced Disneyland as allegory of the addiction of late-twentieth-century culture for the hyperreal (Poster, this volume).

The opposition of the virtual-as-fake to an implicitly authentic real has prompted two types of reactions. One of them is a rejection of the fake, leading to a backlash against electronic culture. A flurry of recent books enjoins us to "get real" by renouncing the so-called virtualizing technologies: *Silicon Snake Oil* (Stoll), *The Gutenberg Elegies* (Birkerts), *War of the Worlds* (Slouka), *Virtual Realities and Their Discontents* (Markley), *Virtual Worlds: A Journey in Hype and Hyperreality* (Woolley), *Resisting the Virtual Life* (Brook and Boal), *Data Trash: The Theory of the Virtual Class* (Kroker and Weinstein). Computers may take us into virtual worlds, but it is on this side of the symbolic screen, these books tell us, that we will find genuine human relations, the outdoors, a body able to move in space without cumbersome contraptions, books that can be read in our bath and authors who can be our partners in an intellectual exchange.

The other reaction is one of skepticism regarding the concept of real life and its alleged authenticity. As Sherry Turkle argues, "[the] context [of the culture of electronic simulation]" is the story of the eroding boundary between the real and the virtual (10). For Michael Heim, the development of virtual realities challenges us to reexamine our sense of reality. Will the development and propagation of VR technologies swallow the real and lend support to the militant anti-realism of postmodern thought, as these technologies create an addiction to their fake worlds? Is RL (the MOO users' abbreviation for real life) "just one more window, and it's usually not [the] best one," as an informant told Turkle (13)? If the answer is negative, as my instinct tells me, what are the criteria for distinguishing computer-generated virtual worlds from the real world?

It used to be that the presence of the body spelled the difference between virtual worlds and reality; but with the development of VR technology, this is no longer true. As Brenda Laurel argues, computer simulations offer the opportunity of "taking your body with you into worlds of the imagination" (14). Common sense suggests a number of other distinctions: Virtual worlds are controlled by rules, the real world behaves unpredictably. Virtual worlds are created by man, the real world is not. Virtual worlds depend on the real world for energy, the real world creates its own. Virtual worlds are immaterial, the real world contains matter. Thomas Laudal, an engineer, refutes all these arguments: virtual worlds are capable of evolving in a way not foreseen by their programmers. This is known as "emergent" behavior. A virtual world capable of emergent behavior is in a state of continuous self-creation, rather than being created once and for all by man. If virtual worlds depend on another world for their energy, so perhaps does the real world: its energy may come from the big bang or black holes speculated by modern physics. And finally, virtual worlds are not totally deprived of matter: as Laudal argues, they contain lots of electrons and photons. Their matter is simply more fluid and less dense than the matter of reality. The last three of these arguments bring to mind an idea developed by J. L. Borges in *The Circular Ruins*. The story depicts a man who dreams another man into reality, only to realize that he may himself be the dream of another mind, and so on *ad infinitum*. By the same reasoning, the real world could be seen as the virtual world of another world, thus losing its centrality in the system of all possible worlds.

To these theoretical arguments, Michael Heim opposes a gut feeling. The difference between real and virtual realities resides in three constraints that "anchor" us in the real world: our inevitable mortality, the irreversible direction of time, and a sense of precariousness arising from the possibility of physical injury (136). It is, in other words, the final character of evil that provides the ontological proof of the difference between real and virtual worlds: if I die or get injured in a computer-generated reality, I can always exit the system, rewind time and start all over again. This argument is valid for currently available simulation systems, but it would not stand against Laudal's objections: one can conceive of a VR system in which time would be irreversible and death final, because users would be locked in. This possibility is suggested by the drama *The Maids* by Jean Genet: when the maids stage the murder of their hated mistress in a play within the play, the one who plays the mistress ingests poison and dies, both in the virtual world of the simulation and in the actual world. The virtual world has been designed in such a way as to prevent escape.

The Virtual as Potential

If the virtual as fake cannot be rigorously distinguished from the real, we may avert the problem by returning to the scholastic definition of the virtual as potential. This alternative is developed by Pierre Lévy, an eminent French theorist of computer culture. Lévy writes:

> Rigorously defined, the virtual has few affinities with the false, the illusory, the imaginary. The virtual is not at all the opposite of the real. It is, on the contrary, a powerful and productive mode of being, a mode that gives free rein to creative processes. . . . (10; all translations are mine)

I will develop here Lévy's theory of the virtual in some detail because it covers texts, writing, electronic technology, and many aspects of contemporary culture without reducing them to virtual realities. (Of the two grammatical forms of "virtual," the noun is much more likely to suggest the potential, and the adjective form the fake and non-real.)

Lévy outlines his idea of the virtual (inspired in part by Deleuze) by opposing two conceptual pairs: one static, involving the possible and the real, and the other dynamic, linking the actual to the virtual.[5] The possible is fully formed, but it resides in limbo. Making it real is largely a matter of throwing the dice of fate. In the terminology of modal logic, this throw of dice may be conceived as changing the modal operator affecting a proposition, without affecting the proposition itself. The operation is fully reversible, so that the proposition p can pass from mere possibility to reality back to possibility. In contrast to the predictable realization of the possible, the mediation between the virtual and the actual is not a deterministic process but a form-giving force. The pair virtual/actual is characterized by the following features:

1. The relation of the virtual to the actual is one to many. There is no limit on the number of possible actualizations of a virtual entity.
2. The passage from the virtual to the actual involves transformation, and is therefore irreversible. As Lévy writes: "Actualization is an event, in the strong sense of the term" (135).
3. The virtual is not anchored in space and time. Actualization is the passage from a state of timelessness and deterritorialization to an

existence rooted in a here and now. It is an event of contextualiza-
tion.
4. The virtual is an inexhaustible resource. Using it does not lead to
its depletion.

These properties underscore the essential role of the virtual in the
creative process. For Lévy, the passage from the virtual to the actual is
not a predetermined, automatic development, but the solution to a problem which is not already contained in its formulation. "Actualization is
. . . the invention of a form out of a dynamic configurations of forces
striving toward a goal [*configuration de forces and finalities*]. It involves
more than the passage of the possible into the real and more than a
choice from a predefined set of alternatives: it is the production of new
qualities, a transformation of ideas, a true becoming which nourishes
the virtual in a feedback process" (15). As this idea of feedback suggests, the importance of Lévy's treatment of virtuality does not merely
reside in its insistence on the dynamic nature of actualization, but in its
conception of creativity as a two-way process involving both a phase of
actualization and a phase of virtualization. While actualization is the
invention of a concrete solution to answer a need, virtualization is a
return from the solution to the original problem. This movement can
take two forms: given a certain solution, the mind can reexamine the
problem it was meant to resolve, in order to produce a better solution;
cars, for instance, are a more efficient way to solve the problem of transportation than horse-drawn carriages. Virtualization can also be the
process of reopening the field of problems that led to a certain solution,
and finding related problems to which the solution may be applied. A
prime example of this process is the evolution of the computer from a
number-crunching automaton to a worlds-projecting and word-process-
ing machine.

The concept of virtualization is an extremely powerful one. It involves any mental operation leading from the here and now, the singular,
the usable once and for all and the solidly embodied to the timeless,
abstract, general, versatile, repeatable, ubiquitous, immaterial, and mor-
phologically fluid. Skeptics may object that Lévy's concept of virtualization simply renames well-known mental operations such as abstraction and generalization; but partisans will counter that the notion is
much richer, and that the significance of the theory resides precisely in
making virtualization at the same time a timeless operation responsible
for all of human culture, and a trademark of the contemporary *zeitgeist*.
In our dealing with the virtual, we are doing what mankind has always
done, only more powerfully, consciously, and systematically. The stamp

of postmodern culture is its tendency to virtualize the non-virtual and to virtualize the virtual itself. If we live a "virtual condition," as Katherine Hayles has suggested, it is not because we are condemned to the fake, but because we have learned to live, work and play with the fluid, the open, the potential.

Lévy's examples of virtualization thus includes both elementary cultural activities and contemporary developments. Among the former are tool making and the creation of language. Tool making involves the virtual in a variety of ways. The concrete, manufactured object extends our physical faculties, thus creating a virtual body. It is reusable, thus transcending the here and now of actual existence. Other virtual dimensions of tools are inherent to the design itself: it exists outside space and time; it produces many physically different yet functionally similar objects; it is born out of an understanding of the recurrence of a problem (if I need to drive *this* nail here and now, I will need to drive nails in other places and at other times), and it is not worn out by the process of its actualization. Language originates in a similar need to transcend the particular. The creation of a system of reusable linguistic types (or *langue*) out of an individual or communal experience of the world is a virtualizing process of generalization and conceptualization; conversely, the use of the system through individual acts of parole is an actualization that turns the types into concrete tokens of slightly variable phonic or graphic substance. Through this actualization, language is contextualized and bound to a spatially and temporally determined referent. Even in its manifestation as parole, language exercises a virtualizing power. Life is lived in real time, as a succession of presents, but through its ability to refer to physically absent objects, language puts consciousness in touch with the past and the future, metamorphoses time into a continuous spread that can be traveled in all directions, and transports the imagination to distant locations.

As examples of more specifically contemporary forms of virtualization, Lévy mentions the transformations currently undergone by the economy and by the human body. In the so-called information age, the most desirable good is no longer solid manufactured objects, but knowledge itself, an eminently virtual resource since it is not depleted by use, and since its value resides in its potential for creating wealth. On the negative side, the virtualization of the economy has encouraged the pyramid schemes currently plaguing the industries of sales and investments. As for the body, it is virtualized by any practice and technology aiming at expanding its sensorium, altering its appearance, or pushing back its biological limits. The inspiration for these practices is the fundamentally virtualizing question: To what new problems can I apply this available resource? As we have seen above, the virtualization of the body begins with the manufacturing and use of tools. In contemporary culture and counterculture, the process is intensified by an array of body-manipulating practices prominently featured in cyberpunk fiction: genetic engineering, cosmetic surgery, sex-change operations, body-building, body art, extreme sports (through which the body becomes fish, bird, or mountain goat), artificial organ implants, performance-enhancing equipment, remote-control devices, telecommunications, and last but not least, VR applications. The development of simulation technologies such as VR illustrates yet another tendency of contemporary culture: the virtualization to a second degree of the already virtual. The purpose of a simulative system is to explore the range of situations that can develop out of a given state of affairs. The knowledge gained by trying out the potential enables the user to manage the possible and to control the development of the real. If all tools are virtual entities, simulations are doubly virtual, since they incorporate the virtual into their mode of action.

The textual domain has not been spared from the virtualizing frenzy of the postmodern age. Consider first the text in its material support. If the virtual is a singularity that produces a plurality, the history of writing technologies is a tale of ever increasing virtuality. The oral text depended on the presence of the body, and the closest thing to duplication was a new performance made possible by memorization. Texts became easily preservable with the invention of writing, and easily copyable with the invention of printing. The electronic medium takes this property to a higher level. Texts can be copied on disk by the stroke of a key; by another stroke, the disk version is copied to the screen. Since the version preserved on disk is invisible to the user, it exists in the virtual mode, waiting for an actualization that will fulfill its potential: being perceived by the eye, being read by the mind. Rather than listening to an original oral performance, or holding one of the many copies of a book, the reader of the electronic text faces one of many screen actualizations of one of many disk copies. Paralleling this exponential ratio of duplication is a loss of volume and solidity of the material support: from the live human body, to thin clay tablets, sheets of paper, minuscule silicon chips, and easily erasable pixels of light flickering on the screen, the text is virtualized by the rarefaction of its substance.[6]

Virtuality is more than a feature of the newly developed material supports of the text; it is also the mode of existence of the text itself as mental object and linguistic artifact. "From its Mesopotamian origin," writes Lévy, "the text has been a virtual and abstract object, independent of any particular support" (33). Paradoxically, this virtual object originates in an actualization of thought. The act of writing taps into (and enriches in return) a reservoir of ideas, memories, metaphors, and linguistic material which contain potentially an infinite number of texts. These resources are textualized through selection, association, and linearization. But if the text is the product of an actualization, it reverts to a virtual mode of existence as soon as writing is over. From the point of view of the reader, a text is like a musical score waiting to be performed; every act of reading constructs the text and actualizes its world in a different way. This potentiality is not just a matter of being open to various interpretations, nor of forming the object of infinitely many acts of perception; otherwise texts would be no more and no less virtual than works of visual art or things in the world such as rocks and tables. The virtuality of texts and musical scores stems from the complexity of the mediation between what is there, physically, and what is made out of it. Color and form are inherent to pictures and objects, but sound is not inherent to musical scores, nor are thoughts, ideas, and mental representations inherent to the graphic or phonic marks of texts. They must be constructed through an activity far more transformative than interpreting sensory data. In the case of texts, the process of actualization involves such highly individualized operations as filling in the blanks in the text with information drawn from the reader's knowledge, memory, and experience; visualizing in imagination the depicted scenes, characters, and events; and spatializing the text by following the threads of various thematic webs, often against the directionality of the linear sequence.

As a generator of potential worlds, interpretations, uses, and experiences, the text is thus always already a virtual object. What the marriage of postmodernism and electronic technology has produced is not the virtual text itself, but the elevation of its built-in virtuality to a higher power. In no form is this exponentiation more obvious then in hypertext. A double one-to-many relation creates an additional level of mediation between the text as produced by the author ("engineered" might be a better term) and the text as experienced by the reader. This additional level is the text as displayed on the screen. In a traditional text, we have two levels:

1. The text as collection of signs written by the author
2. The text as constructed (mentally) by the reader

The object of level 1 contains potentially many objects of level 2. In a virtualized text, the levels are three:

1. The text as written or "engineered" by the author
2. The text as presented, displayed, to the reader
3. The text as constructed (mentally) by the reader[7]

One object of level 1 generates many objects of level 2, which in turn contain potentially many objects of level 3. The additional level is not exclusive to electronic texts. Classical print examples of second-order virtuality are *Hopscotch*, by Julio Cortázar, which can be read according to several reading protocols; or Raymond Queneau's *Cent mille milliards de poèmes*, which are generated by combining the lines of fourteen different sonnets. But the additional level of virtuality is greatly facilitated by the electronic medium. In hypertext, the textual machinery becomes, in Lévy's words, "a matrix of potential texts" (38). As a virtualization of the already virtual, hypertext is truly a hyper-text, a self-referential reflection of the virtual nature of textuality.

As I have suggested above in reference to VR, the development of the virtual as potential usually involves an interactive relation between the user and the system. In textual matters, the concept of interactivity can be interpreted in two ways: figuratively and literally. As might be expected, it is the literal forms that elevate textual virtuality to a higher power. Each of the two manifestations of interactivity may in turn be divided into a weak and a strong form:

Interactivity

	Figural	Literal
Weak	Classical narrative	Hypertext
Strong	Postmodern texts	MOOs, Interactive Drama

Table 4.1

In the weak figural sense, interactivity stands for the collaboration between the reader and the text in the production of meaning. As the phenomenologist Roman Ingarden and his disciple Wolgang Iser have shown, the construction of the fictional world is an active process through which the reader provides as much material as she derives from the text. This activity is intensified by the problematic coherence and self-referential stance of postmodern literature: the postmodern text invites the reader to construct a fictional world not so much to become immersed in it, as for the purpose of observing the process of its construction. Interactivity between text and reader can be literal only if the text undergoes physical changes during the reading process. The interactivity of hypertext is weak because the reader's contribution to the configuration of the text is a choice between predefined alternatives, rather than the actual production of signs. It is only in the performance-oriented environment of MOOs and Interactive Drama, where the user's empowerment involves the power to use language, that interactivity reaches its full meaning of active participation in the creative process.

As important as interactivity is to the development of virtuality, however, it is not the only way to produce an ever changing text. In the visual arts, we have mechanized objects that move like machines, sculptures that chime in the wind, and structures that reflect the light of the sun at different times of the day. All of these artworks present the "many-in-one" quality of the virtualized work. In the textual domain, there are so-called textual machines that use aleatory procedures to produce an ever changing display without intervention by the user. (See "computer-modulated texts" in the introduction to this volume.)

Even when the renewal of the text is obtained through interactive mechanisms, as in hypertext, randomness plays an important role in the process. There is a significant difference between the interactivity of hypertext and of VR systems. In VR, the user can usually foresee the result of her actions. For instance, she can touch a can of yellow paint, then touch the carpet of a virtual living-room display, and the carpet turns yellow. But in most literary forms of hypertext the choices are largely blind. In Michael Joyce's *Afternoon*, we are told that there are "words that yield," words that have special links and branches attached to them, and others that simply lead to the default continuation. The words that yield are not physically marked, and there is really no way for the reader to detect them other than trial and error. The author gives rather cryptic suggestions in the accompanying pamphlet: try pronouns, words that appeal to you, words that have "texture." There is of course no guarantee that a word that has texture for me also will for the author: part of the appeal of the game is to find out where Joyce has hidden links, and whether he and I agree on which words are worthy of special treatment. In this case, reading the hypertext becomes like an Easter egg hunt; the reader clicks on words to find out if more words are hidden underneath. Another function of clicking is to keep the textual machine running. Hypertext theorists claim that interactivity reduces the gap between reader and writer, but the reader's contribution to the production of the text is mostly that of an agent of chance.

It is in non-fictional uses of hypertext that the reader has the greatest control of the textual display. In the World Wide Web, for instance, the highlighted, link-activating key words capture the topic of the text to be retrieved and enable the reader to customize the output to her own needs. In Lévy's words, the screen becomes a new "reading machine, the site where a reserve of potential information is realized here and now for a singular reader through an act of selection" (Lévy 39). As the user of the electronic reading machine retrieves, cuts, pastes, links, and saves, she regards text less as a unified work to be experienced in its totality than as a resource that can be scooped up by the screenful. Electronic technology has not invented the concept of text-as-resource, but it has certainly contributed to the current expansion of this approach to reading. The attitude promoted by the electronic reading machine is no longer "what should I do with texts" but "what *can* I do with them." In a formula that loses a lot in translation, Lévy writes: "Il y a maintenant du texte, comme on dit de l'eau et du sable" (46). (There is now "text," as there is sand and water.) If text is a mass substance, rather than a discrete object, there is no need to read it in its totality. The reader produced by the electronic reading machine will therefore be more inclined to graze at the surface of texts than to immerse himself in a textual world or to probe the mind of an author. Speaking on behalf of this reader, Lévy writes: "I am not interested in what an elusive author put into the text. What I ask of the text is to make me think, here and now. The virtuality of the text nourishes my acting intelligence" (47). The non-holistic mode encouraged by the electronic reading machine tends to polarize the attitude of the reader in two directions: reading becomes much more utilitarian, or much more serendipitous, depending on whether the user treats the textual database as what Mark Nunes calls in this volume a striated space, to be traversed to get somewhere, or as a smooth space, to be explored for the pleasure of the journey, and for the discoveries to be made along the way.

The idea of doing things with text also prevails in the case of electronic writing. The writing process may be the actualization of thought, but word processors and hypertext software promotes a play with "textrons" that maintains the text longer in a virtual state. The ease of manipulation encourages the writer to permute, expand, and edit chunks of text, to reinstate previous versions, and to create databases of potentially usable elements. (As I write this paragraph, I save it in a file called "stuff," not sure whether I'll use it, and if I do, in which one of my current projects.) Writing used to be like weaving on a loom, one word, one sentence after another, as the pen or typewriter carriage moves back and forth like a shuttle.[8] Now, as the pioneers of hypertext software tell us (Bolter and Joyce foremost among them), writing is more like arranging ready-made objects in the metaphorical space of computer memory. We used to think of texts as being made out of words and sentences; now under the conjoined influences of postmodern theory and electronic writing technologies, we think of texts as being made out of text. The loom is still needed to weave the individual elements (unless they are "found objects," lifted from other texts), but organization and linearization is now a two-stage process, the virtual text produced by the first stage serving as input to the second. While the writer remains responsible for the microlevel operations, she may bypass the macrolevel stage, thus offering *du texte* as a freely usable resource to the reader, rather than *un texte* structured as a logical argument aiming at persuasion.

The Virtual Text and Postmodern Theory

The heightened virtuality of the electronic text has been hailed by some theorists as the triumph of the conception of textuality proposed by postmodern literary theory, more particularly by poststructuralism and deconstruction.[9] The subtitle of George Landow's book *Hypertext* is unequivocal about the relationship: *The Convergence of Contemporary Critical Theory and Technology*. There seems indeed to be an "extraordinary convergence"—to borrow the title of a chapter of Lanham's book—between postmodern doctrine and what can be done with electronic textuality. Taking advantage of the inherent reversibility of McLuhan's famous formula, "the medium is the message," theorists of electronic textuality (Lanham, Landow, Bolter) are prone to reading the medium as a message, and this message is invariably the gospel of postmodernism. As Lanham writes: "it is hard not to think that, at the end of the day, electronic text will seem the natural fulfillment of much current literary theory" (130). The passage below (quoted from Landow 3) seems tailor-made for hypertext, but it is actually Roland Barthes's description of the writerly (*scriptible*) in *S/Z*:

> In this ideal text the networks [*réseaux*] are many and interact, without any one of them being able to surpass the rest; this text is a galaxy of signifiers, not a structure of signifieds; it has no beginning; it is reversible; we gain access to it by several entrances, none of which can be authoritatively declared to be the main one; the code it mobilizes extends as far as the eye can reach, they are indeterminable. . . . the systems of meaning can take over this absolutely plural text, but their number is never closed, based as it is on the infinity of language. (*S/Z* 5–6)

Or again, consider this passage from Barthes's essay "The Death of the Author":

> [the text is] a multidimensional space in which a variety of writings, none of them original, blend and clash. The text is a tissue of quotations drawn from innumerable centers of culture. Similar to Bouvard and Pecuchet, those eternal copyists, at once sublime and comic and whose profound ridiculousness indicates precisely the truth of writing, the writer can only imitate a gesture that is always anterior, not original. His only power is to mix writings, to counter the ones with the others, in such a way as never to rest on any one of them. (*Image, Music, Text* 146)

I am singling Barthes out, but theorists of electronic textuality have found parallels with the work of numerous prominent French theorists: Derrida, Foucault, Lyotard, Baudrillard, Deleuze, and Guattari.[10] The aspects of contemporary literary theory that find their fulfillment in hypertext hardly need explanation. The open text. Meaning as reconfigurable network. The slipperiness of the signifier and the deferral of meaning (symbolized by the system of links). Intertextuality. Reading as "exploding the text" and as endless activity. (You never know if you have seen all the lexemes, and traveled all the links of hypertext.) Nonlinearity. The death of the author. The empowerment of the reader. Other points and metaphors of postmodern doctrine are literalized in the role-playing activity of the MOOs: The decentered, multiple nature of the subject. The body and its attributes of gender and race as textual constructs. (Users design their identity through verbal descriptions.) The body inhabited by different selves (who will, on the MOO, grow their own bodies). The self as the performance of roles. In the series of oppositions listed below—through which postmodernism distinguishes itself from earlier periods (mostly from the scapegoat of the Enlightenment)—print texts have been overwhelmingly associated with the left and electronic textuality with the "right" term (in both senses of the word):[11]

Durable	Ephemeral
Linear organization	Spatial organization
Authorial authority	Reader freedom
Predetermined meaning	Emergent meaning
Attention focused on textual world	Attention focused on language
Text experienced as depth (immersion)	Text experienced as surface (surfing)

Centered structure	Decentered structure
Tree structure (hierarchical)	Rhizome (free growth)
Top-down design	Bottom-up design
Global coherence	Local coherence
Reading as goal-oriented navigation	Reading as aimless wandering (*flâner*)
Systematic approach	Tinkering with the heterogeneous
Logical thinking	Analogical thinking
Work	Play
Unity	Diversity
Order	Chaos (self-organizing system)
Monologism	Heteroglossia, dialogism, carnivalesque
Continuous development	Jumps, discontinuity
Sequentiality	Parallelism
Solidity	Fluidity
Text as rhetoric for persuasion	Text as resource
Static representation (of world)	Dynamic simulation (of brain activity, of memory)
Immersive text	Interactive text

Table 4.2

The predominance in electronic texts of many of the features on the right derives to some extent from the inherent properties of the medium. As is the case with all media, electronic writing facilitates certain operations, favors certain structures, and promotes a certain type of writer and reader. It is tempting to interpret this relative determinism as an autonomous "agency of the medium" (Grusin's term, 43). The "extraordinary convergence" of postmodern doctrine and electronic textuality would then be explained by the power of the new technology to create a new subject, as it dictates compelling changes in our mode of thinking. Alternatively, the development of the technology could be attributed to the force of postmodern thought, a force through which ideology would produce the proper tools to fulfill its ideals. Without entirely discounting the possibility of these two explanations (or the possibility of a feedback loop between the force of thought and the force of the technology), the convergence appears much less wondrous if one remembers that already available ideologies affect the *use* as well as the theorizing of already available technologies. The form, content, and mode of action of currently available specimens of hypertext fiction are as much a reflection of general trends in the avant-garde literary production of our time as they are the product of the properties of medium itself. Similarly, the MOO practices of creating new bodies and inventing new forms of sexuality follows the body politics of our age as much as they are promoted by the role-playing facilities inherent to the system. We don't read much in the critical literature about the MOO users who choose to be "just themselves" because they find role-playing too strenuous, "authenticity" more pleasurable, and the self unproblematic; but I have encountered some of these living anachronisms. (They may, of course, have been lying.) In a different age—one that believed in the knowability of reality, and whose literary elite placed value in plot, character, and global coherence—the medium of hypertext could be used for entirely different purposes than it has been so far. For instance, rather than inviting the reader to explode it, the text could present itself as a jigsaw puzzle challenging the reader to put back together a coherent narrative picture. In contrast to Joyce's *Afternoon*, there would then be a definitive answer to the question "what happened," but the reader would have to explore the entire network to find the solution. The system of links could also be used to provide detailed descriptions or background information about the characters and settings. The reader could thus choose to speed through the plot—as in *Reader's Digest* versions of books—or to linger on the scene. Still another possibility would be to use the hypertextual mechanism to tell a tale with parallel plot lines or to narrate events from different points of view. As Jack makes love to Jill, clicking on either character's name would access their private thoughts. None of these conceivable uses would lead to the demise of what Barthes calls the "readerly," nor to its replacement by the "writerly" text.

There is no point in denying the natural and elective affinities of electronic writing for postmodern aesthetics—natural, because of the transient substance of electricity itself, and elective, because of the influence of the cultural climate on what is done with the medium. But if every medium exercises its own power and constraints, and if every medium is inserted within a cultural context, it is nevertheless up to the users to decide how to exploit this potential. Art is as much a matter of resisting, transforming, or expanding the medium as one of taking advantage of its built-in features. In the visual arts, there are watercolor works that imitate oil painting, and oil paintings that imitate watercolor; photographs that imitate paintings and paintings that imitate photographs. In literature, there are print narratives that revive oral storytelling traditions (a significant contemporary trend, as the popular success of Gabriel García Márquez, Isabel Allende, and Toni Morrison suggests), and others that explode the covers of the book and realize in print the possibilities now associated with the electronic medium. It is not unthinkable that electronic writing will one day rediscover (and transform) the forms of literary expression typical of the book medium, or that it will emancipate itself from postmodern doctrine.

Nothing could be more detrimental to the cause of electronic textuality than enrolling it in a war between the left side and the right side of the above table. Hypertext theory has too often resorted to an "End of the Book" rhetoric that doomed to extinction the pleasures and modes of thinking associated with the print medium. This rhetoric has done more to turn off amateurs of literature than to promote electronic textuality. The features on the left may have dominated literature when the book was the main support of texts, but it is also the texts of the late age of print that have familiarized us with the patterns of the other side: postmodern theory has been largely developed in book form. If the resources of the right are accessible to a thought elaborated in the print medium, why should the resources of the left side be banned from electronic textuality? Thought progresses by expansion, not by elimination. If we consider the three major modes of transmitting texts—oral, print, and electronic—from the point of view of efficiency, it is obvious that each mode represents a progress over the preceding one, and that computers should eventually replace books, just as books have replaced storytelling as the dominant way of disseminating knowledge. But if we look at the three modes from the point of view of their literary potential, privileging aesthetic considerations, then each one expands the resources of literary expression, without rendering obsolete the pleasures provided by the other two. It is only by recognizing the legitimacy and aesthetic potential of both the left and the right column of the table that literary theory can approach electronic textuality without turning into a "pleasure police."[12] And while the right side is inherently more hospitable to the virtual than the left one, it is only by remaining open to both sides (and perhaps by developing others) that the texts of cyberspace can fully invest in the resources of virtuality. If the virtual as potential is their essence, postmodernist uses and theorizing are a possibility, not a necessity.

Notes

1. The Greek root *cyber* means "steersman," and cybernetics is the study of the mechanisms controlling the travel of information, but we are accustomed to associating the word with electronic information.

2. In the press, the term "cyberspace" is typically used in titles of articles about the Internet. For instance, an article from the Associated Press about an Internet user feeling suddenly sick, sending a message on the Net and

getting help from other users is titled "Ailing 'Net chess player gets aid from cyberspace" (*Denver Post*, 9/30/96), but the word "cyberspace" is absent from the article itself. Titles, it should be remembered, are selected by the staff of the newspaper, while the article usually comes from a news agency. Since the function of titles is to catch attention, they display a more creative, more metaphorical use of language. In this case, the personification of cyberspace as an agent providing aid lends a supernatural aura to an otherwise fully explainable event.

3. This metaphor is suggested by Lévy, 45.

4. Internet posting by Reuters (C-reuter@clarui.net), 10 April 1996.

5. The relation between these two pairs, as well as between the two components of each pair, leaves quite a few unresolved questions. Is the possible opposed to the real, or does Lévy regard the real as a subset of the possible (as does modal logic: the real world is a member of the set of all possible worlds)? Does the actual coincide with the real, or does the real comprise both the virtual and the actual? One solution would be to regard the real as a subset of the possible, and the actual and virtual as two modes of being within the real.

6. This passage develops ideas borrowed from Lanham and Hayles, as well as from chapter 3 of Lévy's book *The Virtualization of the Text*.

7. Philippe Bootz (237) comes up with comparable categories: *texte-écrit* (text as written), *texte-à-voir* (displayed text), *texte-lu* (text as read).

8. The image of the web is commonly used to suggest non-linearity, but weaving is a fundamentally sequential operation.

9. VR technology has not fared as well with postmodern theory. Its self-enclosed world, ideal of immersive participation, metaphysics of (tele)presence, and striving toward a post-symbolic mode of communication clash with most of the ideas put forward by contemporary literary criticism.

10. See Mark Poster, *The Mode of Information*, on these relations.

11. These oppositions are drawn from various sources, but I would like to single out Turkle's *Life on the Screen* and Lanham, *The Electronic Word*, especially pp. 14ff.

12. I borrow this phrase from the title of David Shaw's book *The Pleasure Police* (New York: Doubleday, 1996).

Works Cited

Barlow, John Perry. "Leaving the Physical World." Loeffler and Anderson 178–84.

Barthes, Roland. *S/Z*. Trans. Richard Miller. New York: Hill and Wang, 1974.

———. "The Death of the Author." *Image, Music, Text*. New York: Hill and Wang, 1977.

Baudrillard, Jean. *Selected Writings*. Ed. Mark Poster. Stanford: Stanford UP, 1988.

Benedikt, Michael. "Introduction." *Cyberspace: First Steps*. Ed. Michael Benedikt. Cambridge: MIT P, 1991. 1–26.

Birkerts, Sven. *The Gutenberg Elegies: The Fate of Reading in an Electronic Age*. New York: Fawcett Columbine, 1994.

Bolter, Jay David. *Writing Space: The Computer, Hypertext, and the History of Writing*. Hillsdale, NJ: Lawrence Erlbaum, 1991.

Bootz, Philippe. "Gestion du temps et du lecteur dans un poème dynamique." *Littérature et informatique. La littérature générée par ordinateur*. Ed. Alain Vuillemin and Michel Lenoble. Arras: Artois Press Université, 1995. 233–48.

Borges, Jorge Luis. "The Circular Ruins." *Labyrinths: Selected Stories and Other Writings*. Ed. Donald A. Yates and James E. Irby. New York: Modern Library, 1983. 45–50.

Bricken, Meredith. "Virtual Worlds: No Interface to Design." Benedikt 363–82.

Brook, James, and Iain A. Boal, eds. *Resisting the Virtual Life: The Culture and Politics of Information*. San Francisco: City Lights, 1995.

Dery, Mark. *Escape Velocity: Cyberculture at the End of the Century*. New York: Grove P, 1996.

Eco, Umberto. *Travels in Hyperreality*. London: Picador, 1987.

Gerrig, Richard J. *Experiencing Narrative Worlds: On the Psychological Activities of Reading*. New Haven and London: Yale UP, 1993.

Gibson, William. "Academy Leader." Benedikt 27–30.

———. *Neuromancer*. New York: Ace, 1994.

Grusin, Richard. "What Is an Electronic Author? Theory and the Technological Fallacy." Markley, 39–54.

Hayles, N. Katherine. "The Condition of Virtuality." *Language Machines: Technologies of Literary and Cultural Production*. Ed. Nancy Vickers and Peter Stallybrass. New York: Routledge, 1997.

Heim, Michael. "The Erotic Ontology of Cyberspace." Benedikt 59–80.

———. *The Metaphysics of Virtual Reality*. New York and Oxford: Oxford UP, 1993.

Joyce, Michael. *Afternoon: A Story*. Cambridge, MA: Eastgate Systems, 1987. Software.

Kroker, Arthur, and Michael A. Weinstein. *Data Trash: The Theory of the Virtual Class*. New York: St. Martin's P, 1994.

Landow, George P. *Hypertext: The Convergence of Contemporary Critical Theory and Technology*. Baltimore and London: Johns Hopkins UP, 1992.

Lanham, Richard. *The Electronic Word: Democracy, Technology, and the Arts*. Chicago: Chicago UP, 1993.

Laudal, Thomas. "One Global Community—Many Virtual Worlds." *Electronic Journal of Virtual Culture* 3.3 (1995).

Laurel, Brenda. "Art and Activism in VR." *Wide Angle* 15.4 (1993), 13–21.

Lévy, Pierre. *Qu'est-ce que le virtuel?* Paris: La Découverte, 1995.

Loeffler, Carl Eugene, and Tim Anderson, eds. *The Virtual Reality Casebook.* New York: Van Nostrand Rheinhold, 1994.

Markley, Robert, ed. *Virtual Realities and Their Discontents.* Baltimore: Johns Hopkins UP, 1995.

Merriam-Webster's Collegiate Dictionary 9th ed. Springfield, MA: Merriam-Webster, Inc., 1991. 1317.

Nell, Victor. *Lost in a Book: The Psychology of Reading for Pleasure.* New Haven: Yale UP, 1988.

Novak, Marcos. "Liquid Architecture in Cyberpsace." Benedikt 225–54.

Pimentel, Ken, and Kevin Texeira. *Virtual Reality: Through the New Looking-Glass.* Intel/Windcrest McGraw Hill, 1993.

Poster, Mark. *The Mode of Information: Poststructuralism and Social Context.* Chicago: U of Chicago P, 1990.

Rheingold, Howard. *Virtual Reality.* New York: Simon and Schuster, 1991.

Slouka, Mark. *War of the Worlds: Cyberspace and the High-Tech Assault on Reality.* New York: Basic Books (HarperCollins), 1995.

Stenger, Nicole. "Mind Is a Leaking Rainbow." Benedikt 49–58.

Stoll, Clifford. *Silicon Snake Oil: Second Thoughts on the Information Highway.* New York: Doubleday, 1995.

Tomas, David. "Old Rituals for New Space": *Rites de Passage* and William Gibson's Cultural Model of Cyberspace." Benedikt 31–47.

Turkle, Sherry. *Life on the Screen: Identity in the Age of the Internet.* New York: Simon and Schuster, 1995.

Walton, Kendall. *Mimesis as Make-Believe: On the Foundations of the Representational Arts.* Cambridge and London: Harvard UP, 1990.

———. "Spelunking, Simulation and Slime: On Being Moved by Fiction." *Emotion and the Arts.* Ed. Mette Hjort and Sue Laver. New York: Oxford UP, 1997, 37–49.

Wexelblatt, Alan. "Giving Meaning to Place: Semantic Spaces." Benedikt 255–72.

Woolley, Benjamin. *Virtual Worlds. A Journey in Hype and Hyperreality.* Cambridge, MA: Blackwell, 1992.

PART II:

CYBERSPACE IDENTITY

5

Women Writers and the Restive Text
Feminism, Experimental Writing, and Hypertext

Barbara Page

It was while reading my way into a number of recent fictions composed in hypertext that I began to think back on a tendency of women's writing which aims not only at changing the themes of fiction but at altering the formal structure of the text itself. In a useful collection of essays about twentieth-century women writers, called *Breaking the Sequence: Women's Experimental Fiction*, Ellen Friedman and Miriam Fuchs trace a line of authors who subvert what they see as patriarchal assumptions governing traditional modes of narrative, beginning with Gertrude Stein, Dorothy Richardson, and Virginia Woolf, and leading to such contemporaries as Christine Brooke-Rose, Eva Figes, and Kathy Acker. They write:

> Although the woman in the text may be the particular woman writer, in the case of twentieth-century women experimental writers, the woman in the text is also an effect of the textual practice of breaking patriarchal fictional forms; the radical forms— nonlinear, nonhierarchical, and decentering—are, in themselves, a way of writing the feminine. (3–4)

Among contemporary writers, women are by no means alone in pursuing non-linear, anti-hierarchical, and decentered writing, but many women who affiliate themselves with this tendency write against norms of "realist" narrative from a consciousness stirred by feminist discourses of resistance, especially those informed by poststructuralist and psychoanalytic theory. The claim of Friedman and Fuchs cited above is

111

itself radical, namely that such women writers can produce themselves—as new beings or as ones previously unspoken—through self-conscious acts of writing against received tradition. A number of the contemporary writers I discuss in this essay make a direct address within the fictive text to feminist theory, rather more as a flag flown than as a definitive discursive marker, in recognition of themselves as engaged with other women in the discursive branch of women's struggle against oppression.[1] For some writers of this tendency, hypertext would seem to provide a means by which to explore new possibilities for writing, notwithstanding an aversion among many women to computer technologies and programs thought to be products of masculinist habits of mind. My argument is not that the print authors I discuss here would be better served by the hypertext medium, but that their writing is in many respects hypertextual in principle and bears relation to discourses of many women writers now working in hypertext.

These women writers, as a rule, take for granted that language itself and much of canonical literature encode hierarchies of value that denigrate and subordinate women, and therefore they incorporate into their work a strategically critical or oppositional posture, as well as a search for alternative forms of composition. They do not accept the notion, however, that language is hopelessly inimical or alien to their interests, and so move beyond the call for some future reform of language to an intervention—exuberant or wary—in present discourses. I focus in particular on writers whose rethinking of gender construction enters into both the themes and the gestural repertoire of their compositions, and who undertake to redesign the very topography of prose. At the most literal level of the text—that of words as graphic objects—all of these writers are leery of the smooth, spooling lines of type that define the fictive space of conventional print texts and delimit the path of the reader. Like other postmodernist writers, they move on from modernist methods of collage to constructions articulating alternatives to linear prose. The notion, for example, of textuality as weaving (a restoration of the root meaning of "text") and of the construction of knowledge as a web that has figured prominently in the development of hypertext has also been important in feminist theory, though for rather different purposes.[2] Like other postmodernist writers, also, many of these women experimentalists are strikingly self-reflexive, and write about their texts in the text. One important difference, though, concerns the self-conscious will among these writers not simply to reimagine writing as weaving but rather to take apart the fabric of inherited textual forms and to reweave it into new designs. For all of these authors, restiveness with the fixity of print signifies something more than a struggle going on under a blanket of established formal meaning. Their aim is to rend the surface of language and to reshape it into forms more hospitable to the historical lives of women and to an aesthetic of the will and desire of a self-apprehended female body that is an end unto itself and not simply instrumental. One frequent mark of this new writing is the introduction of silence, partly as a memorial to the historical silencing of women's voices, but also as a means of establishing a textual space for the entrance of those "others" chronically excluded from the closed texts of dogmatists and power interests.

As my point of departure, I want briefly to describe Carole Maso's 1993 novel, *AVA*, her third book in order of composition, though published fourth. This text unfolds in the mind of a thirty-nine-year-old professor of comparative literature named Ava Klein, who is dying of a rare blood disease, a form of cancer. The book, divided into Morning, Afternoon, and Night, takes place on the last day of Ava's life, the same day in which President George Bush draws his line in the sand of the Persian Gulf states, inaugurating a war. Against this act and all the forces of division and destruction it symbolizes, against the malignancy of cancer and of militarism, Maso poses the unbounded mind of Ava, whose powers of memory and desire abide in the emblematic figure of a girl, recurring throughout the text, who draws an A and spells her own name. Ava's narrative is in fragments that in the act of being read acquire fuller meaning, through repetition, through their discrete placement on the passing pages, through variation, and also through the generous space between utterances that gives a place to silence and itself comes to represent a certain freedom—of movement, of new linkage, of as-yet-unuttered possibilities. Here is how the book begins:

MORNING

Each holiday celebrated with real extravagance. Birthdays. Independence days. Saints' days. Even when we were poor. With verve.

Come sit in the morning garden for awhile.
Olives hang like earrings in late August.

A perpetual pageant.

A throbbing.

Come quickly.

The light in your eyes.

Precious. Unexpected things.

Mardi Gras: a farewell to the flesh.

You spoke of Trieste. Of Constantinople. You pushed the curls
from your face. We drank Five-Star Metaxa on the island of Crete
and aspired to the state of music.

Olives hang like earrings.

A throbbing. A certain pulsing.

The villagers grew violets.

We ran through genêt and wild sage.

Labyrinth of Crete, mystery of water, home.

In a polemical preface to *AVA*, Maso argues that much of current
commercial fiction, in attempting to ward off the chaos and "mess" of
death with organized, rational narratives, ultimately becomes "death
with its complacent, unequivocal truths, its reductive assignment of
meaning, its manipulations, its predictability and stasis." In this preface, Maso traces her resistance to traditional narratives back to feelings
of dissatisfaction with the "silly plots" of stories her mother read aloud
to her as a child. In order to stop "the incessant march of the plot forward to the inevitable climax," she would, she recalls, wander away, out
of earshot, taking a sentence or a scene to dream over. Often she would
detach the meanings from the words her mother read, turning the
words into a kind of music, "a song my mother was singing in a secret
language just to me." Bypassing the logos of stories, then, she walked
into a freer space where she was able to invent, or rediscover, another
tempo and ordering of language felt as a sensuous transmission from the
mother's body to hers. "This is what literature became for me: music,
love, and the body" ("On *AVA*" 175–76).

This is the beginning, but not the end or sum of Maso's fiction.
Rather like Adrienne Rich's "new poet" in her "Transcendental Etude,"
she walks away from the old arguments into a space of new composition,
where she takes up fragments of the already spoken with a notable lack
of anxiety about influence. In the stream of her narrative one hears formal and informal voices of precursors and contemporaries, male and
female, along with patches of fact, history, even critical discourse that
figure as features of the rhythmic text, the writing of a richly nourished
adult mind—Ava Klein never more alive than on the day of her dying:

García Lorca, learning to spell, and not a day too soon.

Ava Klein in a beautiful black wig. Piled up high.

And I am waiting at what is suddenly this late hour, for my ship to come in—

Even if it is a papier-mâché ship on a plastic sea, after all.

We wanted to live.

How that night you rubbed "olio santo" all over me. One liter oil, chili peppers, bay leaves, rosemary.

And it's spaghetti I want at 11:00 A.M.

Maybe these cravings are a sign of pregnancy. Some late last-minute miracle. The trick of living past this life.

To devour all that is the world.

Because more than anything, we wanted to live.

Dear Bunny,
      If it is quite convenient we shall come with our butterfly nets this Friday.

You will have literary texts that tolerate all kinds of freedom—unlike the more classical texts—which are not texts that delimit themselves, are not texts of territory with neat borders, with chapters, with beginnings, endings, etc., and which will be a little disquieting because you do not feel the

Border.

The edge.

How are you? I've been rereading Kleist with great enthusiasm and I wish you were around to talk to and I realize suddenly,

I miss you. (113)

For Ava, thinking and feeling go together, and reading is sensuous, rendering literal the definition of influence, so that whole passages of her text—still unmistakably her own—are washed in the colors of an admired author: Woolf, Garcia Lorca, Beckett, and others. Ava's reading is finally a species of her promiscuous engorgement with life, and of a mind that declines to wall off speaking from writing or to isolate recollection, narration, and description from meditation and analysis. In the passage above, for example, a snatch of a letter to Edmund Wilson ("Bunny") from the lapidary lepidopterist Nabokov stands next to a bit from Hélène Cixous, graphically tailing off into broken borders which in turn begin to enact an expansion of the sort of text that Cixous calls for. The book, curiously, achieves unity in the act of reading, as the rhythmic succession of passages induces a condition approaching trance. The effect is both aural and visual: when spoken, real time must pass between utterances; when read, real space must be traversed by the eye between islands of text.

In an essay that itself intermingles argument and reflection with quotation from her own novels and from precursor writers and theorists, Maso points to images that both ground her ambition and suggest alternatives to linear prose: "*AVA* could not have been written as it was, I am quite sure, if I had not been next to the water day after day. Incorporating the waves." And, "The design of the stars then in the sky. I followed their dreamy instructions. Composed in clusters. Wrote constellations of associations." Attributing independent will to genres, she describes the "desire" of the novel to be a poem, of the poem to be an essay, of the essay to reach toward fiction, and "the obvious erotics of this" ("Notes" 26). The desiring text rebels against the virtual conspiracy between "commodity novelists" and publishers to lock a contrived sense of reality, shorn of its remoteness and mystery, into "the line, the paragraph, the chapter, the story, the storyteller, character." As a lyric artist in large prose forms, Maso explains that

> Writing *AVA* I felt at times . . . like a choreographer working with language in physical space. Language, of course, being gesture and also occupying space. Creating relations which exist in their integrity for one fleeting moment and then are gone, remaining in the trace of memory. Shapes that then regather and re-form making for their instant, new relations, new longings, new recollections, inspired by those fleeting states of being. ("Notes" 27)

She names as precursors Virginia Woolf of the *Waves* and Gertrude Stein, in Stein's remark, "I have destroyed sentences and rhythms and literary overtones and all the rest of that nonsense . . ." (28, 27). In place of plot she aims to "imagine story as a blooming flower, or a series of blossomings," for example, and makes space in the text for "the random, the accidental, the overheard, the incidental. *Precious, disappearing things*" (27; italics in the original). And here the italicized words, from the second section of *AVA*, incrementally repeat a line from the opening of the book— "Precious. Unexpected things"—to underscore the ethical, as well as aesthetic impulse in Maso's fiction (*AVA* 186).

For Maso, the attraction of the novel is its unruly, expansive refusal of perfection. She argues that, because we no longer believe that the traditional stories are true, we can no longer write tidy, beginning-middle-end fiction, even if this means that we must "write notebooks rather than masterpieces," as Woolf once suggested ("Notes" 29). The gain will be "room and time for everything. This will include missteps, mistakes, speaking out of turn. Amendments, erasures, illusions." Instead of the "real" story, we shall have: "The ability to embrace oppositional stances at the same time. Contradictory impulses, ideas, motions. To assimilate as part of the form, incongruity, ambivalence" ("Notes" 30). And for Maso, who has the confidence to found imagination on her own experience, this form of fiction, that does not tyrannize and that allows "a place for the reader to live, to dream," leads not to the "real" story but to "what the story was for me": "A feminine shape—after all this time" ("Notes" 30, 28).

In an essay that is something of a tour-de-force, entitled ":RE: THINKING:LITERARY:FEMINISM: (three essays onto shaky grounds)," poet and theorist Joan Retallack, like Maso, addresses what is—or can be—of particular import for women in the refiguration of writing toward non- or multilinear, de- or recentered prose, by means of a revaluation of the terms traditionally affixed to the subordinated figure of the feminine:

> An interesting coincidence, yes/no? that what Western culture has tended to label feminine (forms characterized by silence, empty and full; multiple, associative, nonhierarchical logics; open and materially contingent processes, etc.) may well be more relevant to the complex reality we are coming to see as our world than the narrowly hierarchical logics that produced the rationalist dream-work of civilization and its misogynist discontents. (347)

In thinking about why for her the writing of women today seems particularly vibrant with potential, Retallack underscores the worth both of productive silence, that gives place to the construction of new images and meanings, and of collaboration, that empowers writer and reader to "conspire (to breathe together) . . . in the construction of a living aesthetic event" (356). While denying a turn toward essentialism, she argues that the historical situation of women now provides a particularly fertile "construction site" for new writing, one important feature of which is its invitation to the active participation of others in an ongoing textual process:

> I'd like to suggest that it is a woman's feminine text (denying any redundancy), which implicitly acknowledges and creates the possibility of other/additional/simultaneous texts. This is a model sig-

nificantly different from Bloom's competitive anxiety of influence. It opens up a distinction between the need to imprint/impress ones mark (image) on the other, and *an invitation to the other's discourse*. . . . (358; my italics)

Against those feminists who despair of entering a language overcoded with misogyny, Retallack argues that "Language has always overflowed the structures/strictures of its own grammars," and that "The so-called feminine is in language from the start" (372). In this regard, Retallack supplies a validation of Maso's ready, unanxious introduction of quotation from male authors in what she calls her feminine text.

That prose writers like Maso and poet/theorists like Retallack do not stand alone is indicated, for example, by the 1992 anthology entitled *Resurgent: New Writing by Women*, co-edited by Lou Robinson and Camille Norton. It brings together a generous selection of writers who mix genres of verse and prose freely and embed manifesto or critique in both the narrative and the topography of the writing. *Resurgent* is divided into two, or perhaps four, parts—"Transmission/Translation" and "Collaboration/Spectacle"—as it moves from single-author texts to collaborative and to performative texts. Lou Robinson writes in the introduction:

Everywhere in these prose pieces I find that unpredictable element in the language which forces consciousness to leap a gap where other writing would make a bridge of shared meaning . . . , a sense of something so urgent in its desire to be expressed that it comes before the words to say it, in the interstices, in the rhythm: Marina Tsvetaeva's "song in the head without noise." . . . This is writing that swings out over a chasm, that spits. (1)

Among the most interesting pieces in *Resurgent* are the collaborations, including one by Daphne Marlatt and Betsy Warland, entitled "Reading and Writing Between the Lines," which undertakes a punning reclamation of the term "collaboration" itself. Their endeavor resembles that of Retallack, when she reclaims the word "conspire" by reminding readers of its root meaning as "to breathe together" and applies it to the notion of opening the authorial text to the discourse of others. In their piece, Marlatt and Warland, "running on together," write their way through the self-betrayal of collaboration in its political sense to a celebration of co-labial play, in the lips of speech and of women's sex:

'let me slip into something more comfortable'
                                    she glides across the

room
labi, to glide, to slip

(*labile; labilis:*
labia; labialis)
    la la la
'my labyl mynde . . . '
labilis, labour, belabour, collaborate, elaborate

. . . . .

slip of the tongue

    'the lability of innocence'

. . . . .

    labia majora (the 'greater lips')
    la la la
       and
    labia minora
    (the 'lesser lips')
not two mouths but three!
slipping one over on polarity

    slippage in the text
you & me *collabi*, (*to slip together*)
labialization!)
slip(ping) page(es)
like notes in class

o labilism o letter of the lips
o *grafting* of our slips
labile lovers
'prone to undergo displacement in position or change in nature,
form, chemical composition; unstable' (159)

This wordplay owes most, perhaps, to Irigaray's feminist displacement of the phallus as the central signifier in the sexual imaginary, particularly as articulated in Lacan. In *This Sex Which Is Not One*, she
writes: "Woman 'touches herself' all the time, and moreover no one can
forbid her to do so, for her genitals are formed of two lips in continu-

ous contact. Thus, within herself, she is already two—but not divisible into one(s)—that caress each other" (24). Although Irigaray's language is open to the criticism that it may lead to biological essentialism, we should bear in mind that all language is shot through with metaphors, many derived from the body, and that some of the boldest interventions by innovative women writers have been through an insistence on speaking the body in new terms as a way of breaking the hold of traditional discourses that denigrate and demonize the female body. This is a move against a crippling inheritance of ideology, as Nicole Ward Jouve points out: "The whole idea of *sex* talking is itself symbolic, is itself discourse; the phrase is a turning around and reclaiming of 'male' discourse" (32). It is also a move, as we have seen in Maso, toward the discovery, in material forms commonly associated with the feminine, of structures capable of inspiring new forms of writing. For collaborative writers Marlatt and Warland, the co-labial slippage between two and one opens the text to a commingling of voices about the unsanctioned commingling of women's bodies, thus enacting a double subversion of the Lacanian Law. The effect is not that of reductive essentialism but rather of the frank erotics Maso refers to, an imaginative discursive enactment of the "desire" of one text for another.

At some points in Marlatt and Warland's text two voices march down separate columns of type in a way reminiscent of Kristeva's antiphonal essay-invocations,[3] but at others, they merge into pronominal harmony and a playful syntactic break-up, reminiscent of Stein, that shakes loose the overdetermined subject:

to keep (y)our word. eroticizing collaboration we've moved from treason into trust. a difficult season, my co-labial writer writing me in we while we are three and you is reading away with us—

who?

you and you (not we) in me and all of us reading, which is what we do when left holding the floor, watching you soar with the words' turning and turning their sense and sensing their turns i'm dancing with you in the dark learning to trust that sense of direction learning to

are you trying to avoid the auto-biographical? what is 'self' writing here? when you leave space for your readers who may not read you in the same way the autobiographical becomes communal even communographic in its contextual and narrative (Carol Gilligan) women's way of

read you in to where I want to go   thinking—and collaborating.
although the connotations you
bring are different we share the
floor the ground floor meaning
dances on. . . . (162–63)

The verbal strategies here are familiar enough to contemporary readers: the deconstructive questioning (whose is "(y)our word"?) that exposes the instability of subject and object; the reclaiming of terms and
unmaking of conventional syntax; the diologism of the blocked texts.
The antiphonal effect of the double columns in fact puts eye-reading
into crisis, just as, conversely, the broken, parenthesized, multiplication
of signifiers baffles a single voice reading aloud in sequence. Unlike
many collaborative writers, Marlatt and Warland refuse to distinguish
between their two voices by use of a different typeface or placement on
the page. In Maso's *AVA*, influences naturalize and borders among texts
break; in Marlatt and Warland, collaboration undermines the notion of
writing as intellectual property: we cannot tell where one leaves off and
the other begins. It is no coincidence, I think, that prose of this kind
floats in generous, unconventional volumes of space, seeking escape, it
would seem, from the rigid lineation and lineage of the print text.

Tendencies of the kind of writing I have been describing receive
fresh realization in the medium of hypertext. One of these, a collaborative fiction called *Izme Pass*, by Carolyn Guyer and Martha Petry,
seems particularly congruent with those in *Resurgent*, both in its politics and in its formal concerns. *Izme Pass* came about as the result of an
experiment in writing proposed for the journal *Writing on the Edge*. The
editors first asked hypertext novelist Michael Joyce, best known for his
hyperfiction *Afternoon*, to compose a story. Then they invited other
authors to revise or augment his text into a collaboration. Carolyn
Guyer and Martha Petry, each of whom had been at work on a hyperfiction of her own, took up the challenge but refused to accept Joyce's
fiction, called *WOE, or a memory of what will be*, as a prior or instigating
text. Recognizing a patriarchal precept in the positing of a master text,
they set about to create an independent construction that would also
transgressively subvert and appropriate *WOE* (79). In an on-screen map
they placed a writing space, containing fragments of Joyce's text, into
a triad with spaces containing parts of their own works in progress,
then added a fourth, new work, called "Pass," woven of connections
they created among the other three texts to produce an intertextual
polylog:

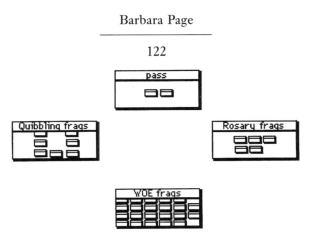

Figure 5.1

As Guyer and Petry explain: "Almost immediately we began to see how this process of tinkering with existing texts by intentionally sculpting their inchoate connections had the ironic effect of making everything more fluid. *Izme Pass* began to affect *Rosary* [Petry's work] which poured its new character back into *Quibbling* [Guyer's work] which flowed over into *WOE* and back through *Izme*" (82). At the level of textual organization and of structural metaphor, *Izme Pass* mocks *WOE*, which graphically emanates from a "Mandala," an Asiatic diagram for meditation supposed to lead to mystical insight:

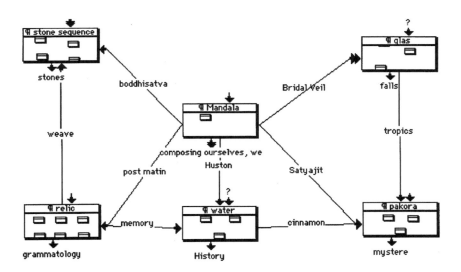

Figure 5.2

Instead, they designed a diamond- or o- or almond-shaped map headed by a "Mandorla," the Asiatic signifier of the yoni, the divine female genital:

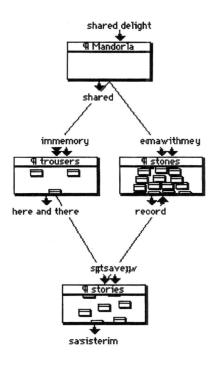

Figure 5.3

Appropriations and revaluations of the sort illustrated here constitute critique as an internal dynamic of this hypertext. Because it is written in the Storyspace program, however, *Izme Pass* takes the further step of opening itself to interventions by readers turned writers, who can, if they choose add to, subtract from, or rearrange the text. In this respect, the politics of hypertext allows for one realization of a feminist aim articulated by Retallack: it provides "an invitation to the other's discourse." It pushes further those disruptions of the "real" story Maso calls for, allowing for effects of the sort she lists, including "missteps, mistakes, speaking out of turn. Amendments, erasures, illusions." Like all hypertexts, *Izme Pass* prohibits definitive reading; the reader chooses the path of the narrative. The graphical device of notating linked words, moreover, sometimes introduces further narrative possibilities. Opening *Izme Pass* through its title, the reading begins with this figure of a female storyteller:

> When a woman tells a story she is remembering what
> will be. What symmetry, or asymmetry, the story
> passes through the orifice directly beneath the
> wide-spread antlers, curved horns of ritual at her head.
> just as it passes through the orifice between her open
> legs. Labrys. How could she not know?
>
> When a woman tells a story it is to save. To husband
> the world, you might say. Thinking first to save
> her mother, her daughter, her sisters, Scheherazade
> tells, her voice enchanting, saving him in the bargain.
>
>
> When a woman tells, oh veiled voice, a story.

Figure 5.4

In *Izme Pass*, words linked to other texts can also signify in the passage on-screen. Here, for example, the linked words: "a story"; "passes through"; "passes through"; "mother"; "daughter"; "her sisters"; "saving him in the bargain," yield a narrative surplus, becoming syntactic in themselves and creating resonant juxtapositions. In this case, the linked words sketch an incipient story having many "passes," constellated around a family of women, that predicates the saving of a man.

Proceeding into the text through the word "story" itself, on a first pass one arrives at a text space, under the title "stones," that gives a definition of "cairns" and suggests one metaphor—or several—for communal story-writing:

> Cairns: the cumulative construction of heaps of stones by
> passers-by at the site of accidents, disgraces, deaths,
> violence, or as remembrances (records) of journeys.
>
> It is as if the stones in their configuration, in the years of
> their leaning against each other, learn to talk with one
> another, and are married.

Figure 5.5

Nested in the "stones" box at the map level is an assemblage of writing spaces that themselves graphically depict a sort of cairn and produce a textual neighborhood, so to speak, of thematic materials associatively linked to the notion of stones:

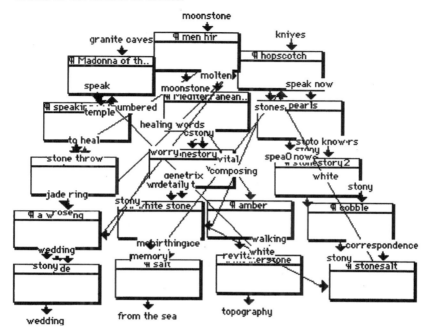

Figure 5.6

Such a rich site as this offers a host of possibilities to the reader. I might, for example, linger at the level of this screen to examine the variety of materials gathered into the cairn. Or I might choose a text and follow the default path where it leads, out of this screen to other locations in *Izme Pass*. If I choose to click on "stonestory 1," at the center of the cairn, I am transported abruptly to a narrative line: "She said, 'When I was little I held stones up to my crotch to feel the coldness.' " Following the default path from this space, I navigate next to a space titled "a wedding," containing this text:

Beside her groom, the cool stone closed tightly in her palm. Just before the ceremony he had given her a small jade butterfly, signal of his intent. He wanted to learn her, and one of the first things he knew was that jade was her stone.

Piedras de ijada, stones of the loin.

Figure 5.7

And then after that to a space titled "delight":

His. Delight. Is what she seeks. In this shade which
she herself creates, his mind turned inward, she might
hold him in her palm so, brief reprieve.

Another, he says. Again.

Figure 5.8

Another click on the default path returns me to "stonestory 1," establishing a tight narrative circle that I realize has moved me swiftly
through ritual passages of a female eroticism that has been symbolically
associated with and mediated by stones. Deciding at this point to investigate the adjacent "stonestory 2," I navigate into the prophetic speech
of a woman, here again unnamed: "She said, 'In order to move moun-
tains you've got to know what stones are about.' " The default path
in this case issues outward into a journal entry about a sort of female
Demosthenes, with the words "She gathered a pearl in her mouth, an O
within an O . . . " and then on to a screen entitled "Scheherazade," one
of *Izme*'s key figures, I realize, recalling the "stories" text with which
my reading began. Backtracking to the journal entry about "an O
within an O," I take note of the growing significance of circles in *Izme*,
and decide to revisit a screen I had previously encountered in my survey
of the cairn, entitled "salt," and I read:

the alchemical symbol was the same for water as for
salt (representing the horizon, separation and/or
joining of earth and sky)

symbol of purification and rebirth

tastes like blood and seawater, both fluids identified
with the womb

Figure 5.9

Within this configuration of *Izme*'s texts, circles have produced associations among: the form of a woman's body, rituals of sexual passage, prophetic speaking, female storytelling and, here, a mystical perception of cosmic order. Because I am exploring *Izme* as an open text, that is, one that allows, even encourages, the reader to intervene as a writer,[4] I now decide—unthinkable in one too well-schooled in reading closed print texts—to make a link and add a new text, by joining the O motif to the passage I quoted above in this essay, from Irigaray's *This Sex Which Is Not One*. But where to place it? In order to answer this question, I find myself attending more closely than I might otherwise do to how the structure of *Izme* and its thematic nodes interact. Finally, I decide simply to nest my new text within the salt, so to speak, by dragging a writing space I create into the interior of the "salt" space, linking it to the Irigaray passage from the alchemical symbol ⊖ on a path that I name "like lips":

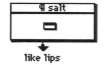

Figure 5.10

In all the texts under discussion here, there is a dynamic relation between feminist thematics and textuality, a relationship that intensifies in a hypertext such as *Izme Pass*, with its complex interweaving of disparate writings and its invitation to the reader to move freely both among texts and between texts and syntactic maps. Not all hypertexts by women are as unconstrained or open as *Izme Pass*, although many nevertheless contain aspects of what one might call hypertextual feminism. Judy Malloy's lyrical fiction *its name was Penelope*, for example, presents only a handful of choices at any given moment of reading, through labels that may be clicked on to carry the reader into sections titled "Dawn," "Sea" (subdivided into four sections: "a gathering of shades," "that far-off island," "fine work and wide across," "rock and a hard place"), and "Song." Because the text screens of the "Dawn" and "Sea" sections have been programmed by the computer to produce a sort of random rearrangement with each successive reading, the contexts and nuances of any given passage change with different readings, even though one's movement through a sequence is relatively linear. Though restrictive by comparison with *Izme Pass*, the structure Malloy adopts strengthens the analogy she intends between the text screens we read and the photographic images her artist-protagonist, Anne Mitchell, is trying to work into assemblages.

The "it" named Penelope in Malloy's fiction is a toy sailboat, the inciting image of her strategic reconsideration of the *Odyssey*. In her story, Anne Mitchell, though a weaver of images like her wifely forebear, does not stay put but rather wends her way through relationships and sexual liaisons, evading "That Far-Off Island," Malloy's version of Calypso, on which, Malloy remarks in her introductory "Notes," "[i]n these days, some married women artists feel trapped" (11). Penelope's compounded, disjunctive structure corresponds with and seems to arise from the narrator's restless splitting off of attention, under the opposed attractions of sexual and aesthetic desire:

That Far-Off Island

On the telephone he told me a story
about working in an ice cream store
when he was 14 years old.
I looked through the box of photos that I keep by my bed
while I listened.

Figure 5.11

Repeatedly in the narrative, the pursuit of art draws Anne away from a lover and the "island" of monogamous, domesticated sex:

That Far-Off Island

We were looking at contact sheets in his kitchen.
My coffee sat untouched in the center of the table.
Where his shirt was unbuttoned,
dark hairs curled on his chest.
I got up and began to put the contact sheets
back into the manilla folder.
"I have to go," I said.

Figure 5.12

Unlike its classical antecedent, Malloy's *Penelope* is spare rather than expansive, made of vignettes rather than continuously developed action or panoramic description. Malloy, however, argues that *Penelope*, a narrabase, as she calls it, is not stream of consciousness, like parts of Joyce's *Ulysses*, though it does bear a resemblance, she believes, to Dorothy Richardson's *Pilgrimage*, "that strove to be the writing equivalent of impressionist painting," just as *Penelope* "strives to be the writing equivalent of the captured photographic moment . . . " ("Notes" 13). The analogy between the on-screen texts of *Penelope* and sequences of photographs prompts the reader's reflection upon the nature of each medium. A photograph can be read as a composed image of visual objects removed from time and stilled into permanence, or as a momentary arrest of motion in time, pointing back toward a just-gone past and forward to a promised future. Similarly, though the lines of any on-screen writing are set (at least in a read-only text), and may seem as isolated as a single photograph found on the street, in the varied sequences one reads, the words of a text screen float on a motile surface, poised for instantaneous change into another, not fully predictable writing.

In light of this interrelation of theme and structure in *Penelope*, Malloy's decision to set the texts in "Song"—which tells a partial tale of a love affair—into a fixed sequence nudges the reader to consider how this differently designed episode relates to the rest of the fiction. "Song" offers something of a romantic idyll, and something of a threat to Malloy's edgy contemporary woman artist, fearful that sexual desire may lead her to yield to a man who would fill all of her space and time with his demand for her attention and care. And so the set sequence of "Song," threaded through with images of a recording tape that is raveled and rewound, comes to an end that allows either for a replay of its looping reverie, in accordance with the textual program, or instead to a new departure, either through the active agency of the narrator within the fiction, who takes up the instrument of her work, or of the reader, who reaches out for a selection other than <Next>:

Song

Across the brook,
three teenage boys sat on a rock,
drinking beer.
I took out my camera.

END OF SONG - if you press <Next>,
the chorus will begin again.

| *Next* | *Sea* | *Song* |

Figure 5.13

Thus, in Malloy's *Penelope*, the interplay of hypertextual freedom and sequential constraint—an artifact of the electronic medium itself—surprisingly produces a variant enactment of the dilemmas and decisions her woman artist struggles with inside the fiction.

In a later work, entitled *Forward Anywhere*, composed collaboratively by Malloy and Cathy Marshall, the authors struggle with questions of structural design produced by their initial decision to compose through e-mail and to edit material in html at an Internet site, deploying both a gathering function and a random function of the program, to emphasize the fluency, associativeness, and disjunction of e-mail correspondence. Midway in their correspondence, the project was shockingly threatened with disruption, however, when Malloy suffered severe injury in an accident. Emerging eventually with "a fresh patchwork of scars," and faced with a long recuperation, Malloy and Marshall decided to incorporate this event and writings about it into the work by letting Malloy's screens about her accident "mark the end of the first phase" of their collaboration. Malloy, from her bed in Phoenix, Arizona, and Marshall, herself in motion between Texas and California, developed a "virtual way of continuing," to blend two very real lives through a "virtual collaboration" which built in both literal and figurative material concerned with accidents, scarring, and patching ("Closure" 67, 68). The "found" title, *Forward Anywhere*, fortuitously derived from text's navigational buttons, suggests momentum, openness, and accidentality in a work that also achieves a surprisingly unified tone of fortitude, even optimism.[5]

In all of the works I have been discussing, the conscious feminism of the writer animates her determination not simply to write but to intervene in the structure of discourse, to interrupt reiterations of what has been written, to redirect the streams of narrative and to clear space for the construction of new textual forms congenial to women's subjectivity. And all of these writers have understood that their project entails both the articulation of formerly repressed or dismissed stories and the rearticulation of textual forms and codes. It is for this reason, perhaps, that feminist theory and textual practice can be of particular pertinence to theorists of hypertext who recognize a radical politics in the rhetoric and poetics of hypertextual writing. And this is why, I believe, hypertext may prove a fruitful site for innovative writing by women, despite a deep-dyed skepticism toward and resistance to some of its claims and demands.

In her hypertext novel *Quibbling*, excerpts of which provided material for *Izme Pass*, Carolyn Guyer embeds passages from a diary that reflect her sense of writing at a critical moment of change in relations between women and men. Importantly, she conceives that where they are placed in the text will affect how they can develop and how they will encounter one another. Here, for example, is one such passage, titled, significantly, "topographic":

8 Sept 90
I wonder what would happen to the story if I changed how I have it organized right now. I've been keeping all the various elements of it gathered separately in his/her own boxes and areas just so I could move around in it and work more easily. But it strikes me that each of the men is developing as himself and in relation to his lover, while the women are developing as themselves but also kind of like sisters. Each man has his own box as a major element, or cove, but each woman has her own box *within* the nun area. Like a dormitory, gynaeceum, or a convent.

I've thought a number of times lately to bring each woman into her lover's box and make each cove then a marriage box, but have not done it. The topography of the story speaks as it forms, as well as when the reader encounters it. I believe what I was (am) doing is helping the women stay independent. Also, giving them access, through proximity, to each other.

Figure 5.14

In many ways, topography is the story of this writing, and it is remarkable that women, so long objectified and imprisoned in male fantasies of the feminine as territory, earth, terra incognita, should incorporate into the struggle to achieve self-articulation the remaking of both the material and figurative space in which they live, or will live after the earthquake that shakes down the myriad symbols and structures that have constructed and constricted them. Even in the handful of hypertextual fictions that have been written thus far, the potential for projects of radical change in representational art is evident. Especially for women writers who self-reflexively incorporate thinking about texts into fiction and for women who wish to seize rather than shy from the technological means of production, hypertext—which peculiarly welcomes and makes space for refraction and oppositional discourses—can be inviting, even though it rightly arouses a suspicion that its assimilative vastness may swallow up subversion.

This suspicion is confirmed provocatively by Stuart Moulthrop and Nancy Kaplan in a discussion of what they regard as the "futility of resistance" in electronic writing: "Where a resistant reading of print literature always produces another definitive discourse, the equivalent procedure in hypertext does just the opposite, generating not objective closure but a further range of openings that extend the discursive possibilities of the text for 'constructive' transaction" (235). The very openness of hypertext, initially appealing to writers of resistance discourses, carries the risk that their voices may simply be absorbed into the medium, precisely because, as Moulthrop and Kaplan explain, "it offers no resistance to the intrusion" (235). The subversions and contestations in *Izme Pass*, however, suggest that resistance is possible at least at the level of syntax or structure. Similarly, as her diary in *Quibbling* indicates, Guyer wishes to structure gender-specific boundaries and communities into her text, in an effort to preserve her fictive women's independence from men while giving them proximity to other women. While the principle of linking perhaps does open a text to limitless discursive possibility, as Moulthrop and Kaplan argue, when a graphic mapping is used, as in Storyspace documents, new possibilities for demarcation and affiliation appear. This protocol, however, carries its own hazard; although any writing in an open electronic text is both provisional and discursively extendible, graphic maps or syntactic displays can reinscribe enclosure and hierarchy.

In differently structuring the text spaces of men and women in *Quibbling*, Guyer moves toward the encoding of difference at the level of structure, but then, through the reflexive interpolation of the diary, she shifts the signification of those spaces into history, by analogy to women's communities in the dormitory, convent, or gynaeceum. Historians of women have viewed such places variously, either as sites of confinement or as places where women have achieved both supportive community and freedom from servitude. While giving scope to the independence of women, in *Quibbling* (and in the collaborative *Izme Pass*) Guyer places emphasis on the importance of women's communities through both structure and story. In *Penelope* Malloy lays emphasis on the development of women's subjectivity. Like the individualistic woman writer in Woolf's *Room of One's Own*, Malloy's Anne Mitchell seeks a place where she can concentrate her attention and do her work, like Maso who wants to write, not the "real" story, but what "the story was for me." There is ample room in feminism for both tendencies, as Malloy's own subsequent writings reveal, and one can easily imagine an Ava or an Anne Mitchell at work within the fictive space of *Quibbling*.

There is room too for re-membering our foremothers, as Woolf urges, in radically new ways, as demonstrated in Shelley Jackson's hyperfiction *Patchwork Girl*, whose putative authorship is a composite of "Mary / Shelley and Herself," "Herself" being an insouciant protagonist who announces: "I was made as strong as my unfortunate and famous brother, but less neurotic!" ("I am"). Patchwork Girl is a composite of body parts which when clicked on disclose their own life stories, playfully fictionalizing a truth of genetic inheritance, just as Jackson—reminiscent of Maso—achieves polyvocality through the importation of text bits from many sources. In a note on sources, Jackson remarks: "At certain places in this web I have lapsed without notice into another's voice, into direct quote or fudged restatement. My subject matter seemed to call for this very unceremonious appropriation" (Title page: "Sources"). One segment of the text, a colorful crazyquilt when viewed on-screen, has been composed entirely of quotation from a dozen sources, ranging from L. Frank Baum (whose *Patchwork Girl of Oz* is, like Shelley's *Frankenstein*, an anchor text), to Cixous, Haraway, Lucretius, and even Klaus Theweleit's *Male Fantasies*. Far from appearing as a hopelessly belated puppet of prior texts, Patchwork Girl achieves a distinctive voice and a refreshing refiguration of female subjectivity through the fictive possibilities enabled by hypertext, in its resistance to definition, ownership, finality. As Patchwork explains:

> Born full grown, I have lived in this frame for 175 years. By another reckoning, I have lived many lives . . . and am much older. . . . I belong nowhere. This is not bizarre for my sex, however, nor is it uncomfortable for us, to whom belonging has generally meant, belonging TO ("I").

In a text area called "rethinking," under the title "what shape" Patchwork reaches a turning point articulated as an analogy between forms of writing and forms of life:

> If I clung to traditional form with its ordered stanzas—to youth, adolescence, middle age and senility—I belonged in the grave. . . .
> I could be a kind of extinguished wish for a human life, or I could be something entirely different: instead of fulfilling a determined structure, I could merely extend, inventing a form as I went along. This decision turned me from a would-be settler to a nomad.[6]

After many adventures, Patchwork Girl sails for the New World, enters time present, and becomes a writer, perched for the moment in Death Valley: "In the mobile home where I live I've set up a writing desk. I'm writing some things down. But often I strap on my laptop computer and go out" ("afterwards"). Patchwork, like her author, a Harawayan cyborg, appropriates for her own use—with striking hardihood and cheer—the technology that enables the open-ended, hypertextual recomposition of her subjectivity.

The direction hypertext and its fictions will take in this volatile moment for textuality and for gender relations is not altogether clear, but if hypertext is to realize its potential as a medium for inclusive and democratic writing, it is profoundly important that women's desire and creative will should contribute to its future shapings. As Guyer writes, "the topography of the story speaks as it forms," and a more hospitable topography will speak a fuller, richer story, one that can, as Retallack argues, invite those former Others into an ongoing shared discourse.

Notes

1. On the matter of "writing the feminine," two questions are likely to be raised right away: (1) does the very term impose an invidious construction of the dyad masculine/feminine, such that the "feminine" locks writers into otherness, lack, and erasure; (2) does "writing the feminine" limit or liberate the writer, or perhaps achieve some other unanticipated result? I intend to take up these questions less in reference to theory than to the practice and professions of women writers who regard themselves as feminist or who regard their texts as examples of writing the feminine.

2. See for example Nancy K. Miller, "Arachnologies: The Woman, the Text, and the Critic."

3. Kristeva's "Stabat Mater," for example.

4. In her essay, "Fretwork: ReForming Me," Carolyn Guyer describes her dismay on finding that someone had taken up her invitation to add writing to a work of hers, because she first judged that it was not good and then felt guilty because she "was imposing cultural values as if they were universal, absolute standards." In this essay she searches for theoretical and figurative means by which to incorporate and embody "the challenges of multicultural communities," uncovering along the way the trap of perfectionism (as Maso has also done in her argument for the messiness of the novel) and, by contrast, the privilege, as she defines it, "in sharing rather than in the owning of knowledge." This leads her to argue for the value of opening art to differences that alter contexts and restore the vitality of dynamic process rather than the stillness of mastery. Guyer's argument calls to mind John Cage's advocacy of aleatory composition.

5. Malloy and Marshall discuss the composing of *Forward Anywhere* in "Closure Was Never a Goal in this Piece," an essay written as a simulacrum of on-screen e-mail correspondence. Another outcome of her accident is Malloy's spontaneous collaboration with friends, entitled *name is scibe*, "written simultaneously on ARTS WIRE and on The WELL" while she was recuperating.

6. Philosopher Rosi Braidotti has theorized the figure of the "nomadic subject," adapting Deleuze and Guattari for feminist purposes. She is thinking in particular of polyglot European intellectuals, who relinquish fixity of place and language for "an identity made of transitions, successive shifts, and coordinated changes, without and against an essential unity"

(22). In place of the polyglot, Jackson playfully offers a polyvocal poly-morph.

Works Cited

Braidotti, Rosi. *Nomadic Subjects: Embodiment and Sexual Difference in Contemporary Feminist Theory*. NY: Columbia UP, 1994.

Friedman, Ellen G., and Miriam Fuchs, eds. *Breaking the Sequence: Women's Experimental Fiction*. Princeton: Princeton UP, 1989.

Guyer, Carolyn. "Fretwork: ReForming Me." 1996. Internet: http://mothermillennia.org/Carolyn/Fretwork1.html

———. *Quibbling*. Eastgate Systems. Software, 1991. Macintosh and Windows.

Guyer, Carolyn, and Martha Petry. *Izme Pass. Writing on the Edge* 2.2 (Spring 1991). Eastgate Systems, 1991. Software. Macintosh

———. "Notes for Izme Pass Expose." *Writing on the Edge* 2.2 (Spring 1991): 82–89.

Irigaray, Luce. *This Sex Which Is Not One*. Trans. Catherine Porter. Ithaca: Cornell UP, 1985.

Jackson, Shelley. *Patchwork girl by Mary/Shelley & herself*. Eastgate Systems. Software, 1995. Macintosh and Windows.

Jouve, Nicole Ward, with Sue Roe and Susan Sellers. "Where Now, Where Next ?" *The Semi-Transparent Envelope: Women Writing—Feminism and Fiction*. Ed. Roe, Sellers, Jouve, with Michèle Roberts. London and NY: Marion Boars, 1994

Joyce, Michael. *Afternoon: A Story*. Cambridge, MA: Eastgate Systems, 1987. Software. Macintosh.

———. *WOE, or a memory of what will be. Writing on the Edge* 2.2 (Spring 1991). Eastgate, 1991. Software. Macintosh.

Kristeva, Julia. "Stabat Mater." *The Kristeva Reader*. Ed. Toril Moi. NY: Columbia UP, 1986.

Malloy, Judy. *its name was Penelope*. Eastgate Systems, 1993. Software. Macintosh and Windows.

Malloy, Judy, et al. *name is scibe*. 1994. Internet: http://www.artswire/interactive/www/scibe/story.html

Malloy, Judy, and Cathy Marshall. "Closure Was Never a Goal in This Piece." *Wired Women: Gender and New Realities in Cyberspace*. Ed. Lynn Cherny and Elizabeth Reba Weise. Seattle, WA: Seal P, 1996.

———. *Forward Anywhere*. Eastgate Systems, 1995, 1996. Software. Macintosh.

Maso, Carole. *AVA*. Normal, IL: Dalkey Archive P, 1993.

———. "On *AVA*." *Conjunctions* 20 (May 1993): 172–76.

———. "Notes of a Lyric Artist Working in Prose: A Lifelong Conversation with Myself, Entered Midway." *American Poetry Review* 24.2 March/April 1995): 26–31.

Miller, Nancy K. "Arachnologies: The Woman, the Text, and the Critic." *The Poetics of Gender*. Ed. Nancy K. Miller. NY: Columbia UP, 1986. 270–95.

Moulthrop, Stuart, and Nancy Kaplan. "They Became What They Beheld: The Futility of Resistance in the Space of Electronic Writing." *Literacy and Computers. The Complications of Teaching and Learning with Technology*. Ed. Cynthia L. Selfe and Susan Hilligoss. NY: Modern Language Association of America, 1994. 220–37.

Retallack, Joan. ":RE:THINKING:LITERARY:FEMINISM: (three essays onto shaky grounds)." *Feminist Measures: Soundings in Poetry and Theory*. Ed. Lynn Keller and Christanne Miller. Ann Arbor: U of Michigan P, 1994. 344–77.

Rich, Adrienne. *The Dream of a Common Language: Poems 1974–1977*. New York: Norton, 1978.

Robinson, Lou, and Camille Norton, eds. *Resurgent: New Writing by Women*. Urbana and Chicago: U of Illinois P, 1992.

6

"The Souls of Cyber-Folk"

Performativity, Virtual Embodiment, and Racial Histories

Thomas Foster

Since the "real" identities of the interlocutors at Lambda
[a text-based role-playing site on the Internet] are un-
verifiable . . . it can be said that everyone who participates
is "passing," as it is impossible to tell if a character's description matches a player's physical characteristics.
      —Lisa Nakamura, "Race In/For Cyberspace" (182)

When I was human, I was pretty assimilated myself. The
only black at work. One of only two families in my neighborhood. And, other than the occasional cutting little reminder, I was pretty comfortable in my illusion. I don't
ever plan to get that comfortable as a *cyborg*.
      —Dwayne McDuffie and Denys Cowan, "The Souls
            of Cyber-Folk," part 1, *Deathlok* #2 (13)

[Cyberpunk fiction] is . . . posthumanism with a venge-
ance, a posthumanism which, in its representation of
"monsters"—hopeful or otherwise—produced by the interface of the human and the machine, radically decenters
the human body, the sacred icon of the essential self, in
the same way that the virtual reality of cyberspace works
to decenter conventional humanist notions of an unproblematical real.
      —Veronica Hollinger, "Cybernetic Deconstructions" (207)

"You Will Be Assimilated"?:
Race in the Integrated Circuit

What value does Donna Haraway's "ironic political myth" of the cyborg
have as a framework for critical race studies (*Simians* 149)? And, conversely, what kind of perspective does critical race studies offer for understanding the political and social implications of the concept of the

137

cyborg? Virtual reality computer interfaces and more generally cyber-space technologies raise questions of the status of embodiment in post-modern, mass-mediated cultures, because VR technologies make visible what Allucquere Rosanne Stone calls "location technologies"—that is, techniques for mapping cultural meanings and representations onto physical bodies. Stone's work on virtual systems theory attempts to account for the ways in which "the accustomed grounding of social interaction in the physical facticity of human bodies is changing" (17). Racial and usually racist traditions often ground racial difference in perceived bodily differences and translate that difference into inferiority. In this context, the relevance of the technocultural changes Stone describes to the analysis of race in contemporary culture seems clear, clearer even than the relevance of Haraway's use of the cyborg or human-machine interface as a figure for changes in the relation of mind and body in Western philosophical traditions. To date, however, the discourse on cyberspace demonstrates a striking lack of engagement with the possible racial implications of such theoretical work.

As the study of "social systems that arise in phantasmatic spaces enabled by and constituted through communication technologies" (37), including but not limited to cyberspace, computer networks, and virtual reality, Stone's virtual systems theory sets out to rearticulate debates about the public sphere and specifically the modern, liberal narrative of the formation of the rational (read, white male) citizen through the transcendence of bodily particularity. This argument would seem to offer an easy opening for the discussion of race as one form of such particularity which troubles this narrative of becoming a citizen. Lauren Berlant, for example, argues that "we can see a real attraction of abstract citizenship in the way the citizen conventionally acquires a new body by participation in the political public sphere" (113). This privilege is, however, available to women and African-Americans only through mimicry or cross-identification with the supposedly more universal position of white men, a process that Berlant describes as the adoption of a full-body "prosthesis" (113, 133). Stone uses this same language to define her object of study as "the spaces of prosthetic communication" created by new technologies like virtual reality (36).

Stone uses the term "virtual systems theory" to encompass not only the new relationships between physical and virtual bodies in cyberspace but also older forms of "warranting," defined as "the production and maintenance of this link between a discursive space and a physical space" (40). This process of warranting, for Stone, is not unique to cyberspace but has always functioned "to guarantee the production of what would be called a citizen," since "this citizen is composed of two major elements": "the collection of physical and performative attributes" that Judith Butler and Kobena Mercer in separate works call the culturally intelligible body and "the collection of virtual attributes which, taken together, compose a structure of meaning and intention for the first part," primarily through discursive means. These two sets of attributes compose what Stone calls "the socially apprehensible citizen" (40), in which becoming a citizen means acquiring a new, virtual body. In other words, for Stone, as for critics like Michael Warner and Berlant, the production of the "citizen" has always involved a process of relative disembodiment, and this history provides the context in which to understand the changes introduced by virtual reality and new technologies of computer-mediated communication.

As Stone's reference to Judith Butler suggests, virtual systems theory also effectively rearticulates the critical discourse on performativity, cultural practices of cross-identification such as drag or butch/femme role-playing, and the gender "subversion" that results from such refusals to treat gender (a set of discursive or "virtual" attributes) as expressive of physical sexual characteristics. Butler's famous argument is that, in humanist traditions, "culturally intelligible bodies" are produced only through the insistence upon such an expressive or one-to-one relationship between sex and gender, or "the physical and the virtual" (*Gender Trouble* 134, 137). As Stone argues, the technological mediation of computer technologies offers new possibilities for redefining this relationship in ways that are not simply expressive or mimetic. Despite the reference to Mercer's work on racial representations in Stone's formulation of "the culturally intelligible body," however, one dominant tendency in both critical and popular narratives of cyberspace and VR has been to emphasize subversive performativity, and therefore also to emphasize gender, at the expense of attention to the racial implications of these new technologies.

This essay will attempt to define both the limits and the benefits of cyborg body politics and cyberspatial embodiments for understanding the persistence of racialized representations in contemporary American culture, as well as the mutations those representations might currently be undergoing. To do so, I will use the example of the rewriting of *Deathlok*, a Marvel comic book about a cyborg, by an African-American creative team who turn *Deathlok* from a typical superhero comic into a narrative about the transformation of an African-American man into a cyborg and the consequences of that transformation (which include the ability to access cyberspace).

To find a model for analyzing racial representation in terms of cyberspace technologies, it is necessary to turn to a work of literary studies, specifically Kimberly Benston's study on the performance of "blackness" in contemporary African-American poetry. In a discussion of a poem by A. B. Spellman, an elegy for John Coltrane, Benston claims that this poem "must be read as a series of provisional or transitional hypotheses linking an actual to a virtual being" (181). The language here, I would argue, is not simply an unintentional echo of Stone's definition of the "socially apprehensible citizen" as a combination of physical and virtual attributes (40). Benston's essay suggests that the problem of representing "blackness" in African-American culture prefigures the way that Stone redefines embodiment in Western culture, as requiring a virtual prosthesis. At the same time, in Benston's formulation, the problematic nature of blackness also involves the acknowledgment that the relation between physical and virtual is not fixed in a one-to-one relationship but instead can be "provisional," or to use Judith Butler's theoretical vocabulary, "iterative"—that is, continually produced and reproduced in successive discursive moments.

Benston's essay also distinguishes two main modes of racial performance in African-American literature, a distinction which evokes the contemporary debates about the subversive potential of performativity. Benston uses Ralph Ellison as a model for the kind of linguistic or discursive performativity that Butler privileges, arguing that for Ellison "the meaning of blackness does not inhere in any ultimate referent but is renewed in the rhythmic process of multiplication and substitution generated from performance to performance" (173). In contrast, Benston associates Amiri Baraka with an essentializing, theatrical notion of performance (as opposed to performativity), in which blackness represents a preexisting "presence that is dissimulated in performance" (173).

The question of the relationship between racial representations and theories of performativity seems to me to offer the best context for understanding the ambivalent relationship of race and cyberspace. As Lisa Nakamura has recently suggested, theories of performativity have the potential to establish connections between race and cyberspace historically and not just by analogy with gender. While theories of performativity like Butler's tend to focus on deessentializing supposedly natural modes of embodied experience (or in a more nuanced reading of Butler, tend to de-essentialize dominant norms for the relationship between physical bodies and frameworks of cultural intelligibility), histories of racial performance complicate the project of deessentializing or denaturalizing embodiment. Eric Lott and Michael Rogin's recent books on blackface performance in the United States, for instance, both emphasize the centrality of such performances in the construction of racial norms for both blacks and whites. ("Blackface" here refers to the minstrel show tradition, in which white performers made themselves to appear "black" in ways that even African-American performers were forced to imitate in order to be publicly recognized as "black"—that is, as conforming to white stereotypes of blackness.) Race has never been constructed *only* through "the corporealizing logic that [seeks] to anchor the indeterminacies of race to organic organization," though the project of the "science" of comparative anatomy was precisely to construct such an expressive relation between observable differences between physical bodies and cultural expectations about different racial norms, capacities, and behaviors (Wiegman 43). Through the vehicle of blackface, for example, racial norms have historically been constructed through the kind of anti-foundational performative practices that have come to be associated with postmodern modes of cross-identification and gender-bending. By "anti-foundational," I mean that in blackface performances it was not necessary to ground racial identity in a black body. Nor was it necessary to occupy a black body in order to be perceived by others as producing a culturally intelligible performance of "blackness." A similar argument can be made about "passing" and the production of "whiteness" as a racial category.

It is precisely in terms of these histories of non-expressive, non-humanist modes of performing and producing "blackness" and "whiteness" that African-American culture might be understood as prefiguring the concerns of virtual systems theory. Dwayne McDuffie and Denys Cowan's *Deathlok* conceptualizes its African-American protagonist's relationship to both cyborg embodiment and cyberspace in terms of the racial problematics of passing, assimilation, and blackface minstrelsy.

"When I Was Human": Narratives of Racialized Posthumanism

Given the relative obscurity of this popular text, it seems worthwhile to begin with a general description of the *Deathlok* comic's most recent incarnation or upgrade. The revisionary narrative of Deathlok as an African-American cyborg was launched in a four-issue limited series published between July and October of 1990. This revision was co-engineered by the writing team of Gregory Wright and Dwayne McDuffie (with McDuffie often writing the actual scripts after collaborating on the plots with Wright), and it was designed to go beyond the tokenism and superficiality of supposedly black superheroes like Marvel's Black Panther, who in the late 1960s and 1970s represented a blatant attempt to reach a black demographic without altering the conventions of superhero comics in any significant way. Denys Cowan took over the job of penciler beginning in the third issue of this series and went on to become the first regular artist on the continuing monthly comic version of *Deathlok*, which followed the success of the limited series. Wright and McDuffie initially alternated as writers on multi-issue story arcs of the monthly comic. Generally, the story arcs produced by the African-American creative team of McDuffie and Cowan focused more on racial issues, however obliquely, while the issues written by Wright tended more toward traditional action narratives and especially toward typical Marvel comics superhero crossovers, with Deathlok either fighting or teaming up with various other Marvel characters.

Cowan left *Deathlok* after issue 15 and McDuffie after 16, though McDuffie returned to write one last storyline, in issues 22–25. After McDuffie and Cowan's departures, Gregory Wright produced two last story arcs, in which *Deathlok* finally turned even further in the direction of a standard Marvel superhero comic. The focus turned to investigating the history of character Deathlok and his previous incarnations by introducing a hideously complicated plot involving alternate timelines. This plot seems designed to appeal mainly to readers who knew the prior history of the comic book character rather than to readers interested in racial issues. As a result, the comic lost its audience and was cancelled after issue 34, ending an almost three-year run.

The narrative of the four-issue limited series establishes how an African-American scientist named Michael Collins has his brain transplanted into an experimental cyborg body, designed as a prototype of a cyborg soldier (see figure 6.1 for the initial full-page image of the Deathlok body, prior to its interface with Collins's brain). Collins is a programmer and software designer at the company responsible for this secret weapons research, Cybertek. When he learns that his own work designing human/machine interfaces for prosthetic limbs is being appropriated for this secret weapons research, Collins confronts his employer, is kidnapped, and his brain is used as "wetware" in the experiment. Collins is also a pacifist, and this new version of *Deathlok* is clearly designed to intervene in the film genre of violent cyborg action heroes, like the Terminator, as well as to rewrite the racial implications of cyborg narratives. (In earlier versions of Deathlok, the brains used to interface with the cyborg body were always taken from white soldiers.)

As part of the hybrid Deathlok cyborg, Michael Collins unexpectedly regains consciousness only to find himself carrying out the commands programmed into the onboard computer that also inhabits his cyborg body and with which Collins carries on a continual internal dialogue

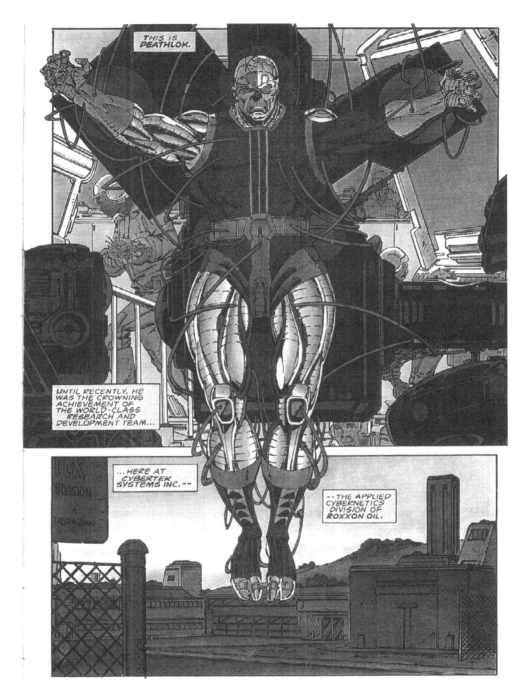

Figure 6.1 *Deathlok* (4 issue limited series, 1990) #1 page 2.
TM & © Marvel Characters, Inc. All rights reserved.

throughout both the limited and monthly series. Specifically, Collins finds himself operating as a counter-insurgency unit in Central America, putting down a peasant uprising. As he puts it, "I'm worse than a monster. I'm a weapon. I've become the walking embodiment of all I despise" (*Deathlok* limited series #1, page 40). In McDuffie and Cowan's first story arc in the monthly series, "The Souls of Cyber-Folk," this process of coming to embody all Collins despises will be associated not only with becoming a cyborg killing machine, but also with the larger process of assimilating into white society.

Collins's brain, however, was not supposed to regain consciousness at all, but was simply supposed to function as an organic storage medium. Almost immediately, Collins discovers how to override the programming installed in his cyborg body, and he institutes a "no-killing parameter" for the onboard computer. As a result of what they perceive as this malfunction, the researchers and programmers bring him back to the lab and try to purge the cyborg system of Collins's personality. Collins fights back by entering cyberspace for the first time, specifically the computer network installed in his own body (see figure 6.2). By doing so, Collins is able to take control of the cyborg and escape.

His next move is to try to visit his wife and son, but his wife's reaction to his new body only convinces Collins that he is now a monster with no possibility of a normal family life. He does, however, go on to contact his son more surreptitiously, by using his cyborg body to plug his nervous system directly into the phone system and his home computer, in this comic's version of a typical cyberpunk trope, of "jacking in" to computer networks. In this manner, Collins is able to appear to his son as a character in a videogame. In fact, Collins gives his son a lecture on avoiding violence and doing what's right, not what's easy (see figures 6.3 and 6.4). In effect, he tries to revise and rewrite the videogame's programming in the same way that he has overridden and overwritten the onboard computer in his cyborg body, and in the same way that McDuffie and Wright are trying to rewrite the conventions of action heroes in the comic book itself.

Collins's lecture to his son inspires him to apply these principles to his own life instead of giving in to despair at his situation. As a result, in issue 2 of the limited series, he returns to Central America to make amends for the actions taken by the cyborg before he gained control of it, and in issue 3 Collins again confronts his former employer, an executive named Ryker, and threatens to shut down Cybertek's weapons research. At that point, on the last page of issue 3, Ryker unveils Collins's organic body, which he has preserved in a kind of suspended animation (figure 6.5). Ryker offers to restore Collins to his original body if

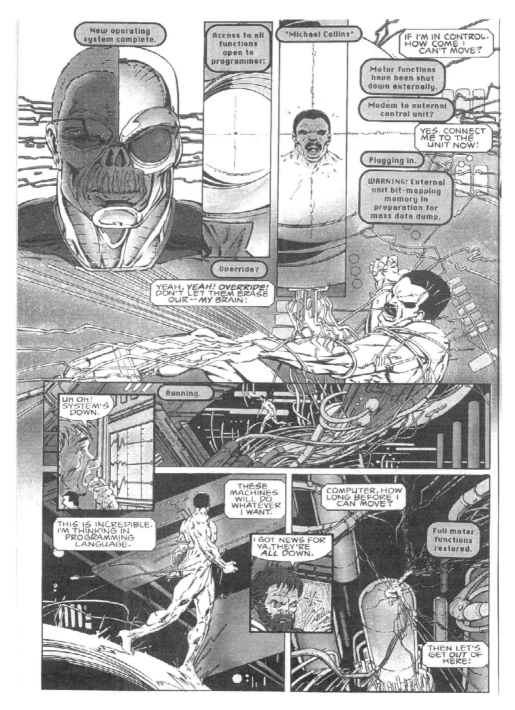

Figure 6.2 *Deathlok* (limited series) #1 page 27.
TM & © Marvel Characters, Inc. All rights reserved.

Figure 6.3 *Deathlok* (limited series) #1 page 42.
TM & © Marvel Characters, Inc. All rights reserved.

Figure 6.4 *Deathlok* (limited series) #1 page 44.
TM & © Marvel Characters, Inc. All rights reserved.

Collins will help Cybertek market their weapons research illegally. The final issue of the series tells the story of how Collins initially agrees to this deal, but ultimately decides that the right thing to do is to turn Ryker in and therefore to choose to remain a cyborg. The narrative of this series then boils down to the story of Michael Collins accepting a new identity as Deathlok, which is how his character is referred to throughout the series, rather than as Michael Collins. But by the same token, Collins undergoes a process of accepting his own posthumanism, his "monstrosity." At this point, however, the distinction between humanity and posthumanity is rendered somewhat ambiguous, given that it is precisely the qualities of commitment to moral principles that mark the cyborg's humanity which also motivate his decision to remain a posthuman "monster."

The other main strand of the Deathlok narrative revolves around the Deathlok cyborg's quest to recover his organic body, and this quest drives the continuing monthly series. Paradoxically, at the same time that Deathlok is presented as learning to be posthuman, the narrative is driven by the continuing relationship between his cyborg and his organic bodies. Both Deathlok's posthumanism and the thematics of his two bodies seem legible enough as an allegory of slavery. From the very first image of the Deathlok cyborg, that cyborg body evokes both the iconography of Christian crucifixion and the imagery of lynching. When Deathlok begins a speech (to another cyborg) with the words "when I was human . . . , " the narrative of an African-American man being forcibly transformed into something that is no longer fully human, at least in the eyes of others, can hardly help but evoke the African diaspora. The possibility of reading the *Deathlok* narrative in terms of U.S. racial histories is reinforced at those moments when other characters joke about the cyborg's ambiguous legal status. At one point, Ryker taunts Deathlok about how the cyborg's testimony against his former employer "was discredited since they couldn't determine if you were sentient or just a piece of hardware"; in a later issue there's a joke about whether Deathlok would have health insurance or a warranty (*Deathlok* monthly series #1, page 16; #13, page 8).

Hortense Spillers points out that the treatment of the "captive body" under slavery means that "we lose any hint or suggestion of . . . relatedness between human personality and anatomical features" (68). While this detachment of human personality from physical bodies seems to echo Stone's definition of the effects of virtual systems, the difference of course is that under slavery the detaching of personality from body was a way of reducing human beings to the status of property, not allowing those beings to multiply their personalities and construct alternate personae, as Stone suggests virtual systems do.

Figure 6.5 *Deathlok* (limited series) #3 page 46.
TM & © Marvel Characters, Inc. All rights reserved.

From this perspective, Deathlok's resistance to completely abandoning his organic body as inaccessible signifies resistance to a history of being legally reduced to the status of property, in this case to a machine rather than to chattel. At the same time, however, this allegorical reading of Michael Collins's tranformation into Deathlok and his acceptance that he must remain a posthuman cyborg also implies the necessity of acknowledging how becoming a cyborg, like the African diaspora, changes possibilities for resistance, both setting new limits and creating new opportunities. Michael Collins's transformation into Deathlok then reads as a repetition of the trauma of the middle passage and the construction of a new hybrid culture on the other side of the Atlantic.

"My New Prosthetic Body": Cyborg Narratives, Racial Assimilation, and Public Citizenship

The *Deathlok* narrative is complicated by the fact that the main character has three bodies, not just two. In addition to the cyborg body he occupies throughout the series and the physical body he spends much of his time trying to retrieve, Deathlok also has a virtual body in cyberspace, or rather a range of body images, sometimes referred to as icons or avatars. In figure 6.2, for example, during Deathlok's first excursion into cyberspace, he resumes the appearance of Michael Collins's naked body, while in figures 6.3 and 6.4, when he accesses his son's video game through the phone system, he appears in the form of the Deathlok cyborg. And finally in figure 6.7, his virtual presence is given the form of Michael Collins's physical, racially marked body surrounded by the floating components of the Deathlok cyborg. The racial significance of these representations of virtual embodiment can be understood only in relation to the significance of Michael Collins's transformation into the Deathlok cyborg and what Deathlok calls "my new prosthetic body" (monthly series #1, page 6).

The narrative function of Deathlok's physical body can be understood on a psychic level as an unattainable object of desire that fuels an ongoing, perhaps never-ending quest. But it can also be understood on a more historical level as retrospectively signifying an originary state of physical and cultural integrity interrupted by Michael Collins's capture; that capture then leads to a reenactment of diaspora on the level of body parts, with the detachment of the brain from the rest of the corpus. In this "diaspora," the physical body signifies the equivalent of an African origin, and the transformation into a cyborg constitutes

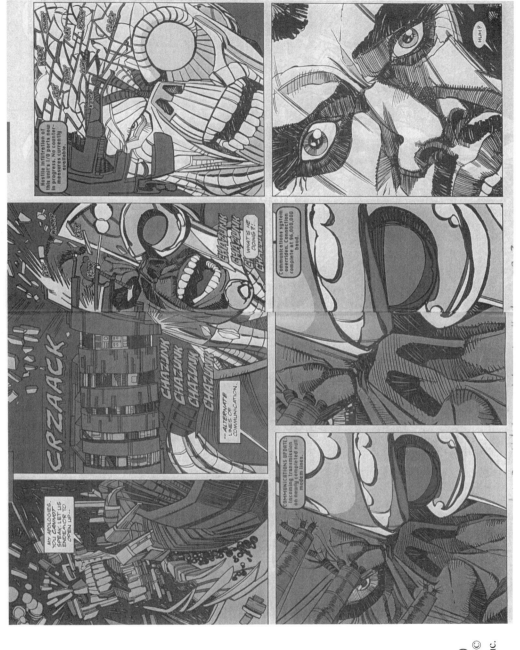

Figure 6.7 *Deathlok* (monthly series) #4 page 4.
TM & © Marvel Characters, Inc. All rights reserved.

Collins's own personal middle passage. *Deathlok's* cyborg narrative also functions as a captivity narrative. African-American organic bodies have historically been taken to signify an absent and possibly inaccessible origin, one associated in U.S. culture with the physical facticity of those bodies, their "nature." Part of the cultural work of the *Deathlok* comic is to work through and denaturalize that fantasy of the pure and untouched physical body as origin, but without simply dispensing with "the body," either.

In Deathlok, the organic body of Michael Collins tends to be associated with the human and specifically with what remains of the cyborg's humanity. That body is first made to reappear with a flourish, as Deathlok's former employer promises, "I can make you human again," in what must be one of the most unusual restagings of the mirror stage in recent popular culture (figure 6.5). In this scene, Deathlok's organic body is being held out to him as exactly the same promise that Lacan argues the mirror image holds out to an infant, the promise of overcoming a sense of bodily fragmentation through the anticipatory unification of diverse physical sensations into an organic whole (4). And, of course, Deathlok ultimately refuses to buy into that promise.

The narrative of the *Deathlok* comic proceeds to trouble the association of the physical body with the human by demonstrating how moral and ethical questions still apply to a cyborg. It does so by attempting to show how a cyborg can be a pacifist (despite the comic's tendency to be overwhelmed by its conventional action plots), thereby suggesting that the posthuman is not synonymous with the inhuman. This process also works in reverse: to the extent that Deathlok's physical body is racially marked, in ways that this relatively privileged, middle-class black man comes to appreciate only after he becomes a cyborg, his relationship to the category of the universally human was already problematic.

The tension between Deathlok's cyborg body and his physical one should be read in relation to Stone's definition of the citizen as a combination of physical and virtual attributes or "both physical and discursive elements" (41). In Stone's model, the physical body is not purely physical, but also consists of "performative" attributes (40), which I take to mean the relationship between physical bodies and the cultural frameworks of gender and racial norms that make those bodies meaningful and intelligible. While Stone does not spell out this implication of her argument, it seems to me that it is this partial overlap between the virtual and the physical *within* the physical, the way in which the category of the physical folds the virtual over into itself, which makes it possible for virtual reality to feed back into the construction of the physical, precisely to the extent that virtual reality and cyberspace can be understood as modes of embodied performance. Both the continuing sense of relation between Deathlok's cyborg and organic bodies and the representations of his embodied perspective in cyberspace indicate that Stone's theory of the relation between the physical and the virtual in virtual systems theory is more useful than traditional mind/body distinctions in understanding what it means for Michael Collins to become a cyborg in the comic book's narratives. Becoming a cyborg and accessing cyberspace are not conceptualized in terms of escaping the body, but rather in terms of a more complex relationship that is both potentially productive and potentially problematic. We need to remember here that Deathlok's cyborg embodiment is associated with his access to cyberspace from the very first issue of the limited series, in which he gains control over the cyborg body only through cyberspace; similarly, in the first issue of "The Souls of Cyber-Folk," Deathlok learns to think of himself as a "cybernet," a phrase that conflates cyborg embodiment and cyberspace networks (monthly series #2, page 6).

In this sense, the *Deathlok* comic seems to endorse computer researcher Randall Walser's definition of cyberspace in contrast to other media: "print and radio tell, stage and film show, but cyberspace embodies" (60). As Katherine Hayles points out, such formulations often seem to assume that virtual reality offers all the benefits of embodiment as a mode of processing information without "being bound by any of its limitations" ("Seductions" 179). In *Deathlok*'s version of VR, however, this statement is hardly true. Access to cyberspace reproduces his transformation into a cyborg, as implied by his appearance in cyberspace in the Deathlok body, while at the same time cyberspace also seems to offer a way of communicating Deathlok's ongoing relationship to an organic body that is visually marked as African-American. Deathlok's cyberspatial body images always encode a sense of bodily limitation, a sense of being subjected to the gaze and the cultural preconceptions of others, as well as a potential for shape-shifting and fluid identifications.

The relationships between Deathlok's various modes of embodiment are complex and include two sets of doubled bodies: first, the Deathlok cyborg and the human body of Michael Collins; and, second, the material body of the cyborg and his virtual presence in cyberspace. No wonder, then, that Deathlok claims he never understood "until just now" why his father made him read and reread W. E. B. DuBois's famous passage on "double consciousness" from *The Souls of Black Folk*. Deathlok reads that passage aloud to another black woman cyborg at the beginning of "The Souls of Cyber-Folk": " 'one ever feels his twoness . . . two souls, two unreconciled strivings, two warring ideals in one dark

body, whose dogged strength alone keeps it from being torn asunder' "
(monthly series #2, page 13; DuBois 215).

Like this passage from DuBois, Deathlok's multiple and multiply
doubled modes of embodiment clearly evoke the history of African-
Americans' vexed relationship to the inclusive ideals of the bourgeois
public sphere and to the category of American citizen. *Deathlok* supports and clarifies the racial implications of Stone's attempt to theorize virtual systems in relation to the dominant narrative of citizenship,
which depends upon a process of abstraction or transcendence of bodily
particularity in order for individuals to accede to the supposedly universal realm of rational decision-making. Of course, this precondition of
suppressing the particularity of the physical body is understood as a
privilege, not a loss, and a privilege reserved historically for those individuals who conform to norms ironically grounded in the experience of
a particular historical situation: white masculinity.

The promise of a new body held out by the democratic public sphere
constitutes a dilemma for minority subjects as much as it does an opportunity, and it is precisely this dilemma that Deathlok experiences
when he becomes a cyborg. This dilemma manifests itself in the contradictory rhetoric the comic uses to define the relationship between
Deathlok's various bodies. On the one hand, the comic often deploys
a humanist rhetoric which privileges the organic body as the site of
Deathlok's humanity, suggesting that the cyborg can be clearly distinguished from the human and that embodiment as a cyborg is or should
be only a detour on the way back to Michael Collins's original body.
The implication of this rhetoric is that both cyborg and cyberspatial
embodiment are relatively superficial experiences that do not significantly revise assumptions about organic embodiment or lead to reflection upon those assumptions. At the same time, this rhetoric is consistently undermined by the narrative's demonstration that returning to
organic form is neither possible nor even desirable. More important for
my argument here, the same point is implicit in Deathlok's attempts
both to conceptualize racial identity in terms of being a cyborg and
to conceptualize being a cyborg in terms of racial identity, as when he
quotes *The Souls of Black Folk*. So, does Deathlok's new prosthetic body
and his resultant direct access to cyberspace replace his physical body
or merely supplement it?

The continuing tension between Deathlok's multiple embodiments
in the comic implies that the process of abstraction from his organic
body is never perfect, and Deathlok himself thematizes that reading of the
comic book in terms of U.S. racial histories of assimilation and resistance to it. As Deathlok puts it, he may have been "pretty assimilated"

when he was human, as "the only black at work. One of only two families in my neighborhood" (monthly series #2, page 13). In this speech,
Deathlok associates assimilation with being "human" and rejects both
as comfortable illusions that he can no longer afford. Inclusion in the
category of the human is understood as a privilege bought only at the
price of accommodating a white norm, and Deathlok's cyborg transformation results in his rejection of being assimilated to those norms under the sign or the alibi of becoming "human" again. The final panel on
this page, however, returns to a humanist rhetoric, with the other cyborg agreeing that she will help Deathlok find his human body.

While it shows Deathlok applying his cyborg existence to the understanding of racial dilemmas and as the basis for rejecting assimilation
in the supposedly universally "human," the comic also warns against
rejecting transcendence altogether, for fear of finding oneself trapped in
immanence and particularity and thereby denied inclusion and participation in public life. This would result in being rendered truly invisible.
"The Souls of Cyber-Folk" ends with the artificial intelligence that the
cyborgs have been battling explaining its reasons for capturing them.
The AI describes itself as being in a condition of "philosophical agony"
because it is "incapable of transcending" itself and can only follow its
program (monthly series #4, page 15). The level of both philosophical
and political sophistication here is quite high. Deathlok explicitly con-
nects his situation as both a cyborg and a black man to that of the AI,
in an extraordinary speech at the end of the final issue in which he and
his partner, a black woman cyborg, defend the AI. This woman, Misty
Knight, claims that the AI "reacted violently to a world that defined
him by a stereotype" as *different*—then held him to the ridiculous
limitations *inherent* in that false definition. All [the AI] really tried to do
was assimilate" (monthly series #5, page 17). Deathlok goes on to qual-
ify that argument, by suggesting that the AI was actually both "afraid
of being too *different*" and also "afraid of being too much the *same*"
(#5, page 19). The AI's dilemma is how to negotiate between assimilation and separatism, transcendence and immanence, abstraction and
particularity, disembodiment and the behavioral determinism of a
physical form "hard-wired" with programming constraints the AI can
never change.

This question of the relation between physical and virtual often takes
the form of a rhetoric of location organized by the spatial metaphors
of interiority and exteriority, as when Deathlok is referred to as pilot-
ing a cyborg body rather than being a cyborg (monthly series #1, page
12). The question of who Deathlok is becomes a question of where he
is, once he can no longer locate himself securely in Michael Collins's
physical body. As Stone puts it, the dislocation of self and body made

possible by new computer and communications technologies poses new questions, "not simply problems of accountability (i.e., who did it), but of *warrantability*" or "is there a physical human body involved in this interaction *anywhere*" (87). Collins's initial reaction to finding himself firing on civilians in the body of a cyborg soldier that he cannot control, is one of recognition or possibly misrecognition: "It's *me*! I'm shooting people. *I'm* responsible for this" (limited series #1, page 21). This statement suggests both Deathlok's initial failure to understand the epistemological and ontological changes he has undergone, and also his resistance to understanding his situation as one of disembodiment, in which the question of responsibility would be displaced by warrantability, the problem of locating subjectivity in a physical body. While Stone may only be suggesting the need to defer questions of responsibility until the connection between bodies and selves can be established, there seems to be an inherent tendency in such formulations not only to defer but to fantasize about eliminating questions of responsibility entirely in favor of a disembodied, transgressive situation of boundarylessness. It is this tendency that *Deathlok* seems to resist.

In the final analysis, only the identity of his organic brain, transplanted in the cyborg body, can prove that Deathlok is not what Cybertek plans to explain him as: a machine who thinks he's Michael Collins (limited series #2, page 11). But the possibility of distinguishing Deathlok's cyborg and human components is undermined by the assertions that Deathlok's brain has been turned into wetware, used as a computer storage medium, and interfaced with an onboard computer. The scene in which he gains control of the cyborg body also represents that body itself as a computer network. So what distinguishes his brain from his cyborg body? This same undecidability is stressed in the joke about whether he would have a warranty or health insurance, and it is precisely this undecidability which marks the difficulty of conceptualizing Deathlok as either "same" or "different"—that is, which marks the limits of a simple spatial metaphor, organized around the opposition between "inside" and "outside," for defining his relationship to his body. And it is precisely the limitations of such a metaphor or model that Stone argues are foregrounded by new computer technologies and virtual systems.

"Computer, Where Are We?":
Relocating the Body in Cyberspace

The cyberspace scenes in *Deathlok* reinforce the complexity and ambivalence of Deathlok's relationship to his different bodies. There are two main types of representations of cyberspace in the comic. In the first, Deathlok accesses the computer inside his own body (figure 6.2) or has that computer network accessed by someone else, to create a "shared communication environment" within his own onboard computer, plugged directly into his brain (figures 6.6 and 6.7). In these scenes, Deathlok's virtual presence is typically represented by an image of his organic body; he becomes Michael Collins again. The second set of representations depict Deathlok accessing other computer networks, outside his own body, as if they were part of his own extended nervous system, to use Marshall McLuhan's phrase (figure 6.3 and 6.4). In these scenes, Deathlok's virtual body image is typically a version of the Deathlok cyborg.

How are we to read these different representations? Does Deathlok "return" to his organic form when he uses cyberspace to access and control his cyborg "self"? Does this act reveal the essential core of his humanity that remains within that mechanical body, the ghost in the machine? In this reading, cyberspace would serve as a vehicle for literally expressing Deathlok's "true" "inner" self, and cyberspace would therefore also reinforce the humanist rhetoric of Deathlok's cyborg transformation as only a superficial change that could potentially be reversed without affecting his humanity. The representation of his virtual body in its organic form as naked (figure 6.2) might be taken to imply that the cyborg body is to be associated with clothing that can be removed at will to reveal the organic body, unaffected by the cyborg components. Similarly, the two-page spread that depicts the AI infiltrating Deathlok's onboard computer to generate a virtual communications environment inside Deathlok (figure 6.6) seems designed to suggest a reversal of the cyborg transformation, as the closeups of Deathlok's face grow progressively larger from panel to panel, until it becomes hard to decipher the image as a face. At that point, in the final panel, Deathlok's face is suddenly juxtaposed with a black and white graphic of Michael Collins's organic facial features, as the image shifts to cyberspace. This sequence of images recalls the reference in Ralph Ellison's *Invisible Man* to the racial project of "creating the *uncreated features of his face*" (354; italics in the original), as well as to Deleuze and Guattari's discussion of "faciality" as a sign of the universally human (167–91). The *Deathlok* comic is remarkable for its willingness to risk presenting a protagonist whose features are inhuman enough to make it impossible to read his expressions, though this is perhaps more conventional in superhero comics than in other media.

Even in this two-page spread, however, the reading of cyberspace as a return to an untouched organic state is undermined by the black and white representation of the virtual body image and also by the juxtaposition of the organic face with the image just above it, a schematic rendering of the inside of the cyborg's head, showing I/O ports that allow access to Deathlok's brain—that is, an image of body invasion that has already taken place and has altered Deathlok's organic brain and which therefore undermines the illusion that he might return to a purely organic state.

The illusory nature of that desire to retrieve the organic without having been affected by becoming a cyborg is also indicated by the simple fact that Deathlok does not always appear in organic form in cyberspace, as he might be expected to do if cyberspace were understood as a traditionally expressive medium. Such an understanding of cyberspace would contradict Stone's definition of new computer technologies and their implications for multiple "articulations of physical and virtual space" and the resulting technosocial evocation of "unruly multiplicity as an integral part of social identity" (42). In an African-American context, however, such formulations also tend to evoke Ralph Ellison's figure of Rinehart and his "world of fluidity," without boundaries (*Invisible Man* 498), where Rinehart figures an "identity" which is purely performative, as the narrator discovers when he is repeatedly mistaken for Rinehart simply by taking on the appearance of a hipster.

Deathlok's transformation back into Michael Collins in cyberspace is also qualified by the image that follows that transformation (figure 6.7). Here we see that the organic body has not been simply extricated from its infiltration by mechanical parts, but that those parts continue to hover around the organic body. This image is ambiguous, since it could be read as establishing the spatial metaphor of the organic body as the true inner self of the Deathlok cyborg. But it can also be read as indicating how even the organic body remains unavoidably connected to these mechanical parts and computer networks, just as this illusion of repossessing an organic body is made possible only by the AI "infiltrating" Deathlok's body and flooding him with outside information at the rate of 96,000,000 baud. This second image then typifies the double meaning of c-space in the *Deathlok* narrative. Cyberspace signifies a freedom and fluidity of embodied existence, allowing Deathlok to re-traverse the boundary between human and posthuman, man and cyborg, but that freedom is never complete for Deathlok, at least. In the same way, in *Invisible Man*, Rinehart's "world . . . without boundaries" is made possible only by his having been rendered invisible through stereotyping; "his world is possibility" only because he accepts the impossibility of having any social existence other than what is conferred on him by others' perception of him (498).

Similarly, in figure 6.7, Deathlok's onboard computer gives him a quick lecture on the epistemology of virtual reality. The computer emphasizes that VR constitutes the "organic brain's subjective interpretation of non-visual data," and it points out that the word "looks" is an "inappropriate description" of this process of interpretation. Robyn Wiegman has analyzed the extent to which naturalizing ideologies of racial difference depend upon presenting visual evidence (such as skin color) as adequate verification for cultural ascriptions of inferiority, an ideology which the discipline of comparative anatomy tried to elevate to the level of a science in the nineteenth century (6–14). This ideology is one example of the "conventional humanist notions of an unproblematical real" that Veronica Hollinger suggests are "decentered" by "the virtual reality of cyberspace" (207). In other words, Deathlok's experience of virtual reality reveals that seeing is not believing but instead is interpretation.

More specifically, the computer claims that such interpretive processes inherent in visual perception are "hard-wired" into the organic brain, in the same way that Deathlok has managed to hard-wire a no-killing parameter into the onboard computer. The implication is that even if visual perceptions are denaturalized and shown to be cultural constructs, those constructs may nevertheless be hard-wired into our perceptions and will not simply disappear, even if such a disappearance were desirable. Cyberspace may mean that we can assume whatever form or identity we wish, regardless of whether it matches our physical embodiment, but we still cannot escape the possibility that some types of preconceptions are likely to be hard-wired into the people we interact with in cyberspace. One reason for the persistence of such preconceptions may be that virtual reality privileges vision as a mode of information processing, and visual perception remains inextricably linked to a history of racial stereotyping.

It is important to point out, however, that the entire narrative of *Deathlok* is premised on the notion that it is possible to overcome and to rewrite this kind of hard-wired programming, which is more recognizable as such within a technosocial context than within the naturalized context of purely organic bodies. In fact, *Deathlok* shares this premise with William Gibson's paradigmatic cyberpunk novel, *Neuromancer*, as I have argued elsewhere. Deathlok's story really begins when his organic brain takes over control of the cyborg body and reprograms it. But Deathlok also applies the same process to the violent video game his son is watching, taking over one of the characters to suggest that his son try to find a way to win the game without violence. At that point, the thematics of hard-wiring and resistance to it starts to function in cultural and not just technological contexts; Deathlok tries to rewrite the hard-wired tendency to associate violence with masculinity (and possibly with African-American men specifically). The metaphor of cultural hard-wiring also defines the whole project of the comic, which set out to revise the conventions that now seem to come built-in to superhero comics. I would like to argue that the centrality of this trope of rewiring hard-wired conventions or expectations also applies to the representation of race in *Deathlok*. The cyborg and the racial thematics converge around the possibility of intervening in the ways that cultural constraints take the form of limitations imposed on particular types of bodies, with those constraints coming to seem "built-in" or "hard-wired" to those bodies.

Even if readers choose to view Deathlok's organic body image in cyberspace as an expression of the real person, the question remains whether readers will perceive Deathlok's true self as human or black, as too much the same or too much different. It is in this sense, perhaps, that Deathlok applies DuBois's idea of double consciousness to the transformation of a black man into a cyborg and a cyberspace participant. Cyberspace is hardly immune from the "peculiar sensation, this double consciousness, this sense of always looking at one's self through the eye's of others" (monthly series #2, page 13; DuBois 215). As critics of DuBois have pointed out, the idea of double consciousness represents DuBois's revisionary intervention in medical discourse on multiple personality disorder, with DuBois's goal being to redefine that condition as something more than just a pathology (Wald 176–77; Bruce). As DuBois puts it, the goal is to "merge" this "double self" without losing either "of the older selves" (215). Stone similarly uses multiple personalities as a way to conceptualize the new possibilities for the relationship between self (or selves) and body in virtual systems, going so far as to claim that "some forms of multiple personality are useful examples" of an emergent technosocial modality; "the multiple," she argues, "is the socializer within the computer networks, a being warranted to, but outside of, a single physical body" (43). DuBois's account of "two souls, two thoughts, . . . two warring ideals in one dark body" strongly suggests that the potential of virtual systems to multiply personalities should also be understood in relation to the historical situation of African-Americans and their modes of social existence, and this is just what *Deathlok* sets out to do. The value of working out this relationship lies in the way that it both qualifies the more extreme celebrations of cyberspatial fluidity and freedom of self-fashioning and also helps to specify the ways in which new technologies might function to facilitate genuine changes in the construction of cultural identities.

The fictional representation of cyberspace computer networks locates them both outside and inside the Deathlok cyborg body. Collins's status as a cyborg is largely constituted by the interface between Michael Collins's organic brain and the Deathlok cyborg's onboard computer. This popular narrative of becoming a cyborg then situates the effects of new computer technology in relation to the construction and performance of embodiment, and in this narrative embodiment is understood primarily in racialized terms. The Deathlok narrative thus helps define the relevance of emergent computer and communication technologies to the understanding of how race has been and can be performed. At the same time, this fictional narrative also defines the relevance of already existing histories and traditions of racial performance to the understanding of virtual systems theory.

Works Cited

Benston, Kimberly W. "Performing Blackness: Re/Placing Afro-American Poetry." In *Afro-American Literary Study in the 1990s*. Ed. Houston A. Baker, Jr., and Patricia Redmond. Chicago: U of Chicago P, 1989.

Berlant, Lauren. "National Brands/National Body: *Imitation of Life*." In *Comparative American Identities: Race, Sex, and Nationality in the Modern Text*. Ed. Hortense J. Spillers. New York: Routledge, 1991.

Bruce, Dickson D., Jr. "W. E. B. DuBois and the Idea of Double Consciousness." *American Literature* 64 (June 1992): 299–309.

Butler, Judith. *Bodies That Matter: On the Discursive Limits of "Sex."* New York: Routledge, 1993.

———. *Gender Trouble: Feminism and the Subversion of Identity*. New York: Routledge, 1990.

Deleuze, Gilles, and Felix Guattari. *A Thousand Plateaus: Capitalism and Schizophrenia*. Trans. Brian Massumi. Minneapolis: U of Minnesota P, 1987.

DuBois, W. E. B. *The Souls of Black Folk*. In *Three Negro Classics*. Ed. John Hope Franklin. New York: Avon, 1965.

Ellison, Ralph. *Invisible Man*. New York: Vintage, 1989.

Foster, Thomas. "Meat Puppets or Robopaths?: Cyberpunk and the Question of Embodiment." *Genders* 18 (Winter 1993): 11–31.

Gibson, William. *Neuromancer*. New York: Ace Books, 1984.

Haraway, Donna. *Simians, Cyborgs, and Women: The Reinvention of Nature*. New York: Routledge, 1991.

Hayles, N. Katherine. "Boundary Disputes: Homeostasis, Reflexivity, and the Foundations of Cybernetics." In *Virtual Realities and Their Discontents*. Ed. Robert Markley. Baltimore: Johns Hopkins UP, 1996. 11–37.

———. "The Seductions of Cyberspace." In *Rethinking Technologies*. Ed. Verena Andermatt Conley. Minneapolis: U of Minnesota P, 1993.

Hollinger, Veronica. "Cybernetic Deconstructions: Cyberpunk and Postmodernism." In *Storming the Reality Studio: A Casebook of Cyberpunk and Postmodern Fiction.* Ed. Larry McCaffrey. Durham: Duke UP, 1991. 203–18.

Lacan, Jacques. *Ecrits: A Selection.* Trans. Alan Sheridan. New York: Norton, 1977.

Lott, Eric. *Love and Theft: Blackface Minstrelsy and the American Working Class.* New York: Oxford UP, 1993.

McDuffie, Dwayne, and Denys Cowan. "The Souls of Cyber-Folk." *Deathlok* #2–5 (August–November 1991). New York: Marvel Comics.

McDuffie, Dwayne, and Gregory Wright, et al. *Deathlok* limited series #1–4 (July–October 1990). New York: Marvel Comics.

Mercer, Kobena. *Welcome to the Jungle: New Positions in Black Cultural Studies.* New York: Routledge, 1994.

Nakamura, Lisa. "Race In/For Cyberspace: Identity Tourism and Racial Passing on the Internet." *Works and Days* 13.1/2 (1995): 181–93.

Rogin, Michael. *Blackface, White Noise: Jewish Immigrants in the Hollywood Melting Pot.* Berkeley: U of California P, 1996.

Spillers, Hortense. "Mama's Baby, Papa's Maybe: An American Grammar Book." *Diacritics* 17.2 (summer 1987): 65–81.

Stone, Allucquere Rosanne. *The War of Desire and Technology at the Close of the Mechanical Age.* Cambridge, MA: MIT Press, 1995.

Wald, Priscilla. *Constituting Americans: Cultural Anxiety and Narrative Form.* Durham: Duke UP, 1995.

Walser, Randall. "Spacemakers & the Art of the Cyberspace Playhouse." *Mondo 2000* 2 (summer 1990): 60–61.

Warner, Michael. "The Mass Public and the Mass Subject." In *Habermas and the Public Sphere.* Ed. Chris Calhoun. Cambridge, MA: MIT P, 1992. 377–401.

Wiegman, Robyn. *American Anatomies: Theorizing Race and Gender.* Durham: Duke UP, 1995.

7

The Disturbing Liveliness
of Machines
Rethinking the Body in
Hypertext Theory and Fiction

Christopher J. Keep

In their attempts to coin a new critical vocabulary for the practices of reading and writing hypertext, theorists have had a surprisingly regular recourse to somatic metaphors. J. Yellowlees Douglas, for example, describes reading Michael Joyce's *WOE* as "being a little like watching yourself undergo an upper G. I.":

> You peer at the display, uncertain exactly what the map of light and shadow represents, then you notice the tube of your esophagus rippling with long swallows as you tip the stuff down your throat. You roll onto your left side and the gritty image shows you an inert bag filled with liquid. (112)

WOE is part of the emerging genre of "hypertext fiction": it is an electronic text composed of "lexia," individual blocks of text (though it might just as well have contained graphics, video clips, or sound recordings) which are connected to other lexia through a system of programmable links. The reader uses his or her mouse to click on words which take him or her from one block of text to another and in this way is allowed to move through the narrative in a non-linear and associative manner. For Yellowlees Douglas, hypertext radically disturbs the largely autonomic act of reading: her image of a gastrointestinal examination draws attention to the way in which electronic texts make visible the complex machinations of an activity largely taken for granted. In "The Grotesque Corpus," Terence Harpold employs similar tropes in order to foreground the social dimension of hypertextuality. Taking up

Bakhtin's concepts of heteroglossia and the carnivalesque, he argues that the peristaltic action of reading an electronic narrative shapes and informs the reader's subjectivity. In reading a hypertext, the reader is caught up in a web of utterances, of voices and narrative possibilities, which blur the lines of monadic subjectivity and compel us to confront the social nature of all utterances. Harpold concludes that "[t]he heart of the hypertextual corpus lies in its Pantagruelesque belly: the gullet, the stomach, the tripe—all the knotted and labyrinthine forms of this heteroglot form" (7).

This convergence of interest in the deep workings, the rumblings, gurglings, and squelchings, of the physiological processes attests to something other than a simple metaphorical relationship between hypertext and the body. In what follows, I want to treat Yellowlees Douglas's symptoms of physical discomfort as indicative of the ways in which the reader's sense of him- or herself as an embodied subject is disturbed by this involvement with the machine. Reading, as Roger Chartier claims, "is not just an abstract operation of intellection: it is an engagement of the body, an inscription in space, a relation to oneself and others" (20). To read is not to withdraw from the body so much as to occupy it differently. Conversely, the body, too, is configured and altered by our perceptions of it, perceptions which are themselves constituted in the ensemble of gestures and actions which we perform. "The body must be regarded," writes Elizabeth Grosz, "as a site of social, political, cultural and geographical inscriptions, production, or constitution. The body is not opposed to culture, a resistant throw-back to a natural past; it is itself a cultural, *the* cultural, product" (*Volatile Bodies* 23). Reading is one such social and political inscription, a writing of the body which reveals its culturally and historically contingent character. Bodies, or more precisely, our different senses of inhabiting a physical self, are as variable as the texts that they read.

Hypertexts refigure our perception of ourselves as closed systems: sitting before the computer monitor, mouse in hand, and index finger twitching on the command button, we are engaged in a border experience, a moving back and forth across the lines which divide the human and the machine, culture and nature. Such skirmishes into the digital terrain must, at least at this historical moment in which such actions appear relatively novel or "alien," remind us of the alterity of electronic texts. Contrary to those who claim that a hypertext allows the reader to become its "author," the reader has no *a priori* subjectivity that he or she brings to the screen. Subjectivity, in this sense, is formed in relation to our bodily sense of occupying a specific space and time: it is constituted and reconstituted from moment to moment as the reader responds to the various challenges and opportunities of reading an electronic narrative. This is not to say that the *person* reading the hypertext does not "exist" before turning on the computer, only that our individual and unique stores of experiences, knowledges, and memories are differently instantiated in the reading of a hypertext. The fiction of links and lexia requires a different engagement of the body, an alternative inscription in space, and a variable relation to oneself and others.

Hypertext fiction has demonstrated an acute awareness of the ways in which electronic textuality pressures the category of the "human." Allowing the reader to pursue a path of his or her own making through its narrative possibilities, hypertext both answers to the intentions of the reading subject and exceeds them. Its openness to the reader, its ability to adapt to his or her every decision, masks the degree to which it is also informing and participating in this process of narrative "making." While the Codex book provides a comforting mirror for the unity of the reading subject, hypertext fiction delights in its opacity, its irreducible alterity. It opens a new space of reading, a dialogue between self and self, and between self and other, in which such distinctions are increasingly called into question. Gilles Deleuze and Félix Guattari describe such conjunctions as "assemblages." "An assemblage," they write, "has neither base nor superstructure, neither deep structure nor superficial structure; it flattens all of its dimensions onto a single plane of consistency upon which reciprocal presuppositions and mutual insertions play themselves out" (90). In reading a hypertext novel such as John McDaid's *Uncle Buddy's Phantom Funhouse*, one becomes an "assemblage," an unstriated plane of intensities and exchanges between the human and machine. McDaid's text, I argue, can serve as a case study of how hypertext fiction effectively exploits the ways in which electronic textuality perforates the integrity of the body image of the reading subject, opening it out to new combinations and connections. Free of the nostalgia for some lost wholeness to which the virtual appears to herald the end, this hyperfiction embraces the possibilities of dispersal, dissemination, and scattering that are the very condition of the electronic sign.

The Book and the Body

If books have become, as Geoffrey Nunberg puts it, our most "implausible objects of desire," it is perhaps because they act as a mirror of the ego's own illusory sense of totality (17). According to Lacan, the child's earliest sense of itself is as a *corps morcelé*, a "body in pieces," which lacks any formal coherence or identity of its own (2). Physiologically incapable of controlling its own motor activities, the infant is "an unco-ordinated *aggregate*, a series of parts, zones, organs, sensations, needs and impulses, rather than an integrated totality" (Grosz, *Jacques Lacan* 33). In this stage of its development, the child does not distinguish between itself and the world around it. The pre-oedipal subject exists in an undifferentiated state until first observing itself, in Lacan's paradigmatic instance, in the mirror. Only in reaction to seeing itself as a specular whole, as an object discrete from the mother, does the ego come into being. Our sense of self is thus formed out of an experience of absence: the image the ego (mis)takes for itself is fundamentally *other* than itself, an optical illusion formed by the convergence of light rays on a reflective surface. And it is in response to this originary loss that the ego may entertain nostalgic phantasies of a lost wholeness, or fetishize objects with which it would paste over the gap at the heart of subjectivity.

The codex book is an exemplary fetish object: apprehendable as a single, bounded, and discrete form, its apparent completeness recalls the image of totality in relation to which the ego first "discovers" its autonomy.[1] Held in the hands, its pages caressed and turned, or even flung away like a lover scorned (and it is significant in this regard that one of the most oft-repeated complaints about electronic texts is that "you can't take them to bed"), the book is a reassuring comfort to the ego's deep-seated concerns for its own illusory integrity. In his mournful memoir of book culture, *The Gutenberg Elegies*, Sven Birkerts recalls his own earliest feelings of embodiment and their relationship to the book: "I remember the sensation of reading (Freudians can note this) as one of returning to a warm and safe environment, one that I had complete control over. When I picked up a book it was as much to get back to something as it was to set off to the new" (88). The nostalgia for the book, then, is indistinguishable from the longing for the infant's sense of security and belonging, for the "warm and safe environment" prior to our inscription in the symbolic order, of which, paradoxically, the book is an eminent sign. Birkerts repeatedly draws our attention to the "spatiality" of the book, that one reads not for what is written, nor for the story or the facts, but for the sense of self-possession it affords. The ability to read a book from beginning to end provides much the same sense of a mastery as the child experiences when it first masters its bodily processes, when its developing muscle coordination allows it to effect action in the world. A book can be "finished": it allows one the sense that it has given itself over completely to the reader, surrendered all its secrets.

The realist novel provides an exemplary illustration of the relationship that obtains between the book and the bodily pleasures it offers. A genre whose cultural fortunes were co-extensive with the rise of the printing press and movable type, the realist novel is in many senses the fullest realization of the material conditions of the codex book. The realist text exploits the inherently teleological nature of the book, the fact that its pages are bound to a center spine and thus most easily perused by reading one after another, by making it integral to a determinately linear plot. In *S/Z*, Roland Barthes demonstrates that the "readerly" text moves inevitably toward closure, the moment at which its initiatory enigma (a murder, for example) is resolved and the ideological status quo both reinstated and reaffirmed. Rendering the text "fully intelligible," closure lends the reader the illusion of absolute comprehension, and thus reasserts the autonomous individual as "the origin of meaning, knowledge and action" (Belsey 67). The sense of mastery afforded by closure is significantly amplified by the fact that it coincides with the turning of the last page, with the *physical* mastery of the text. The satisfactions of the realist text thus recall those of the mirror-stage; its pleasures are made possible by the ways in which the book functions as the double of the body.

Of course, many writers, from Laurence Sterne to James Joyce and Vladimir Nabokov, have sought ways to explode the materiality of the codex book. Milorad Pavić, for example, sees the book as engendering a kind of readerly lethargy. In casting his *Dictionary of the Khazars* as series of densely interlinked dictionary entries, he challenges his readers to make the kind of connections and choices that hypertext favors:

> No chronology will be observed here, nor is one necessary. Hence each reader will put together the book for himself, as in a game of dominoes or cards, and, as with a mirror, he will get out of this dictionary as much as he puts into it, for you . . . cannot get more out of the truth than what you put into it. (13)

To this end, the novel contains not just one "dictionary," but three, one for each of the major religions which had a stake in the interpretation of the dream which anticipated the end of the Khazar empire. Many of the terms are repeated in each of the three dictionaries, but the content of the entries varies according to the religious context. Various key terms are coded with colored icons, a cross, a star, and a crescent moon, to aid in cross-referencing. The book can thus be read in any number of ways. Each section can be read separately in a linear fashion. Conversely, the reader might consult the text randomly, as one might leaf through a dictionary, or proceed diagonally, following one term from one section to another, to gauge its different transmutations. And, finally, one can choose between a "male" and "female" version: the novel was issued in two separate editions, one for each gender.

Experiments such as Pavić's remind us that the challenges posed to the codex book by hypertext are not necessarily unprecedented. But their very novelty as readerly objects should also remind us of the cultural hegemony enjoyed by realist narrative. As Catherine Belsey notes, classic realism is "still the dominant popular mode in literature, film, and television drama" (67). This hegemony, I would argue, is not only part and parcel of the continuing prestige of the book as fetish object, but of the specific relationship that obtains between the book and the values of humanism. As much an unrepentant apologist for realism as the codex book, Birkerts writes:

> The characters and situations, products of the author's creative intention, are knit together into a larger wholeness. . . . As readers we take this in, unconsciously, and we may begin to conceive of our own actions under this same aspect of fatedness. . . . Our lives feel pointed toward significance and resolution; we feel ourselves living toward meaning, or at least living in the light of its possibility. I don't know that this more sustained self-charge is available anywhere else but in books. (90–91)

The realist novel, in this sense, is not simply another cultural commodity, but an instrument of selfhood, the preeminent means by which our culture reproduces its highest values. The "self-charge" it affords is one which assumes that the world is an orderly and knowable space, that its multiplicities are reducible to some underlying pattern and that this pattern obtains not by chance but through some volitional action of higher agency. The world of the realist novel, in short, is reassuringly *knowable*.

An electronic text, by contrast, provides no such assurances. It is an unsilvered looking glass which stymies the subject's narcissistic desires. Detached from the materiality of the codex book, the text escapes to the other side of the computer screen. Here it is inaccessible, remote, and provides none of the tactile pleasures of a bound volume. Even when the reader enters his or her own words onto the screen, they seem divorced from their source. Rendered in a computer typeface constituted by the underlying software program and placed against a pixilated background, they take on a fascinating (in the sense of both alluring and terrifying) otherness. As Mark Seltzer says of the typewriter, the computer "replaces, or pressures, that fantasy of continuous transition [which is the hallmark of the act of writing by hand] with recalcitrantly visible and material systems of difference: with the standardizing spacing of keys and letters; with the dislocation of where the hands work, where the letters strike and appear, where the eyes look, if they look at all" (10). The radical decentering of the subject effected by earlier writing technologies is accelerated in the age of digital reproduction, for now our words move to a virtual space where they shine back at us with an uncanny light all their own.

The incunabula of the digital revolution, hypertexts carry with them both the fear and pleasures of the *corps morcelé*, of the time before the sense of oneness. In a very real sense, there is no such "thing" as a hypertext, an object one can hold in the hands, a single, identifiable construct which would mirror the subject's own fragile sense of autonomy. Hypertexts exist *in potentia*, as a skittering of electronic impulses which take no determinate form until invoked by the computer's operating system. Even then they do not cohere into a stable object, but are dependent for their "shape" upon the set of interactions between the underlying software program and the person at the keyboard. As the exact nature of this interaction will vary from reading to reading, and from reader to reader, hypertexts cannot be known in the same way one "knows" material objects. It is impossible to speak of Stuart Moulthrop's *Victory Garden* with the same ontological precision as one speaks of, say, *Hard Times*; not every reader of Moulthrop's hypertext will have read the same words, in the same order, as will the reader of Dickens's novel. Moreover, if, as seems increasingly likely, it comes to pass that all texts are placed on-line so that they may be browsed through the kind of global hypertext search routines now available through World Wide Web, even the local sense of coherency afforded by the user's own "copy" of the text will fade. That is to say, not only will a text not exist as a material artifact on a bookshelf, it will not even exist, as is now often the case, on a floppy disk in your computer. It will reside on a mainframe which the reader has access to only through phone lines or fiber-optic cables. And there it will be linked with all the other html-encoded documents on the Web.

The consequences of this removal of the text from a proximity to the reader's body will be manifold. According to R. Howard Bloch and Carla Hesse, "Genres until now considered to be discrete suddenly will mingle indiscreetly on the screen; any text will be able to mate electronically with any other text in what looms as the spectre of a great miscegenation of types brought about by digitization, and whose ultimate fantasy is the evaporation of boundaries, the decomposition of a textual corpus that carries the charge of physical decomposition as well" (4). The end of books brings with it a general collapse of the bounds which once kept intact not only literary genres, but those between "author" and "reader," and "artist" and "critic." And, as Bloch and Hesse argue, the fears surrounding this biblio-apocalypse cannot "be detached from a fear of loss of bodily integrity" (4).

The Disturbing Liveliness of Machines

Hypertextuality challenges the very possibility of totality upon which the codex book depends. It demands, in short, a new body, one which finds its pleasures not in the satisfactions of completion and enclosure, nor in the stately assurances of the Cartesian *cogito*, but in the possibilities of connectivity and openness. The computer must be understood as something more than a prosthesis, an extension of the somatic sensorium. It is a force in its own right, the uncanny autonomy of which threatens the sovereignty of the human. As Donna Haraway points out, "Late twentieth-century machines have made thoroughly ambiguous the difference between natural and artificial, mind and body, self-developing and externally designed, and many other distinctions that used to apply to organisms and machines. Our machines are disturbingly lively, and we find ourselves frighteningly inert" (176).

Haraway describes this amalgam of human and machine as a "cyborg." In an effort to conscript the bastard offspring of the military-industrial complex into the service of 1980s-style socialist feminism, she defines the cyborg as "a creature of the postgender world; it has no truck with bisexuality, pre-Oedipal symbiosis, unalienated labour, or other seductions to organic wholeness through a final appropriation of all the powers of the parts into a higher unity" (175). The image of the cyborg, however, seems ill-adapted to her ideal of "lived social and bodily realities in which people are not afraid of their joint kinship with animals and machines, not afraid of permanently partial identities and contradictory standpoints" (179). For a cyborg, at least as it has been imaged by filmmakers and novelists, subordinates the machinic, the animal, the other, to the human; from Victor Frankenstein's "monster" to Arnold Schwarzenegger's "Terminator," the cyborg has always appeared in a distinctly anthropomorphic form. As Claudia Springer writes in her analysis of the spate of cyborg films which followed in the wake of Haraway's essay, "these films represent cyborgs as aggressive bulging bodies. The cyborg's physical prowess is heightened, not abandoned, and its strength is muscular not cerebral. What these cyborgs do best is kill" (88). The cyborg, as Haraway emphasizes, is as much a creature of the imagination as of technology and, as such, it can never quite escape the ideological undercurrent of the popular imagery from which it was born. With its emphasis on "a final appropriation of all the powers of the parts into a higher unity," I would argue, Haraway's cyborg is too easily reducible to a hypermasculinized and newly unified subject. And, as such, it is an inadequate model for the hypertext reader. What is required here is not an image which would subsume the machinic to the bodily outlines of the human, but something more akin to Deleuze and Guattari's concept of an "assemblage." Hypertext readers are not cyborgs, not glisteningly metallic man–machines, but something altogether less "finished" and less "whole." In speaking of them we need an image which would confound the very idea of an image as an object fixed in time and space and would capture instead the assemblage's sense of flux and indeterminacy. We need, in short, something more *disturbing*.

Hypertext author Richard Gess offers such a vision. In his account of the writing of *Mahasukha Halo*, Gess records his growing sense of the autonomy of his hypertext:

> Then came a fierce period, diving in every night, writing it up, . . . and the thrill of growing the thing, watching it behave like a life-form. Stitched and spliced into busy systems, lit with current, the inert lines of text became sentient, reacting to stimuli, changing their shape, growing. ("Magister Macintosh" 39)

The hypertext novel differs from its book-bound counterpart in that it appears to happen "out there" rather than "in here." As the web of interconnections grows from node to node, they begin to manifest a logic of their own, a logic of oblique associations and chance linkages quite distinct from the sense of orderliness and teleology in which Birkerts finds the delights of realist narratives. Such a logic appears as distinct from that of the authoring consciousness even as it owes its existence to that consciousness. "That was what I thought I'd get if I made [my novel] a hypertext," writes Gess. "I wanted to make a mind, feverishly free-associating, that would use that illusion to invade that dark space in each reader's skull and take it over. Something alive" ("Magister Macintosh" 41). Straddling the lines between culture and nature, the hypertext assumes a viral form: in the very act of answering to the reader's decisions, the hypertext quietly imposes its own "feverish" logic, possesses his or her mind even as it is possessed by his or her intentions. The relationship is a parasitic one in which the invading organism is as important to the host as *vice versa*, the two intermingled in an economy of mutual exchange and transformation. As if in response to this sense of ruptured identities, Gess's text is full of images of genetic chaos, gender confusion, and somatic interference: "Everything left me through all my holes"; "Men blistered with gesturing vulvas, women with erect penis noses"; "Neighbour genetics of gender mutate cyclically." The normative human body has been infiltrated, taken over, and translated into something multiform and transgressive, the very "spectre of a great miscegenation of types brought about by digitization."

Gess's emphasis on the otherness of his hypertext is salutary. While it is true, as Jay David Bolter writes, that the computer is "intelligent only in collaboration with human readers and writers," we should not let such "common sense" occlude from us the importance of the computer's relative autonomy in the process of this collaboration (193). This is the paradox of hypertextuality: while linked electronic texts have no material or ontological existence of their own, they are nonetheless more than the sum total of their readers' desires. Hypertexts may depend on their readers, but so too do their readers depend on them. They are active forms which obey their own programming code. Moreover, their database structures and navigational tools largely determine the exact nature of the degree of interaction which the reader will be allowed, the kinds of links he or she may traverse or create, and how he or she will do so. This deep structure constitutes the alterity of the hypertext, the unassimilable excess upon which signification depends.

In many hyperfictions, the possibility of controlling the reader's access to certain lexia is central to the text's narrative design. Eastgate System's Storyspace authoring system (the program of choice for many creative writers working in the medium), for example, offers the option of using "guard fields" which require that the reader have visited certain lexia before others can be read. The text most often cited as the first "classic" of this new genre, Michael Joyce's *Afternoon: A Story*, makes notable use of guard fields: it radically reconfigures itself during the course of reading in response to the reader's decisions. Choosing one link can potentially foreclose the possibility of ever visiting another, while the text of a lexia once read may, on being reencountered, seem subtly altered to reflect earlier decisions. Even in a text such as Carolyn Guyer's *Quibbling*, which allows the reader full access to its underlying structure, the spatial arrangement of lexia partly determines the context(s) in which any one lexia may be read. Like most Storyspace "webs," *Quibbling* is organized in a series of imbricated "clusters" which group lexia into identifiable groups (see figure 7.1). Within these clusters, individual blocks of text may be linked into default "paths" so that the reader is more likely to read them consecutively. The effect these organizing principles have on a reading is increased when, as is usually the case, the reader uses the navigational palette, an interface which depends on the spatial relationship between lexia in order to move from one to the next. The otherness that results from the use of

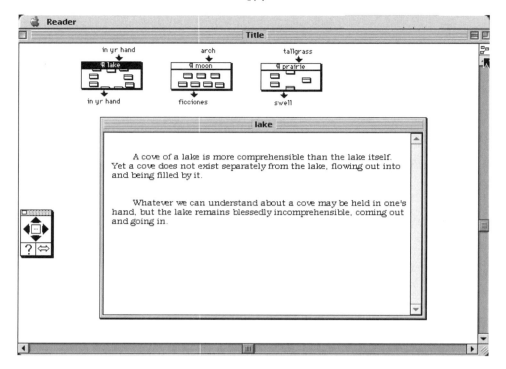

Figure 7.1

guard fields, clustering, and other means of organizing lexia is a site of resistance. It mediates between the user and his or her desires, and, like any intermediary, necessarily alters those desires in the process. Hypertexts inscribe themselves onto the skin of the human as deeply as the human writes itself into the machine. They are interactive in the truest sense, reconfiguring their readers even as they are reconfigured by them.

The Active Reader

The relative autonomy of the machinic component of hypertext reading has been uniformly downplayed by its theorists. Seeking, apparently, to reassure those who may be put off by the prospect of interacting with a computer, most critics have presented hypertext as a kind of triumph of humanist individualism. George Landow, for example, regularly rehearses what has become one of the dominant myths of electronic textuality, the unrestricted "freedom" of the reader. Endowed with the ability to move through the text in a non-sequential fashion through the facility of links, the reader, Landow claims, becomes an active participant in the "writing" of the text. Authority for the text's meaning thus passes from the "author" to this new reader/writer, whose decisions physically alter not only the text's "meaning," but the material conglomeration of signs by which it is constituted. "Hypertext," Landow concludes, "provides an infinitely re-centerable system whose provisional point of focus depends upon the reader, who becomes . . . truly active" (11).

Underlying this attractive claim for the ways in which hypertext "empowers" the reader, however, is a consumerist ideology that allows for the reappearance of the self-knowing subject of *laissez-faire* capitalism in the world of "de-centred" hypertextuality. An electronic text may be severed from the proper name of an "author," it may lack the material unity once assured it by the form of the codex book, but the reader's "choices" will nonetheless allow him or her to "re-centre" it. Landow gives us the hypertext reader as supermarket shopper, "freely" moving about a world of endless lexical commodities, picking and choosing those which best suit the color scheme of his or her research interests. Organic unity and internal coherence may have been routed from the text by the advents of the poststructuralist literary theory, but they reappear in the undisturbed totality of the person sitting before the computer screen. Thus closure is no longer a property of the text, but of the reader: when the reader decides to stop reading, Landow writes, "he or she ends, kills, the story, because when the active reader, the reader-author, stops reading, the story stops, it dies, it reaches an ending" (118). This image of a reader who may "freely" shape the text according to his or her "intentions" assumes a self-knowing, undivided subject, free of the internal contradictions which are the condition of embodied subjectivity. Moreover, it effaces the obdurate quality of hypertext, the ways in which its organizational structure necessarily mediates between the reader and his or her desires, just as surely as the supermarket forces its desires on the shopper. The sense of "freedom" in both instances is an illusion maintained by the very fact of "choice."

There is, however, in Landow's dramatic insistence that the reader, like Victor Frankenstein, retains the power to kill that which he or she has brought into being, a discernible note of fear. His attempt to assert the absolute sovereignty of the autonomous subject over the text seems to emerge here from a sense that the reader is not alone in being able to lay claim to "life." The otherness, the disturbing liveliness of electronic texts appears as a threat to the ego's belief in itself as occupying a self-coherent body. It is reminded of the void upon which it is uneasily perched, the condition of fragmentation from which it emerged. There is danger here, Landow seems to say, a danger which must be turned out, suppressed, slain. A number of "creative," or "artistic" hypertexts, however, have turned this danger to their advantage. Far from fearing the loss of bodily integrity, they commit themselves to it, and, by extension, to the most productive energies of hypertextuality itself. It is to one such text, John McDaid's *Uncle Buddy's Phantom Funhouse*, that I now turn.

Lost in the Funhouse

Heralded by Robert Coover as "the most ambitious hyperfiction yet attempted by a single author" (11), McDaid's *Uncle Buddy's Phantom Funhouse* consists of the contents of one Arthur "Buddy" Newkirk's estate to which the reader has been made heir. Newkirk, it seems, has either died or simply gone missing, leaving behind a vast collection of personal memorabilia. The "home" card, the screen to which the reader may most readily return and initiate new explorations, is an image of a house, each room of which represents a different HyperCard stack, a different repository of Arthur Newkirk's prodigious artistic output (see figure 7.2). Each "room" of the house contains a different kind of literary remains that one may choose to explore. Choosing the "Sooner or Later" room, for example, allows one to peruse the contents of Newkirk's film script concerning a group of young physicists caught up in the political intrigues of university funding; "Source Code" contains an issue of an electronic magazine for writers who use computer code to write poetry; "Final Cuts" is a portfolio of lyrics and other memorabilia from Newkirk's days in an acid rock band; "Fictionary of the Bezoars" is an elaborate parody of Pavić's *Dictionary of the Khazars*; "Art Gallery" contains a slowly shifting series of photos that follow Newkirk from infancy to middle age; and "Oracle" is a series of Tarot-like cards, the prophecies of which point obliquely to the missing man's fate. Each of these rooms contains "passage ways" to the other rooms, some of which, of course, open only when the right password is provided. These and other electronic elements are supplemented with tapes of Newkirk's music, and page proofs for a short story. The text is thus less a narrative to "follow" than a space to explore: the teleology of the book gives ways to an architectonics of identity.

Focusing on the life and mind of one man, *Uncle Buddy's* takes up anew the realist novel's fascination with interiority and psychological verisimilitude. Vastly expanding the range of materials available to the

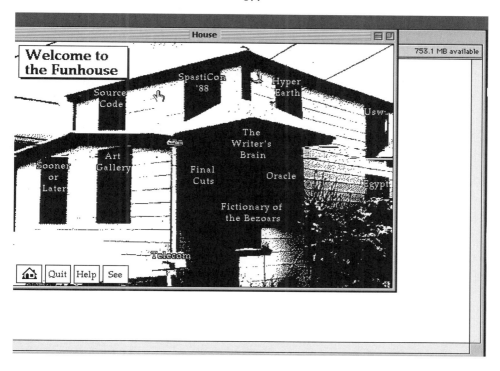

Figure 7.2

author, hypermedia seems to make possible the realist's dream of capturing on the page the always absent traces of a life lived, the ineffabilities of character that make a "person" into an individual, a proper name, a unique point of reference. Indeed, one of the largest of the Funhouse's "rooms" is entitled "The Writer's Brain," a collection of diary entries and notebook marginalia that minutely register the changing character of Newkirk's thinking. But for all the encyclopedic range of the Funhouse's archives, Newkirk himself remains missing. The hypertextual form of the Phantom Funhouse reveals in ever greater detail the molecular substrata of its subject, but also reminds us that there is no limit to this descent into the body. Newkirk changes each time we encounter him, each time we enter the Funhouse from another angle, or glimpse him through the distortions of another mirror.

The opening lexia of the "Art Gallery" makes a telling reference to John Barth's well-known short story "Lost in the Funhouse." In this story, an adolescent boy ventures into a funhouse and becomes hopelessly lost among "the endless replication[s] of his image in the mirrors" (90). These mirrors, like the myriad narrative forms and genres which one finds in McDaid's own funhouse, are figures of the conventional tropes (e.g., the descriptions of physical appearances and mannerisms that create a sense of "character," omniscient narration that provides access to the thoughts and feelings of those characters, etc.) by which the realist novel "mirrors" reality. But, as Barth writes of the use of blanks as substitutes for proper names, "Interestingly, as with other aspects of realism, it is an *illusion* that is being enhanced, by purely artificial means" (69–70). The reader of McDaid's text quickly becomes as "lost" among the endless representations of Arthur Newkirk, as the boy in Barth's story becomes lost among the labyrinthine corridors of realist literary conventions. The "deep structure" of McDaid's text, the dense web of hypertext links that connect one room and one memory with another, lead the reader deeper and deeper into its hidden recesses, confounding any easy sense of "progress." "A book," writes Nunberg, "doesn't simply contain the inscription of a text, it *is* the inscription. . . . This property is crucial to the way we read any book whose content is essentially linear or narrative, as we subconsciously register the external boundaries of the volume in the terms of the space between our thumb and forefinger, and reckon our text accordingly" (18). Where the reader of the codex book may note his or her steady advancement through the pages, the "assemblage" that is the hypertext reader, by contrast, has no "place," and thus necessarily experiences a sense of disorientation, the loss of proprioceptive coherence which the bound volume so carefully maintains. This is especially so when the reader encounters a text like McDaid's either on the Internet or in tandem with an Internet session. Moving back and forth, for example, between "Principia Cybernetica," the cybernetics website, and Newkirk's own ruminations on thermodynamics, or between one's own e-mail and that found in the Funhouse's "Telecom" room, serves to fissure not only McDaid's text but the reader's own sense of occupying a single apprehendable space. Dispersed among the hypertextual links of the Net, the ego's sense of itself as embodied, as comprising a discrete entity, is eroded, broken up, and scattered as surely as is the textual body of Uncle Buddy himself. The lines separating the "human" from the "machine" and the "fictional" from the "virtual" give way to an unstriated space of linkages and associations, an always expanding field of connections, voices, and bodies which know each other only in the intimacy of their electronic extensions.

Arthur Newkirk is both everywhere in this text and nowhere; the very means by which we might, like Borges's infamous cartographers, produce a perfect map of his being is also that which most dramatically attests to his absence, which, in effect, divides us from him. This, however, is a productive loss, for it is precisely the absence of a determinable center that allows the reader to discover pleasures other than those of closure and comprehension, to imagine bodies as something other than monadic. We are, in effect, invited to play among the ruins of identity, to piece together bits of Newkirk's e-mail with lyrics from a song or entries in his diary that allow us some sense of "revelation" or of "discovery": we may form conclusions about how Newkirk disappeared or whether he ever found his great love, Emily, again. But such conclusions are always provisional. We can just as easily put those same pieces together with yet others, including other texts that were not written by John McDaid, and in so doing, come to a different reading, a different understanding of the missing man. McDaid's bricolage of text, graphics, and sound delivers us to a world in which the body overcomes the paranoia attendant to the ego's sense of itself as a whole through the playful affirmation of multiplicity and otherness. Here, the reader is no longer a fixed totality, but a mutable site of connection and change, consumption and production, being and non-being.

An assemblage, write Deleuze and Guattari, comprises two segments, one of content, the other of expression. "On the one hand, it is a *machinic assemblage* of bodies, of actions and passions, an intermingling of bodies reacting to one another; on the other hand, it is a *collective assemblage of enunciation*, of acts and statements, of incorporeal transformations attributed to bodies" (88; italics in the original). Assemblages are opposed to all totalizing gestures such as the "active reader." The heterogeneous elements of which they are composed do not harken back to some original plenitude that has been lost nor do they constitute in their aggregate form some *telos*, some moment of completion. They are, rather, "lines of flight" which serve to erode the distinctions between subject and object, self and other, which subtend the humanist subject. The reader of electronic narratives is just such an "assemblage": the otherness of hypertext, the way in which nodes are grouped, links are formed, or interfaces designed, forces the reader to engage dialectically with the computer. He or she thus ceases to be a site of fullness in his or her own right and becomes an extended space of production, a series of flows, energies, intensities, discontinuities, and desires which refuse the (en)closure of the normative body. The electronic sign, by its very nature as a dematerialized pulse, pushes beyond the bounds of structure and it is this anarchism which texts such as McDaid's embrace. Hypertext fiction offers the reader the opportunity to "get lost," to suppress the desire to always know where one is inscribed in the text and to wander free of such landmarks. The reader moves through the text in a complicated interaction between machine and self that privileges the pleasures of traveling over those of arriving. Such traveling necessarily reconfigures the body: the alterity, the unknowability of Arthur Newkirk is emblematic of the otherness of hypertext itself, and it is through our relationship to this alterity that we, as readers, may become not the masters of the text, but collaborators in its writing, participants in the process of our own becoming.

Notes

1. A fetish is an object which the fetishist uses to ward off or compensate for his awareness of the threat of castration. Freud describes it as "a substitute for the woman's (mother's) phallus which the little boy once believed in and does not wish to forego" (199). It commemorates the moment at which the child first becomes aware of his lack, which precipitates his painful awakening from the undifferentiated condition of the *corps morcelé* and his entry into the Symbolic order.

Works Cited

Barth, John. "Lost in the Funhouse." *Lost in the Funhouse.* New York: Bantam, 1968. 69–94.

Barthes, Roland. *S/Z: An Essay.* Trans. Richard Miller. New York: Hill and Wang, 1974.

Belsey, Catherine. *Critical Practice.* London: Methuen, 1980.

Birkerts, Sven. *The Gutenberg Elegies.* London: Faber and Faber, 1994.

Bloch, R. Howard, and Carla Hesse. "Introduction." *Representations* 42 (1993): 1–12.

Bolter, Jay David. *Writing Space.* Hillsdale, NJ: Lawrence Erlbaum, 1991.

Chartier, Roger. *L'Ordre des livres.* Aix-en-Provence: Alinca, 1992.

Coover, Robert. "Hyperfiction: Novels for the Computer." *New York Times Book Review* 29 August 1993: 1–12.

Deleuze, Gilles, and Félix Guattari. *A Thousand Plateaus: Capitalism and Schizophrenia.* Trans. Brian Massumi. Minneapolis: U of Minnesota P, 1987.

Freud, Sigmund. "Fetishism." *Collected Papers.* Ed. James Strachey. Vol. 5. New York: Basic Books, 1959. 198–204.

Gess, Richard. "Magister Macintosh." *The Drama Review* 37 (1993): 38–44.

——. *Mahasukha Halo.* Storyspace hypertext software supplement to *Perforations* 1.2 (1992).

Grosz, Elizabeth. *Jacques Lacan: A Feminist Introduction*. London: Routledge, 1990.

——. *Volatile Bodies: Toward a Corporeal Feminism*. Bloomington: Indiana UP, 1994.

Guyer, Carolyn. *Quibbling*. Computer software. Cambridge, MA: Eastgate Systems, 1993. Macintosh Plus, System 6.0, 2MB RAM.

Haraway, Donna. "A Manifesto for Cyborgs: Science, Technology, and Socialist Feminism in the 1980s." *Coming to Terms: Feminism, Theory, Politics*. Ed. Elizabeth Weed. London: Routledge, 1989. 173–204.

Harpold, Terence. "The Grotesque Corpus." *Perforations* 3 (1992): 1–8.

Joyce, Michael. *Afternoon, A Story*. Computer software. Cambridge, MA: Eastgate Systems, 1988. Macintosh Plus, System 6.0, 2MB RAM.

——. *WOE*. Computer software. *Writing on the Edge* 2 (1991). Macintosh Plus, System 6.0, 2MBRAM.

Lacan, Jacques. *Ecrits: A Selection* London: Tavistock, 1977.

Landow, George P. *Hypertext: The Convergence of Contemporary Critical Theory and Technology*. Baltimore: Johns Hopkins UP, 1992.

McDaid, John. *Uncle Buddy's Phantom Funhouse*. Computer software. Cambridge, MA: Eastgate Systems, 1993. Macintosh Plus, HyperCard 2.0, 2MB RAM.

Moulthrop, Stuart. *Victory Garden*. Computer software. Cambridge, MA: Eastgate Systems,1991. Macintosh Plus, System 6.0, 2MB RAM.

Nunberg, Geoffrey. "The Place of Books in the Age of Electronic Reproduction." *Representations* 42 (1993): 13–37.

Pavić, Milorad. *Dictionary of the Khazars*. New York: Vintage, 1989.

Seltzer, Mark. *Bodies and Machines*. London: Routledge, 1992.

Springer, Claudia. "Muscular Circuitry: The Invincible Armored Cyborg in Cinema." *Genders* 18 (1993): 87–101.

Yellowlees Douglas, J. "Understanding the Act of Reading: The *WOE* Beginner's Guide to Dissection." *Writing on the Edge* 2 (1991): 112–27.

8

Postorganic Performance
The Appearance of
Theater in Virtual Spaces

Matthew Causey

> Performance's only life is in the present. Performance can-
> not be saved, recorded, documented, or otherwise partici-
> pate in the circulation of representations: once it does so,
> it becomes something other than performance.
> —Peggy Phelan, *Unmarked* (146)

> There is nothing more illusory in performance than the
> illusion of the unmediated. It can be a very powerful illu-
> sion in the theater, but it *is* theater, and it is *theater*, the
> truth of illusion, which haunts all performance whether
> or not it occurs in the theater, where it is more than dou-
> bled over.
> —Herbert Blau, *The Eye of Prey* (164–65)

The Metempsychosis of Performance
through Postorganic Fields

In March of 1929 Bertolt Brecht, explaining how the traditional realist
drama was inadequate as a representational device for the industrial age,
wrote that "Petroleum resists the five act structure." He insisted that
"it is impossible to explain a present day character by features or a present day action by motives that would be adequate in our father's time"
(30). If you substitute the word "virtuality" for "petroleum" in the
above sentence you will understand the simple thesis of this paper. A
self-titled "child of the scientific age," Brecht asked in *A Short Or-
ganum for the Theatre*, "what ought our representations of men's life together look like?" (*Brecht on Theatre* 185). Although *affirmative representations* have been problematized through the poststructuralist critique
of the linking of signifier and signified through resemblance, Brecht's

question regarding theatrical representations must still drive us. As we begin to consider performance in virtuality, and the underlying ideology of the will to virtuality, what aesthetic gestures (if any) will seem appropriate to our hypermediated, simulated, televisual culture?

How do we understand the processes of performance in virtual domains? Before I outline my questioning it is important to position the term "performance" in its concrete manifestation (I will discuss ontological matters later) and isolate the areas of new media under consideration. My discussion of performance concerns itself with the category of aesthetic theater that includes, according to Richard Schechner's useful "Performance Time/Space/Event Chart" (*Performance Theory* 252–53), both theater and performance art. I exclude the larger models of performance, as developed in the field of performance studies, that address the phenomena of secular and sacred ritual, sports, and social drama, even though these categories of "restored behavior" are being similarly effected in their convergence with the always already mediated postmodern environment of *televisuality*. Acknowledging the severity of the infection brought on by the televisual and the virtual in all aspects of postindustrial culture, and noting the border crossings between art, performance, and popular culture, I will nonetheless confine my examinations to aesthetic theater.

It is, perhaps, the phenomenon of the televisual and its *worlding of the world as picture* that has most radically affected the ontology of performance. The televisual, of which VR is the latest advancement, has become a primary repository for cultural memory and knowing enacting "a partial transference of metaphysics into techno-cultural systems" (Fry 12), which has led to a "reshaping of ways in which we see . . . [with] repercussion on the way that we think" (Fry 104). Richard Dienst indicates the endgame of televisuality when he writes that "television, then, is the perfect end point, more perfect and complex than either the Bomb or cinema, a pure will-to-vision that everywhere leaves things ready but unseen" (123). The trajectory of such theories of televisuality leads to the suspicion that our notions of art and performance, our methods of thinking, are essentially televisual. The tendencies of televisual art and televisual thinking could be characterized as an incessant picturing that makes "everything" visible but nothing accessible—a simulation machine whose technological alchemy brings forth the creation of the signifier in advance of the signified, warping time, memory, and critique. It is my impression that VR and the myriad of computer communication tools are merely extensions of the televisual world picture. The question that remains is whether the interactive properties of VR and its potential for the exploration of both social constructions and the nature of the mind/body relation will transcend the tendencies of the televisual. Or, is VR interactivity merely televisual multiple choice that offers only the illusion of freedom and exploration? These alternatives open up into broader issues: Can VR technologies be configured as a poststructuralist diremption machine undoing the sense of a unified self in known space, or does VR necessarily sustain the Cartesian mind/body duality and the conception of the self as steady and central, thus representing—as Simon Penny puts it—"the completion of the Enlightenment project" (231)?

The performance sites I will cover are the *virtual* territories of cyberspace created by the *concrete* technologies of computer networks interfaced with the human subject. It is, of course, the human-computer interface (HCI) that dictates the production and the aesthetics of virtual spaces. As technological advancements move us past the constrictors of keyboards, head-mounted displays, and datagloves, toward more open immersive spaces, the HCI will disappear in a joining of body and machine. The prosthetic body of future HCI will extend itself through the machine into distant and imaginary spaces and reordered time. At this point the performative technologies of cyberspace include e-mail, video conferencing performances via CUSeeMe or fiber-optic transmissions, electronic museums, hypertext novels, multimedia interactivity, telepresence technology, interactive immersive virtual environments, virtual reality, artificial intelligence, artificial life, and robotics. Performances on the World Wide Web are now commonplace, and virtual theater companies have formed and are performing and improving across the net. There are ongoing fantasy role-playing worlds of MUDs and MOOs. Discussion lists such as Collab-l and Ars.digit-l facilitate the collaboration and discussion of cyber-performance. *Cyber-stage*, a magazine dedicated to exploring issues surrounding mediated performance, is now published in Canada. The first stage of mediated art has passed. Video, performance, and theater artists such as Nam June Paik, Laurie Anderson, The Wooster Group, and the popular entertainments of Broadway, Las Vegas, and theme parks, continue to incorporate various media, including computer-controlled interfaces for video, film, audio, and lighting into live performance. Experiments in mediated performance, live performance that incorporates advanced imaging technologies, is being undertaken by artists at such theaters as *George Coates' Performance Works*, the *Stanford Arts and Technology Initiative*, and Georgia Tech's *Performance and Technology Research Lab*. The future of postorganic and mediated performance will include "Smart Rooms" with embedded technologies to enable audience interactivity through the body and voice, "virtual characters" generated from computer graphics, artificial intelligence–driven robotics, and digital scenography. What is obvious is that the performativity of cyberspace is being explored and colonized. What is less apparent are how these experiments and power moves will alter our knowledge of performance, theater, and art within and without the new technologies.

The questions to be explored in this chapter and in the practice of virtual theater are the following: How do the appearances of theater *happen* in virtual spaces? What is the "future of illusion" in the technologies of the simulated real? What are the possibilities for performance aesthetics in the virtual domain? Can the fundamental and visceral property of the theater, what Tadeusz Kantor calls "the revelatory message from the realm of death, the metaphysical shock" (114), take place in virtual worlds? In a simulated state of hyperrealism, what of the "sex and death of the flesh" that seems to have always phenomenologically marked performance? What is the ideology of the will to virtuality, the desire for disappearance in cyberterritories?

I will argue two issues: 1) Performance theory fails postorganic performance. I dispute the ontological claims made for performance which regard the essence of performance as a non-repeatable phenomenon of the "now." I call for an expanded performance theory that can address the issue of digital media performance and theater. What the mediated technologies afford performance theory is the opportunity to think against the grain of traditional performance ontology, including the claims to "liveness," "immediacy," and "presence." 2) Postorganic performance fails performance theory. My concern is that postorganic performance, playing out the will to virtuality, may in fact void itself of the capacity to realize the appearance of theater, the presence of the fleshy other. The trajectory of my article works from a call for a new perspective on the nature of performance so as to include the virtual, yet extends itself to a critique of that notion of postorganic performance.

The appearance of theater in the virtual space of the computer establishes a unique aesthetic object, a paraperformative teletheatrical phenomenon wherein the immediacy of performance and the digital alterability of time, space, and subjectivity overlap and are combined. I term the resulting aesthetic acts "postorganic performance."[1] The adjective "postorganic," for the purposes of my model for performance, reflects the transition from the privileging of presence, the authentic aura, the immediacy of the live to the exploration of issues surrounding the circulation of representations through a medium capable of temporal, spatial, and subjective manipulation. The postorganic maps the stage that is revealed through the confrontation of the "live performer" against the various media of digital audio, video, film, and the computer. In the model of postorganicism, performance is not what it was once theorized, a time-dependent disappearing act, for it no longer resides solely in the present moment of the theater, screen, or text.

The technologies of virtual realities, from chatrooms to interactive immersive virtual environments, can allow the performer/operator to explore a host of postmodern actions that demonstrate the textualization of the body and "the reconception of machine and organism as coded texts through which we engage in the play of writing and reading the world" (Haraway 194). The staging of transgender shifts, ethnic morphing, temporal and spatial reconfiguration, constructs a cyborgian utopia, or dystopia, depending upon your perspective, that signals the wholesale subversion of boundaries between man and animal and machine, wholeness and fragmentation, natural and artificial, origin and telos.

According to theories such as Haraway's, we have entered a new stage in evolution in which man and machine become biologically and technically symbiotic. In this context, Bruce Mazlish, in *The Fourth Discontinuity: The Co-Evolution of Humans and Machines*, cites Freud's model of the three great shocks to subject-centered conscious: Copernicus's rejection of the earth as the center of the universe; Darwin's depriveileging of mankind's place in nature by aligning us with the animals; and Freud's own discovery that the ego was not even "master in its own house, but must content itself with scanty information of what is going on unconsciously in the mind" (Mazlish 3). The fourth discontinuity, according to Mazlish, is that "humans and the machines they create are continuous and that the same conceptual schemes that help explain the workings of the brain also explain the workings of a 'thinking machine' " (4). With the advent of the digital worlds of virtual environments, artificial intelligence, and the televisual, as well as the medical advances of mechanic and electronic alteration of the body in devices such as pacemakers, electronic ears, and silicon chips implanted in the peripheral nervous system to interface with robotic limbs, mankind is not what it once was. Western culture in the late twentieth century is undergoing a "posthuman phase," as William Gibson has named and Haraway theorized. A "posthuman" culture will create "postorganic" art.

The sticking point of this posthuman theorization of technology in regard to my thesis on performance is, if we are arriving at the posthuman, what need will we have of the performance of the flesh of the Other? Wouldn't a posthuman be at home in the simulacrum without referentials? Taking my cue from Katherine Hayles, who steadfastly argues for the material base of all cyberexperiences, and countering the theory of the obsolete body as practiced by body artists Orlan and Stelarc,[2] who argue from different positions that technology has rendered the body limited and "problematic," it is safe to assume that the material body radically grounds all of cyberculture despite the science fictions and facts of telepresent space and virtual timings. The notion of the posthuman, the postorganic, should not be construed as a totalizing paradigm that denies the authentic (mortal) nature of each operator.

Performance, configured with technological interventions which disrupt the spatial and temporal texts, literalizes what performance has never been but always has been in theory: "here" and "not here," "now" and "not now" simultaneously. The actor who simultaneously appears "live" on stage and "represented as live" on video or computer monitors, who appears both "live" at point A and through telepresence extends the technological body to appear "as if live" at point B, concretizes the new mediated body and the dreams of the theater. Televisual or virtual performance, not unlike the Cubist rethinking of representational space on canvas, acts as an agent of transformation, altering the manner in which we construct and perceive narrativity, subjectivity, spatial and temporal images.

The ontological nature of performance being "in the now" (the PLAY function) is altered through analog and linear technology (magnetic audio- and videotape played on motor-driven cassettes) into a sequentially alterable but real-time dependent structure (the REVERSE, FAST FORWARD, PAUSE functions). Performance, through digital technologies, enters the simultaneous (INTERACTIVITY, RANDOM ACCESS) whereby the virtual image appears concurrently with or precedes the production of its referent. Performance, in the digital medium, has taken on the ontology of the technological.

The issues that will continue to raise themselves for performance in virtual spaces surround the questions of the "universals of performance" (161). If, as Peggy Phelan theorizes, the ontology of performance is its orbiting disappearance which resists the technology of reproduction, one is left wondering what takes place upon the collision of the televisual and the virtual. How does the maniacally regenerating "now" of performance interact with the reproducible flow of the televisual and its economy/circulation of representations? The performative territory of the technological allows for a variety of spatial, temporal, and subjective configurations that are non-linear, held in reserve, so as to be reordered, replayed, held in abeyance from the tyranny and disappearance of the present. It is my contention that the "now," the immediate, has become one of the "accidents" (the mere appearance) of the *transubstantiation* of performance into the technological.

Postmodern theory, in particular the writings of Jean Baudrillard and Philip Auslander, has critiqued the concept of "liveness" as an unmediated and present event. What we experience as "live" is always already mediated. Herbert Blau writes that "there is nothing more illusory in performance than the illusion of the unmediated" (164). In developing my model of postorganism I am not suggesting a *transfiguration* of performance, wherein the properties of liveness change significance so as to *symbolize* the regeneration of the simulations of technology. Instead I am suggesting a transubstantiation wherein the elements of the "now" are "*changed*," through the contemporary consecration of the new Eucharist, the linkage of human and machine. In the traditional Eucharist the elements of bread and wine are altered, mysteriously, to the flesh and blood of Christ, leaving only the accidents or appearances of bread and wine. The accidents of liveness, the appearances of the now, are all that remain in the passage of the ontology of the body of performance (now dead), now driven into the body of technology. And yet, I argue that theater and performance can still appear in both live and virtual spaces (the same thing only different).

If my suspicions are accurate (that the theater and performance in technology are still theater and performance) the question remains: Are there any "universals of performance" that can be isolated? What are they, and will they reoccur in virtual sites? Herbert Blau in his essay from *The Eye of Prey*, "Universals of Performance; or Amortizing Play" (easily the most important article written in the second half of this century on the nature of performance), creates a sort of particle physics of performance, which can help us think through some of the issues of virtual performance.

By addressing Blau's "universals" I am trying to resist the Situationist paradigm of spectacle and simulation which posits that in postmodernity, discerning the power of performance in the dispersion of the "performative instinct into art and everyday life" (Blau 185) is difficult if not impossible. In the "cultural logic of late capitalism," it has become increasingly difficult to conceptualize performance as an act of resistance or transgression. The period of hypercommodification and simulation strategy that typifies our "society of the spectacle," reconfigures experience as performative commodity. Nonetheless, I feel comfortable that an argument can be made isolating a performative aesthetic gesture which operates simultaneously and within the society of the spectacle. In fact, it is the mediatized, simulated culture that performance and theater need to attend to in virtual environments.

Blau's "universals" are areas of potentialities rather than a frame of ontological restrictions, and therefore are easily co-opted into my model of postorganic performance. Blau considers the *determining of time, consciousness of performance*, and the *transformative nature of performance* as basic to all performance. Although time can be aggressively manipulated, the *marking of "real time"* through cyberspace is possible. The human in the HCI can only pretend to move outside time's relentless motion. *Consciousness of performance*, "the marks of punctuation which are inflections of consciousness" (Blau 162), would seem to be able to operate similarly whether in virtual or real territories. The *transformative nature of performance*, the power to reorder all that enters its sphere, whether text, subjectivity, or ideology, would seem to remain intact in virtual environments. Given the digital flexibility of computer environments, transformation may very well be the essence of the medium. The fragility of the digital artifact (as my colleague Terry Harpold has taught me) disregards stability in a field of constantly shifting manifestations. What is performance in such a field?

The most troubling notion of Blau's universals, in relation to my theory of postorganicism, is considering the *distancing effects of performance* (the splendid isolation of actor and audience) in the fleshlessness of the digital. In order to understand the operations of theater in virtual spaces we need to understand what happens at the first appearance of theater. Blau, as have many others, notes the "essential aloneness" and "the sense of removal or distance" at the occurrence of the theater moment. On stage I watch someone dying. In the darkened "house" decomposing bodies wait for the appearance of the Other. Tadeusz Kantor wrote in his manifesto/essay, *The Theatre of Death*, that the "first actor" brought with him "the revelatory MESSAGE, which was transmitted from the realm of DEATH, [and] evoked in the VIEWERS . . . a metaphysical shock" (114).

Kantor understands that when a moment is metamorphosed from "not theatre" to "theater," there stands difference, there stands the shock of presence, the awareness of death, the lure of the flesh, and the joy of time passing. Although I can easily discount the ontology of performance as being "in the now," present and live, I hesitate at the lack of flesh in virtual performance. If all one can witness or perform in virtual environments is the scopic drive (the privileging of vision to the exclusion of other epistemological modalities) and the manic dance of picturing, where all presence is deferred to bodies in repose at keyboards or tragically isolated in an HMD interface, what have we left? Kantor, calling for a rediscovery of the art of the theater, wrote, "it is necessary to recover the primeval force of the shock taking place at the moment when opposite a man (the viewer) there stood for the first time a man (the actor) deceptively similar to us, yet at the same time infinitely foreign, beyond an impassable barrier" (114).

The promise of interactivity in virtual environments is the breakdown of the isolation of the viewer and actor that can define the theater. In what Jaron Lanier has called "post-symbolic communication" there is no need to watch Hamlet, since you can be Hamlet (Heilbrun 108). Like the classic question of science fiction, am I real or am I a simulation, the issue turns from witnessing the other to being the other. What is theater in such a field?

Two thoughts: 1) The birth of the virtual signals the death of the recent invention of *Man* (Foucault's erased face in the sand), and therefore these romantic notions of semblance, presence and the body, are nothing more than misty nostalgia. If man is uninvented, so will the theater be undone as the sighting of the Other will remain impossible and unnecessary. 2) Undreamed-of technologies, advanced human-computer interfaces, will take us past the isolated body-typing technology toward the time of total immersion, which may, in its simulated state, signal the difference that is the big bang of the theater. When placed in a liquid and invisible interface, what will become of the human face? A machine? A new human?

In the "liquid architecture" of the new computer technologies—to use Marcos Novak's expression—the concept of performance will raise a host of new theoretical questions. Three topics appear particularly urgent:

Performativity of Cultural Constructions

Within the virtual environment, the spectator is transposed into a digital space in which culturally based identities such as ethnicity, class, and gender are volatile, not fixed categories. User/operators are free to perform within the virtual system with any identification they choose; and gender, race, and class become performative differentiation, not fixed, hierarchical assignments within a social order. Certain theoretical strategies recognize that while sexual differentiation, genetic structure, and age are biological phenomena, gender difference, ethnicity, and class are cultural determinations that appear natural only because of the processes in which the ideological is absorbed into the perceptual. Because in the potentially open interactivity of cyberperformance, categories of gender, race, class may be selected and transformed at will, we need theoretical structures that base themselves upon the performative nature of these schemes of differentiation.

Non-Affirmative Sign Systems

In *The Order of Things* and more succinctly in *This Is Not a Pipe*, Foucault narrates a history of the sign from semblance (signifier is similar to the signified), to difference (signifier is contrasted to the signified), and simulation (the signifier and the signified lose their positions and hieratic relations). Although this genealogy of the sign is now canonical in poststructuralist thought, the biases of the designers of virtual environments have already demonstrated distinct realist (semblance) tendencies. How are our notions of theatrical-dramatic performance redefined in a virtual staging? Not unlike Racine and the neoclassical dramatists of the seventeenth-century French theater, some contemporary theorists working on models of human-computer interaction (foremost among them Brenda Laurel) have drawn upon Aristotelian theories of drama to create a formalistic, scientific, and irrefutable structure for uniformity. The interest in recuperating Aristotle, while avoiding more current thought on narrativity and performance, may be due to the fact that the *Poetics* posits the possibility of a comprehensive understanding of human action and the possibility of its representation whereas poststructuralism and postmodernism suppose an unending play between possibilities that is not subject to the same kind of artificial collaboration and objective agreement. This is why one can position VR as an extension of the Cartesian model of space and subjectivity; why else a name like "virtual reality"? Non-affirmative sign systems forgo semblance and difference and work within the system of simulation wherein the sign is marked by its status as negotiable. In both theorizing and designing cyberterritories it is desirable, given my tastes, to approach these "new" fields from contemporary perspectives rather than replicating baroque and classic sign systems.

Chronic/Crystalline Image Regime

Given that VR is a machine of computer imagery shaped by the practice of cinema, animation, and the televisual, it is important to understand the types of theories that can trigger our imaginations to create new visual fields rather than duplicate the same. I would like to suggest that Gilles Deleuze's binary paradigm of image production is useful for this purpose. Postmodern theory, in foregrounding the notion of indiscernibility, the unpresentable, the unnameable, the impossible, the unknown, suggests that aesthetic image-manufacturing is no longer concerned with movements of stabilizations/destabilizations wherein difference between subject and object, the real and the imaginary is maintained, but rather with the "problem of repetition, of false continuities, of disappearing, requiring the invention of a new and different kind of image altogether" (Abbas 183). In *Cinema 2*, Gilles Deleuze, working from Henri Bergson's paradigm of the movement-image and C. S. Peirce's outline of images and signs, constructs two regimes of the image. The first, the organic/kinetic regime, consists of descriptions which assume the independence of the object of discourse. Inside the organic regime, the real is known by its chronological progression and the principles which determine order. In contrast to the organic/kinetic regime, the chronic/crystalline regime includes the unreal, such as dreams, memory, and the imaginary. In this model the imaginary and the real operate as oppositions, each substantiating the other's presence.

Within a representation of the organic regime, narration is truthful, "developed organically, according to legal connections in space and chronological relations in time" (Deleuze 133). Within the crystalline/chronic regime, on the other hand, descriptions replace their object, substitute, actuate, eliminate, and are subsumed by other descriptions, and bring about "the coalescence of an actual image and its virtual image" (Deleuze 127). Narration becomes an ostentatiously falsifying discourse, operating in "a chronic non-chronological time which produces movements necessarily 'abnormal,' essentially 'false' " (129). The actual is cut off from its "motor linkage," and the real is cut off from its "legal connections."

I would want to challenge the implementers of virtual environments to go beyond the model of the Cartesian space and subject and work within the postmodern paradigms of falsity (the spaces and image regimes of non-chronological time and fluctuating subjectivities).

The Practice of the Virtual

It is important to ground the headiness and enthusiasm of the discussion surrounding virtual technologies. For many the immediate experience of donning an HMD and dataglove is deflation. The poor resolution of the LCDs, the awkwardness of the dataglove interface makes one painfully aware that VR technologies are in a primitive stage of development, not unlike the magic lantern in the history of cinema. In addition, the interactivity of the unencumbered human mind and the text of *Hamlet*, for example, far exceeds the multiple choice of interactive software. The theory has passed the possibilities. In that sense VR theory has a unique opportunity to set the agendas for VR experimentation.

Perry Hoberman, an artist working with virtual environments, recently (1994) developed a work titled *Bar Code Hotel* as part of the Art and Virtual Environments Project at the Banff Centre of the Arts in Canada. Since 1991 the Banff Centre has supported research into the artistic uses of virtual reality technologies and hosted the Fourth International Conference on Cyberspace. *Bar Code Hotel*, avoiding the isolating HMD and datagloves of most virtual reality configurations, is an interactive installation. Hoberman uses the Universal Product Code or bar code and laser pen (bar code reader), which we have become accustomed to in our supermarket checkouts, as interface. "An entire room is covered with printed bar code symbols, creating an environment in which every surface becomes a responsive membrane, an immersive interface that can be used simultaneously by a number of people to control and respond to a projected real-time, computer-generated, stereoscopic, three-dimensional world" (Hoberman 289). A guest entering the gallery space installed with *Bar Code Hotel* is given a pair of 3-D glasses. On one wall of the installation space is a video projection screen for the 3-D graphic. In front of the screen are tables on which bar codes are affixed to the surface. Additional bar codes are placed on hand-sized movable cubes and along the walls. From the ceiling are suspended five cables that reach down to the tables and are connected to laser pens accessible for the "guests" to scan the codes. The bar codes on the cubes, when scanned by the laser pen, cause a computer-generated object to appear on the projection screen. The objects include a bowling ball, camera, paper clip, hat, suitcase, glasses, scissors, light bulb, and shoes. The surface bar codes, when scanned, "modify objects' behaviors" (290) in the object, with such commands as "jitter," "bounce," "breathe," "contract," "expand," and "suicide." Another category of bar codes control the interaction between the objects with commands such as "avoid," "chase," and "punch." A set of bar codes is dedicated to the virtual environment that the objects inhabit, and control the "rooms" p.o.v. and the sky with such commands as "earthquake" and "loop the loop." A final set of bar codes, inaccessible to the spectator/operator, and assumed to be inoperative, are placed high along the walls of the gallery space. They read, "think," "remember," "believe," and "accept."

The objects in *Bar Code Hotel* are controlled by and are interactive with the spectator but are also autonomous. "Each object develops different capabilities and characteristics, depending on factors like age, size, and history" (Hoberman 290). The objects have individualized life spans and are responsive in an anthropomorphic manner. As a young object they react speedily to commands, and as they age their response time is eroded. Each object does die leaving a momentary ghost.

Having operated (or checked into) the *Bar Code Hotel*, I can attest to the delight in the interactive play of the 3-D objects. The work as an end in itself is impressive, but the future performative uses of the technology is intriguing. The objects in *Bar Code Hotel* could be replaced with colors, sounds, abstractions that would allow configuring artworks. Replace the objects with representations of dancers, and human figures with a variety of embedded texts, and one can begin to envision a truly interactive theater.

Hoberman may have had something else in mind for his installation beyond an enthusiasm for technology. The object of *Bar Code Hotel* may reside in the inaccessible codes that would command us to think, remember, believe, or accept, and which are placed out of reach of the spectator/operator. The operator can control the technological object to a somewhat limited degree after waiting her turn for the laser pen. Like check-out clerks at the market we are merely assigning a name or price to set the object in dance in the economy of representations. The capacity to think or remember or believe or even accept is out of reach. Hoberman, in *Bar Code Hotel*, avoids the mimetic replication of the surface real while offering a representation of Baudrillard's "fatal strategy" (185–206) of the postmodern object emancipated from the subject.

The Ideology of the Virtual, or Speeding Toward Immobility

This section title is partially named "The Ideology of the Virtual," but it could be transposed to "Virtual Ideology" or abbreviated to "The Id of the Virtual." The former follows the transparency of ideology, ever shifting, a roving opportunistic virus probing, infecting, restructuring, unseen but material; the latter acknowledging the fury and rage suppressed in the orderliness of tired and often unconscious politics, as well as the political unconscious now newly projected onto the vacuous screens of cyberculture. To what end does the will to virtuality drive us? What is this desire for disappearance in cyberterritories? How is the eros and thanatos of performance reinscribed through technology; the displaced body transposed, mutated; the wired flesh masturbating with one hand typing out "hot-chat" with the other? Woman/man machines ecstatically racing in non-time to nowhere. If there is no off switch to the technological, as Avital Ronell has suggested; if, as Marshall McLuhan theorizes, we have become the sex organs for machines; if, as philosophized by Heidegger, the only "revealing" within technology is a "self-revealing" of technology for itself; if we have become contiguous with our machines, as Mazlish writes; if we have entered a postgendered world, as Haraway imagines, then in what manner, if any, can the art of technologized performance respond that will allow for critique, resistance, and revealing of the ideology at work within this closed, homeostatic system?

The contemporary discourse surrounding technology, culture, and performance has to a large extent relied on Martin Heidegger's lecture/article/book "The Question Concerning Technology" as a primary philosophical argument. Avital Ronell's *The Telephone Book*, the anthologies *Rethinking Technologies* and *R U A/TV?: Heidegger and the Televisual*, are exemplary of this tendency. My own theoretical strategy is no exception. Heidegger's model, applied to virtual environments, can help us think of and through the problems. It is ironic that so many theorists attempting an understanding of the politics, ethics, and aesthetics of "answering the call of technology" have appropriated Heideggerian thought given his response to his own "call" from technology (National Socialism). The above books all confront the problem in similar fashion by questioning whether or not Nazism is inherent in Heideggerian thought. Are the strategies of logocentrism and thinking in essentialist terms of Being, essence, and truth fascistic? Avital Ronell counsels that it is important to remember where Heidegger's thinking took him: "the asserted origin of Heidegger's relation to National Socialism began with the call of technology that has yet to get through to us" (8). Answering the call of the technological, like that of any other endeavor, has its ideological effects and ethical ramifications. This is sometimes forgotten in the giddy enthusiasm of technophiles for whom the technology is a displacement for thought, a drug. The technological utopias of freed subjectivities and dispersed borders of cyberspace, VR/VE, AI, that many heralders of the info age proclaim, are often misguided fantasy, void of cultural or political critique, absent of accurate information concerning the actual possibilities of the new technologies, floating in a decontextualized science fiction.

The central thesis of "The Question Concerning Technology" is that nature and humankind have become "standing reserve," the necessary fuel for the "bringing forth" and the revealing of modern technology in its own "interlocking path," its "regulated course" (293, 298). Humankind, in the Heideggerian paradigm, is lost to itself as it stands ready to serve technology. The TV calls for our steady gaze (PLEASE STAND BY) and we answer by sitting ready. "The revealing that rules in modern technology is," Heidegger writes, "a challenging [*Herausfordern*], which puts to nature the unreasonable demand that it supply energy which can be extracted and stored as such" (296). In the contemporary human-computer interface *we are* the standing reserve for technology. Our memory and knowledge housed in the televisual, our disembodied voices in fiber optics, our dematerialized bodies transported through the datasphere and represented on the net, lay testament to our home and responsibilities in the technological.

As we confront our position in the technological and the processes of theorizing and creating mediated and postorganic performance, Heidegger's questioning becomes a central concern. Can there be a revealing outside the interlocking path and regulated course of technology? Or must performance forgo the human in order to play out the demands of technology? My thesis is tied to yet another question: Have the human being and the being in technology collapsed in on one another, requiring the unconcealment of each to uncover the other?

Heidegger argues that the *essence* of technology is something quite distinct from what we normally consider to *be* technology. He defines the essence of technology as a "bringing forth," a way of allowing that which is not yet present to arrive into presencing. The essence of technology, according to Heidegger's text, is similar to art, to *poiesis*, as an act of bringing forth "truth" from the concealed to the unconcealed. But for modern technology, Heidegger constructs a very different model. Modern technology does not enact a bringing forth, the presencing of the human or objects of nature, but operates as a challenging that demands of nature to supply energy which can be extracted and stored. In this manner technology regenerates itself for itself through the fuel of nature.

> Such challenging happens in that the energy concealed in nature is unlocked, what is unlocked is transformed, what is transformed is stored up, what is stored up is, in turn, distributed, and what is distributed is switched about ever anew. Unlocking, transforming, storing, distributing, and switching about are ways of revealing. But the revealing never simply comes to an end. Neither does it run off into the indeterminate. The revealing reveals to itself its own manifoldly interlocking paths, through regulating their course. (298)

Heidegger terms this essence of modern technology *Gestell* or Enframing. Energy in nature, in the process of enframing, is processed for the purpose of satisfying the revealing of technology. What transpires is an unconcealment of technology that perpetuates itself. In this model the "real" is subjugated to a "challenging forth" and "setting upon" by technology as a "standing reserve" for the revealing of technology. The only accessible real is technological. Heidegger argues that nature and humankind have become "standing reserve," the necessary fuel for the "bringing forth" of modern technology in its own "interlocking path," its "regulated course." Humankind, in the Heideggerian paradigm, is lost to itself as it stands ready to serve technology. The Heideggerian notion allows little choice for performance to be revealed in any manner that is not shaped through technology.

In attempting to *think*, which is an attempt to *learn* to think, which is to admit I don't know *how* to think, in thinking on and in the virtual, I want to return to a classic work in modern drama. For the will to virtuality, the will to be replaced, duplicated, removed from the real and delivered up to fantasy, to smash the material and elevate interiority, to suppress the political and hold to the metaphysical, cycling out of the eternal recurrence of the same thing into a wired world where technology demands revealing, is not a computer-age compulsion alone, but a transhistorical phenomeonon. As Herbert Blau reminds us, the battle over symbolic presence versus real presence is not new. In calling on the ideas of Kantor and Genet to argue that the ideology of the virtual is tied to a falling into inauthenticity, an attempt to catapult over the "shock" of the body in performance toward a self-replicating absent body, I recognize the journey away from the theater's message of doubling, of cruelty, of absence, of death, toward technology has already taken place.

The words "Speeding Toward Immobility," quoted from Genet's *The Balcony* (503), comes closest to my perspective regarding the tendency toward virtualizing the real. The phrase suggests that instead of the metaphysical shock from the realm of death in the theater, we have created in the virtual, a falling into inauthenticity wherein death is displaced, deferred indefinitely in favor of a painless fleshless existence where the art process that runs from cruelty to absence to death concludes not with the "excruciating magical relation to reality and danger" (89), as Artaud put it, but is replaced with a "longing toward immobility." The closure of representation sought after in the cruelty of art is replaced with replicating mirror images, eternal reflection, where the demarcation of the unknown is unknown, undesired, as all is Apollonian imagery that voids the Dionysian transition. The picture we have taken of the world of virtuality, which is a virtual world, is the postmodern flat surface of depthless images circulating in an economy of late capital, reified.

The Balcony by Jean Genet narrates the action of a fictional brothel where men play out the fantasies of power through the iconography of Bishop, Judge, General, Chief of Police. An emissary from the aristocracy enlists the Madame and her "johns" to help quell a revolution that is underway in the city outside the brothel by bringing their "roles" into the light of day. The play works like two mirrors held toward one another: no one—no thing—escapes the replicating scopic drive of the image-obsessed subject. I want to focus on the moment when the gasman takes on the role of the Bishop and question how his sojourn into virtuality operates. It is the first speech of the play, spoken by the gasman/Bishop as he is being dressed by a whore, that displays the map of both the path into virtuality and the process of radical art.

> In truth, the mark of a prelate is not mildness or unction, but the most rigorous intelligence. Our heart is our undoing. We think we are master of our kindness; we are the slave of a serene laxity. It is something quite other than intelligence that is involved. . . . (He hesitates) It may be cruelty and beyond that cruelty—and through it—a skillful, vigorous course towards Absence. Towards Death. God? (smiling) I can read your mind. (486)

It is the trajectory of desire from cruelty to absence to death that I want to discuss in relation to thinking through virtuality and performance. Genet, in *The Balcony*, defines the essences of art (coming to be) and performance (magical/ritualistic transformation) in the theater, by way of a sadomasochistic religiosity, as a process through *cruelty*. The cruelty of *The Balcony* echoes both Artaud's paradigm of the Theatre of Cruelty and Kant's philosophy of sublimity: violence against the imagination and understanding, which demonstrates the limits of knowledge while unfolding the mind's capacity for the supersensible as the moment of the sublime appears. The sublime is not the beautiful, which exists as the harmonious appearance and recognition of object and subject. The beautiful comes to be when the faculties of cognition are experienced by the subject as similar to the attributes of the object. The sublime is the border at which point the unpresentable confounds the faculties of the mind, setting out the limits of knowledge while calling forth the unknown. The sublimity of performance and art within the theater lies in their capacity, as Lyotard theorized it, "to put forward the unpresentable in presentation itself" (81). The cruelty of the theater is the moment of the collapse of the ontotheological structure of the stage. Text is no longer the legislative arm controlling desire. However, the virtual Bishop will miss the reordering of the body, of the mind, of consciousness and desire, in his fetishization of the object.

Genet extends his model of the borders of art and performance in the theater beyond "cruelty and through it, a skillful, vigorous course towards *Absence*" (italics mine). The moment of absence contains the wrapping of the subject into the image. In *The Balcony* the invention of subjectivity is represented as the fetishizing of the object, in this case, the Bishop's miter. The subject, in order to define itself, stages its own disappearance by taking on the signs of identity, which mimics the simulation strategy of substituting the signs of the real for the real itself. It is here that we have the creation of the virtual through the desire to avoid (the fear of), the authentic, the sexual, mortal human machine. The process of radical art, according to Genet, begins with cruelty (violence to the faculties of cognition) through absence (loss of subjectivity) toward death, the appearance of the border of art, performance, and theater: the unpresentable. Death is the impossible, the falling into continuity (Bataille), the dissolution of borders (Nietzsche), a reordering of the psyche and the body (Artaud), the sublime (Kant). It is this process that must be resisted at all costs in the establishment of the virtual.

As the gasman/Bishop begins his aesthetic leap into the sublime claiming to read the mind of God, he stops that revealing of the unknown and speaks to the miter perched on his head. He addresses the virtual signs of identity:

Mitre, bishop's bonnet, when my eyes close for the last time it is you that I shall see behind my eyelids, you, my beautiful gilded hat . . . you, my handsome ornaments, copes, laces. . . . (486)

The signs and simulation of God contained in the Bishop's bonnet, handsome ornaments, copes, laces are what hold the gasman's fantasy. He will not complete the process into art through cruelty: the violence against rationality, the destruction of the conscious mind, the desire to undo that which structures and congeals, toward absence and the removal of the self into the images. Absent, he defers eternally death, the impossible, the falling into continuity, the dissolution of borders, the reordering of the psyche and the body, for his desire is to maintain his orbit in virtuality, masturbating, always watching the screen for glimpses of the known, for dissolution into power, for an always ecstatic image duplication and repeatability never darkened by the possibility of death. The screen is a mirror, but it could be the cathode ray tube as well. The Bishop's moment of sustaining inauthenticity has become virtual culture's nightmare. Our world has been worlded as virtual and we cannot change that.

Brief Afterword

Thinking through performance in virtual environments may indeed prove to be unsatisfactory, but it is what we will have to address. The process may indeed be a continuation of the revealing of inauthenticity to point of indifference, where "all is visible but nothing available." Although the process of redeeming the theater in hyperrealism may seem impossible, it is, as Herbert Blau reminded me, the nothing to be done that has to be done.

Notes

1. "Postorganic" is a term currently in use among anthropologists to designate areas of research that explore the cultural and structural impact of digital technologies and the contingent mediascapes. In "Old Rituals for New Space" David Tomas writes, "one might envisage . . . the outlines of another postorganic form of anthropology developing in the context of cyberspace, an anthropology specifically engaged in addressing the problems of engineering cyberspatial forms of intelligence as opposed to the more conventional humanistic, more or less reflexive, study of premodernist, modernist, or postmodernist humankind" (33).
2. On this topic see Paffrath with Stelarc.

Works Cited

Abbas, Ackbar. "Review of Cinema 2, the Time-Image." *Discourse.* Summer 1992.

Artaud, Antonin. *The Theatre and Its Double.* New York: Grove Press, 1958.

Baudrillard, Jean. *Jean Baudrillard: Selected Writings.* Ed. Mark Poster. Stanford: Stanford UP, 1988.

Benedikt, Michael, ed. *Cyberspace: First Steps.* Cambridge: MIT P, 1991.

Blau, Herbert. *The Eye of Prey: Subversions of the Postmodern.* Bloomington: Indiana UP, 1987.

Brecht, Bertolt. *Brecht on Theatre.* Ed. John Willet. New York: Hill and Wang, 1964.

Deleuze, Gilles. *Cinema 2: The Time-Image.* Trans. Hugh Tomlinson and Robert Galeta. Minneapolis: U of Minnesota P, 1989.

Dienst, Richard. *Still Life in Real Time: Theory after Television.* Durham: Duke UP, 1994.

Foucault, Michel. *The Order of Things: An Archaeology of the Human Sciences.* New York: Vintage Books, 1970.

———. *This Is Not a Pipe*. Trans. and ed. James Harkness. Berkeley: U of California P, 1983.

Fry, Tony. "Introduction." *R U A / TV?: Heidegger and the Televisual*. Ed. Tony Fry. Sydney: Power Publications, 1993.

Genet, Jean. *The Balcony*. In *Modern Drama: Plays / Criticism / Theory*. Ed. William Worthen. Fort Worth: Harcourt Brace College Publishers, 1995.

Haraway, Donna. "A Manifesto for Cyborgs." *Feminism / Postmodernism*. Ed. Linda J. Nicholson. New York and London: Routledge, 1990.

Hayles, N. Katherine. "The Seductions of Cyberspace." *Rethinking Technologies*. Ed. Verena Andermatt Conley. Minneapolis: U of Minnesota P, 1993. 173–190.

Heidegger, Martin. *Basic Writings*. Ed. David Farrell Krell. San Francisco: HarperSanFrancisco, 1977.

Heilbrun, Adam. "Virtual Reality: An Interview with Jaron Lanier." *Whole Earth Review* 84 (Fall 1989): 108–19.

Hoberman, Perry. "Bar Code Hotel." *Immersed in Technology: Art and Virtual Environments*. Ed. Mary Anne Moser with Douglas MacLeod. Cambridge: MIT P, 1996.

Kantor, Tadeusz. *A Journey through Other Spaces: Essays and Manifestos, 1944–1990*. Ed. and trans. by Michal Kobialka. Berkeley: U of California P, 1993.

Land, Nick. *The Thirst for Annihilation*. London and New York: Routledge. 1992.

Laurel, Brenda. *Computers as Theater*. Reading, MA: Addison-Wesley, 1993.

Lyotard, Jean François. *The Postmodern Condition: A Report on Knowledge*. Trans. Geoff Bennington and Brian Massumi. Minneapolis: U of Minnesota P, 1984.

Mazlish, Bruce. *The Fourth Discontinuity: The Co-Evolution of Humans and Machines*. New Haven: Yale UP, 1993.

Novak, Marcos. "Liquid Architecture in Cyberspace." Benedikt 225–54.

Paffrath, James D., ed., with Stelarc. *Obsolete Body / Suspensions / Stelarc*. Davis, CA: J.P. Publications, 1984.

Penny, Simon. "Virtual Reality as the Completion of the Enlightenment Project." *Culture on the Brink: Ideologies of Technology*. Ed. Gretchen Bender and Timothy Druckrey. Seattle: Bay P, 1994. 231–48.

Phelan, Peggy. *Unmarked: The Politics of Performance*. London and New York: Routledge, 1993.

Ronell, Avital. *The Telephone Book: Technology, Schizophrenia, Electric Speech*. Lincoln: U of Nebraska P, 1989.

Schechner, Richard. *Performance Theory*. New York: Routledge, 1988.

Scheibler, Ingrid. "Heidegger and the Rhetoric of Submission: Technology and Passivity." *Rethinking Technologies*. Ed. Verena Andermatt Conley. Minneapolis: U of Minnesota P, 1993. 115–42.

Tomas, David. "Old Rituals for New Space: *Rites de Passage* and Gibson's Cultural Model of Cyberspace." Benedikt 31–47.

PART III:
CYBERTEXT CRITICISM AS WRITING EXPERIMENT

9

Artificial Life and Literary Culture

N. Katherine Hayles

Something has crept up on us while we were not looking. It insinuated itself into chaos theory, where it lay concealed amidst the more visible and highly publicized topologies of strange attractors, Mandelbrot sets, and bifurcation points. More subtle than these, it consisted of a changed idea of what it means to model a system. Precisely because of the extreme complexity of highly non-linear dynamical systems, chaos theorists find it impossible to construct a model that stands in one-to-one correlation with the phenomenon.[1]

Take data from wildly different systems—eye motion in schizophrenics, lynx fur returns, cotton market prices—plot them in phase space, and the familiar butterfly shape of the Lorenz attractor emerges. Now imagine generating the same shape from a set of non-linear differential equations. What is the relation between the equations and the systems? Since we did not arrive at the equations by considering how schizophrenics roll their eyes, or what motivates Canadian fur trappers, or why cotton grows better some years than others, the equations do not model the system in the sense, say, that a revolving mobile with varying-sized spheres models the solar system. Different complex systems produce the same kind of shapes within phase space because they incorporate recursive feedback loops that give them certain mathematical properties. The equations also express these properties. The equations are not so much models, then, as programs that run along parallel lines to the natural phenomena. Not one-to-one correspondence, but mappings that follow parallel evolutions. Not mimesis, but simulation.

Running in real time on massively parallel units, literary criticism during the same period was undergoing a radical transformation. Let us tell this story in a different voice (and a different typeface) than the one above, to signify that it proceeds within a different discourse system. This story begins with a familiar narrative about how defining a text as a sign system greatly expanded the idea of textuality, opening the entire field of cultural signs to literary criticism. Not just Rabelais and Shakespeare but fashion and horse racing became the provenance of the literary critic, until it seemed that anything whatever could be justified as falling within literary studies. Three implications of this transformation are relevant here. First, significance was understood to emerge from the play of differences, so that differences became generative structures creating meaning rather than dissonances requiring resolution. Second, because meaning was generated internally, the tie between language and reference was understood in a weak sense or denied altogether. Third, with signification increasingly constituted as a play of signifiers rather than as a relation between signifier and signified, texts achieved a hermetic closure (or from a point of view inside, an infinite expansion) so that Derrida could proclaim there is no outside to the text. What then do texts model? Not a reality exterior to themselves—there is no place exterior to language from which to speak—but their own operations as linguistic structures. Not one-to-one correspondence between word and object, but parallel evolution to other cultural formations. Not mimesis, but simulation.[2]

Traditional accounts of science liked to imagine it as a seamless advance toward truth. Newton wasn't wrong, he was only partially right. His gravity can be neatly fit inside Einstein's gravity like one Russian doll inside another. Thomas Kuhn was one of the first to argue successfully against this view; Mary Hesse and Michael Arbib perhaps said it best. Redescription is never *merely* redescription. To say something in other words is to say something different. *Calling* Sarrasine *a system of signs may not change the ink marks on the page, but it does change the interpretive context that helps to constitute meaning.* Calling complex non-linear systems chaotic may not change their dynamics, but it does change the interpretive context that links them with traditional ideas of chaos as a space of primal creation, a swirling vortex out of which the new can emerge. The same characteristics that make it impossible to build one-to-one models of chaotic systems also make them capable of self-organization. But wait. Are we talking about the phenomenon here, or the model? Consider: if we cut self-organization *within the model* loose from mimesis, what do we have? Not self-organization in the natural world but artificial self-organization. Or, as a provocative redescription would have it, artificial life.

Many of the principal players in the game of artificial life are associated with the Santa Fe Institute for the Study of Complex Adaptive Systems, a research center whose modest quarters in an office building on the outskirts of Santa Fe belie the major impact it is having on initiating and developing the field of artificial life.[3] Its creators call it A-Life (already mutated to alife), leading to many bad puns (get alife) and fascinating programs. As a neologism, alife slyly alludes to AI, the artificial intelligence project that alife proponents say has stalled because it is starting at the wrong end, that is, at the top of an intelligent "I" rather than at the bottom of life. Listen to Christopher Langton *redescribing* in "Artificial Life" the computer programs that he and his colleagues are creating. "The principle [*sic*] assumption made in Artificial Life is that the 'logical form' of an organism can be separated from its material basis of construction, and that 'aliveness' will be found to be a property of the former, not of the latter." A thesis Lévi-Strauss would approve: capture the logical structure of a process, and you have its essence, regardless of the material medium in which it is expressed. Processes encoded in silicon are on an equal footing with those in protein; neither has proprietary rights to the claim of life. The evolutionary processes exhibited by an alife program are therefore not models of evolution, but evolution itself. "Artificial Life," as Langton defines it, "is the study of man-made systems that exhibit behaviors characteristic of natural living systems. It complements the traditional biological sciences concerned with the *analysis* of living organisms by attempting to *synthesize* life-like behaviors within computers and other artificial media. By extending the empirical foundation upon which biology is based *beyond* the carbon-chain life that has evolved on Earth, Artificial Life can contribute to theoretical biology by locating *life-as-we-know-it* within the larger picture of *life-as-it-could-be*" ("Artificial Life" 1; italics in the original).

Conventionally, the field is divided into three research fronts. Wetware is the creation of artificial biological life through such techniques as cloning, DNA recombination, and *in vitro* fertilization and incubation. Hardware is the construction of robots and other embodied artificial life forms. Software is the creation of computer programs instantiating evolutionary processes. In this chapter, I will be discussing hardware and software *(although wetware may perhaps enter in another voice and at another site)*. The software and hardware share common properties that are constitutive of the field as a whole. Alife researchers use a "bottom up" approach, starting from the rudimentary components of life rather than from the top of cognitive thought and sophisticated behavior. They build structures that are highly recursive, involving complex feedback loops in which the output of a system is repeatedly fed back in as input. They subscribe to parallel architectures, distributing control throughout the system rather than localizing at the highest level.

Finally, they achieve complexity through the system's ability to engage in self-organization. Generally only a few simple local rules are given at the outset. Then complexity *emerges* globally as the result of many recursive interactions at the local level. It is this emergent complexity that gives the field its punch, for it is little short of amazing.

Hans Moravec has a dream. In Mind Children *(109–10), he imagines a fantastic scenario in which a robot surgeon excavates brain tissue. The information embodied in the tissue is transferred into a computer; the tissue itself is destroyed. When the operation is over, the skull is empty and "you," the hypothesized patient, find your consciousness unchanged, seamlessly continuous with your previously embodied mind. Now you have no organic body, only the silicon circuits of the computer, along with its peripheral sensing apparatus. Moravec sees the transformation as the next logical step in the evolution of consciousness. Once one conceded that silicon-based intelligence is life, it seems obvious (to Moravec) that the advantages of silicon life forms will make them our evolutionary successors. The days of intelligent wetware are numbered. But humans need not despair, because they can transfer their consciousness into computers. The evils of the flesh are left behind, and immortality is an achievable goal.*

Let me be clear: I consider this a pipe dream. Human mind has evolved over millennia in such complex symbios with specific biological structures that it is inconceivable consciousness could exist in anything like its present form apart from the physical processes that constitute it. The interesting question, then, is not whether such a transformation can take place, but why it is a compelling imaginary at this cultural moment. What does it mean to lose your body, or more precisely to fantasize that you can lose your body and inhabit a computer? What cultural formations speak to this question, and through what dynamics are their responses generated and structured?

One site deeply involved in these issues is contemporary literature. Like Moravec's hypothesized patient, books are in the process of losing their bodies and inhabiting computers instead. Literary critics, nearly all of whom learned their craft by reading print books, have been slow to grasp the implications of this transformation. To explore its complexities (to help constitute its meanings), *I will* redescribe *a text as a space of encoding and decoding. The formulation is deceptively similar to calling a text a system of signs, but bootlegged within it are important implications. Constituting a text as a sign system emphasizes the play of differences within the text; calling it a space of encoding and decoding links it with an operator outside the text who performs the coding operations. The redescription I propose sets up suggestive parallels between texts and computers by creating a common vocabulary that can be used to talk about what happens within the representational space of the text—the fictional world the text creates—and within the representational space of the computer—the cyberspace the computer creates to display the text and permit users to interact with it. The shift from* system *to* space *points toward issues of embodiment, for the kind of space constituted by the informational patterns of a computer is very different than that defined by the material corpus of a print book. Finally, the redescription foregrounds coding operations, hinting that they may be more interesting than reductive one-to-one correlations. In fact, coding operations have a fecundity and creative power not unlike chaotic systems. If the program is structured in the right way, that is, if it has complex recursive feedback loops within and between different layers of code, it may be capable of self-organization.*

So what does this all mean for someone who likes to read fiction? Who fantasizes about moving through the computer screen into the "bodiless exultation" of cyberspace? Who has seen Robocop, The Fly, The Terminator, Tron, *and* Lawnmower Man? *Who increasingly reads and generates texts through a computer? Who knows the pleasures of cruising the net and assuming alternate identities? Who is beginning to think of texts as flickering lights on the screen instead of ink marks on a page? Who suspects that self-organizing processes have already begun while we weren't looking? Since I cannot explore fully the implications of these developments in the encoding/decoding space allocated to this voice, let me make a virtue of necessity and be cryptic instead.* (Self-organizing processes may take over and generate unsuspected complexities out of a few simple rules.)

The present cultural moment is marked by a pervasive belief that information is more real than matter or energy. If you possess the informational pattern of an object, you can generate the object at will. Like the transporter in Star Trek *or in* The Fly. *So information is primary. Everything else flows from it. But what is information? Although it is carried by material markers (ink marks on paper, magnetic polarizations of silicon, strings of bases in protein), it is conceptually distinct from the material in which it is embodied. In fact, it is pattern rather than presence. As deconstruction has taught us, presence is never self-evident by itself; it achieves definition only in a dialectic with absence. Similarly, pattern is never self-evident by itself; it achieves definition only in a dialectic with randomness. We know a pattern exists because something is repeated, but this repetition can be understood as such only because it is foregrounded against a background of randomness or non-pattern. These assertions point toward an important conclusion.* As first-world culture moves from an industrial base to an information society, presence/absence is displaced by pattern/randomness as a generative dialectic for cultural forms. *There's a simple rule for you.*

What does a literature and a literary theory informed by a dialectic of pattern/randomness look like?[4] *Or more precisely, what does a literature and literary theory* redescribed *through a dialectic of pattern/randomness look like? The Lacanian (and deeply gendered) emphasis on castration, which derives from a play of absence/presence projected onto a male body, is displaced by the corresponding moment of crisis in the randomness/pattern dialectic. The Fly tells us what this moment is; so do* Terminator I *and* II *and a host of other popular media. The moment occurs when the plenitude of pattern is disrupted by a deviation so decisive that it can no longer be assimilated into the same. At this moment randomness asserts itself as always already there, and the dialectic stands revealed. The moment is named by mutation. On one level, mutation occurs within the representational space of the text. It is what happens to the body of the scientist in* The Fly, *to Robocop, to the Terminator, to the Terminator's Terminator. On another level, it is what happens to the body of the text as it moves from print to computer. On still another level, it is what happens to the body of the user as neural pathways and synaptic closures are rearranged to accommodate new patterns of tactile, kinesthetic, visual, and auditory interactions with the computer. All of these levels, and others latent within the encoding/decoding spaces of the computer, interact with each other through complex feedback loops. Self-organization of this entire complex system is a definite possibility.*

The hardware side of artificial life is exemplified in the work of Rodney Brooks, a maverick at MIT's Artificial Intelligence Laboratory. He argues that conventional AI has got it all wrong, that the place to start is not at the top of cognition but where evolution started, at the bottom with simple life forms that can robustly interact with their environments. During my recent visit there, he demonstrated his robots and talked about his initial inspiration for building them. In a delicious irony, it came when he was Hans Moravec's roommate in college. Moravec had built a robot designed to be able to cross a room. According to Brooks, it took the robot several hours to complete this task. It would move a couple of feet, compute for fifteen minutes, move another couple of feet and stop to compute again. If anyone crossed its path, it was hopelessly thrown off, so the experiment could be done only in the wee hours when everyone else was in bed. Rodney, a loyal roommate, stayed up to help Hans with the robot. On one of these late nights it occurred to him that a cockroach could not possibly have the computing power dedicated to the robot, yet the cockroach could cross the room with no trouble in a few seconds. He decided that something was seriously amiss in Hans's approach and resolved to try a different way.

In the robots he builds, there is no central representation of the world. "The world is its own best model," he is fond of asserting, by which he means that the robot finds out about the world through its interactions with the environment rather than through a preprogrammed representation.[5] (Moravec's glacier-speed robot had to stop so often to compute because it was operating from a central representation that it periodically had to update.) Brooks's robots are built using what he calls "subsumption architecture." Each layer in the architecture is composed of a "fixed-topology network" of finite state machines. These machines are simple; each has a "handful of states, one or two internal registers, one or two internal timers, and access to simple computational machines, which can compute things such as vector sums" ("Intelligence without Representation" 151). Each finite state machine communicates with the others minimally or not at all. Thus the different subsystems "see" the world in completely different ways. If a conflict between subsystems interferes with behavior, a higher system kicks in to resolve the discrepancy, but only for as long as the immediate situation calls for it.

His description of Herbert, a robot that goes around collecting soda cans from the offices, illustrates the technique. "The laser-based table-like object finder initiates a behaviour which drives the robot closer to a table. It does not communicate with any other subsumption layers. However, when the robot is close to a table there is a better chance that the laser-based soda-can-like object finder will trigger. In turn, it centers the robot on the detected object, but does not communicate anything to other subsumption layers. The arm control behaviours notice that the robot is stationary, and reaches out looking for a soda can. . . . In a similar vein, the arm and hand do not communicate directly either. The hand has a grasp reflex that operates whenever something breaks an infrared beam between the fingers. When the arm locates a soda can with its local sensors, it simply drives the hand so that the two fingers line up on either side of the can. The hand then independently grasps the can."[6] There is some dispute about how successful Herbert has been—rumor claims it operated successfully once and only once—but other robots built later are undeniably robust. They include Genghis, an insectoid six-legged rover that he hopes to sell to NASA for planetary exploration; Squirt, a tiny robot that, cockroach-like, scuttles around searching for darkness; Polly, a robot that shows visitors around the laboratory, casually announcing midway through the tour, "By the way, I don't understand anything I am saying"; and Attila, who crouches on a desk until it senses a human nearby, and then attacks (fortunately for the human, in slow motion).

Subsumption architecture takes advantage of interactions between subsystems to produce behaviors that are not explicitly programmed in. The gait of Genghis works on this principle. Each of the robot's six legs operates independently, running a program that checks its position and keeps it standing. When the central processor sends a "Walk" signal, individual legs begin their motions without "knowing" about the others. At first the robot stumbles around, but as each leg interacts with an environment that includes what the other legs are doing, a smooth coordinated gait emerges. No direct communication has taken place between the legs, and their coordination is not programmed into them in advance.[7] Rather it is an emergent behavior, or as Brooks calls it informally, a "cheap trick." Human observers, seeing these emergent behaviors, frequently attribute complex motivations to the robots that they do not have. Observing the observers, Brooks noticed that the faster a robot moves, the more likely people are to attribute intelligence to it.

Brooks believes that "cheap tricks" must have surfaced often in natural evolutionary processes. When they were successful, they continued because they bestowed an adaptive advantage on the organism. Consciousness itself may be the ultimate "cheap trick," he speculates, an emergent behavior that reflexively attributes motivation to its own embodied processes. But surely we are unlike the robots because we do have a central representation, namely our picture of the world? Not necessarily, he claims. Just because a representation is available to consciousness does not mean that it is also present to our distributed subsystems. Rather, it may be an artifact of consciousness, "an output coding for communication purposes." As evidence for this thesis, he instances the fact that most humans "go through life never realizing that they have a large blind spot almost in the center of their visual fields." This elision suggests that the internal states which actually exist may be quite different from the consensual representations we communicate to ourselves and others ("Intelligence without Representation" 144).

So far his research has concentrated on creating robots with the equivalent of insect intelligence. Which, he is quick to point out, is nothing to sneer at. He illustrates by sketching a quick chronology of life on earth. Single-celled entities appeared 3.5 billion years ago; 550 million years ago saw the first fish and vertebrates; 450 million, insects. "Then things started moving fast," he notes, with reptiles at 370 million years, dinosaurs at 330 million, primates at 120 million, and humans at 2.5 million. The dates imply that by the time insects arrived, evolution was already 90 percent of the way to the human. "Problem solving behavior, language, expert knowledge and application, and reason, are all pretty simple once the essence of being and reacting are available," he argues. That essence is "the ability to move around in a dynamic environment, sensing the surroundings to a degree sufficient to achieve the necessary maintenance of life and reproduction. This part of intelligence is where evolution has concentrated its time— it is much harder" ("Intelligence without representation" 141).

Recently he has moved toward creating a humanoid robot, "Cog," which will include sensors for vision, sound, and kinesthetic manipulation. "The resulting system," he and co-author Lynn Andrea Stein claim, "will learn to 'think' by building on its bodily experiences to accomplish progressively more abstract tasks. Past experience suggests that in attempting to build such an integrated system we will have to fundamentally change the way artifical intelligence, cognitive science, linguistics and philosophy think about the organization of intelligence."[8] What is this changed way of thinking? To summarize: first, there is no central representation; second, control is distributed throughout the system; third, behaviors develop in direct interaction with the environment rather than through an abstract model; and fourth, complex behaviors emerge spontaneously through self-organizing, emergent processes.

Hypertext illustrates how self-organizing processes are relevant to the encoding/decoding spaces of texts. As you probably know, a hypertext is a document stored in a computer that permits a user to interact with it. Certain words or symbols within a hypertext are interactive; when the user clicks on them, the screen changes, moving the user into a different block of text. For example, a hypertext version of Paradise Lost *created by John Huntley and his students links the text of the poem with other texts giving information about Milton's life, expanding on relevant social contexts, explaining etymologies of words, suggesting critical interpretations, and so forth. Diagrams of hypertext documents show a multiplicity of paths connecting various blocks of texts. A convenient way to think about this structure is as a series of windows that the user can open on the computer, with the pathways indicating navigational possibilities between windows.*

The Paradise Lost *hypertext has a central text, but this need not be the case. In Michael Joyce's hypertext novel* Afternoon, *all the textual nodes have equal claim to be "primary." In a narrative such as this, there is no predetermined plot. Rather, there are potential pathways that are actualized when a user traverses them. The actual narrative comes into existence* (emerges globally) *in conjunction with a specific reading. For example, one path apparently tells of the death of the narrator's son and former wife; another permits them to escape this fate. The feedback loops connecting different levels of texts include the user as an integral part of the circuit. Consider what happens when Peter, the narrator, makes a series of telephone calls to determine whether his son has been killed. Afraid of what he might learn, he does not call the people most likely to know, but rather others who could have indirect information.[9] When he calls the hospital to see if his son was taken there, he uses an automated computer telephone program to interrogate the receptionist and nurse, leading (not surprisingly) to ambiguous results. Within the represented world of the text, the calls are aural-electronic texts, transmitted across fiber-optic cables, that Peter must encode and decode. The user interprets the significance of the calls through the decoding/*

encoding operations that constitute reading, and as a result, chooses to activate one pathway or another to the next window of text. Her responses thus constitute a space interactively linked with the spaces within the computer that store and generate the text windows, as well as with the encoding/decoding spaces within the represented world of the fiction that guide her responses and help to generate the next sequence of text. In a deeper, more interactive sense than is true of most print texts, the reader, writing technology, and text simultaneously produce and are produced by each other.

A critical theory of hypertextuality is already well underway. In Writing Space: The Computer, Hypertext, and the History of Writing, *Jay Bolter remarks that hypertext makes many of the seemingly arcane ideas of deconstruction into everyday experiences. The author ceases to be a reified identity and becomes a function distributed throughout the system. The text is similarly distributed, existing nowhere and everywhere at once. (Bolter 195–206). In* Hypertext: The Convergence of Contemporary Critical Theory and Technology, *George P. Landow discusses the reconfigurations of text, author, narrative and literary education that hypertext is initiating. In* The Electronic Word: Democracy, Technology and the Arts, *my colleague Richard Lanham calls for a "digital rhetoric" to explore the implications of a hypermedia in which images, sounds, and print texts freely intermingle. And in "Writing Cyberspace: Literacy in the Age of Simulacra," Stuart Moulthrop extends hypermedia to virtual reality, discussing it as an immersive writing technology. The contribution I would like to make to this emerging body of theory is to* redescribe *hypertextuality as a self-organizing system.*[10]

From another space of encoding/decoding, along a circuitous pathway, let us retrieve the characteristics that allow systems to engage in self-organization: different levels of systemic organization, connected by recursive feedback loops; local rules that, through repeated application, result in emergent global structures; control distributed throughout the system; no central representation; a "bottom-up" approach that starts with the rudiments and lets complexity emerge spontaneously; behaviors developed in direct interaction with the environment rather than through an abstract model. *In a hypertext fiction such as* Afternoon, *there is no central representation. Whereas in a novel like Faulkner's* The Sound and the Fury *it is possible to coordinate the different narrative voices to arrive at a coherent picture of what happened, the diverse pathways in* Afternoon *do not resolve into a unified account. As if to flip the finger at Schrödinger's cat, Peter's son both dies and does not die.*[11] *Hypertexts, like other complex systems, are organized into different levels connected by multiple pathways and recursive loops. The local rules from which complex global structures emerge in hypertext documents are nothing more complicated than reading protocols, combined with the instructions that tell the computer what block of text to display in response to the user's click. Control is distributed throughout the system. The author creates blocks of text, the computer displays them in the appropriate windows, and the user decides which windows to activate and in what order. Complexity emerges when the user interacts directly with the environment provided by the hypertext program.*

This last point deserves fuller exploration. As E. D. Hirsch documented in Cultural Literacy, *the way information is stored in human memory depends on how quickly it enters neural pathways. When information enters in a short time frame—a few seconds—it can be stored as a block. When it enters more slowly, much more effort is required to integrate it with existing information. For example, someone who is just learning to read might take several minutes to decode a sentence. By the time this naive reader reaches the end of the sentence, he has forgotten what the first part said, and the meaning is apt to elude him. Only when the time frame can be speeded up enough so that the entire block can be stored in short-term memory at once does it come together to make sense. This is why beginning readers often repeat aloud a sentence they have laboriously decoded. By saying it over quickly, they are better able to connect it with other information they know and so to grasp its meaning.*

Confronted with the theory and practice of hypertextuality, many people insist that it is nothing new. After all, they say, Paradise Lost *was published in print books with appendices and footnotes long before hypertext appeared on the scene. Nothing has changed with the hypertext version, these people argue, except for the speed of access. But for human memory, speed of access is crucial. It often makes the difference in whether self-organizing processes spontaneously emerge or not. A recondite reader may of course do for herself what the naive reader does when he repeats the sentence—mentally rehearse the footnote on page 497 while looking at the text on page 216 so that both are held in short-term memory together. This takes effort, however, and most readers will make it only occasionally, if at all. By facilitating these juxtapositions, and especially by shortening the time it takes to make them, hypertext encourages self-organization. Moreover, although some print texts are structured so as to encourage or demand self-organization— witness Ts'ui Pên's fantastic novel in Borges's "Garden of Forking Paths," Cortázar's* Hopscotch, Pavić's Dictionary of the Khazars— *the payoff in redescribing spaces of encoding/decoding through the dynamics of self-organization is obviously greater for electronic media rather than for printed words. When the words have lost their material bodies and become information, they move fast.* Brooks noticed that the faster the robot moves, the more likely people are to attribute intelligence to it. Evolution moves fast once species have the ability to move around in a dynamic environment. *I have the feeling that from now on, things will be moving very fast.*

One of the first successful alife software programs was created by

Thomas S. Ray, an evolutionary biologist who left behind the tropical forests of Costa Rica for the silicon ecosystems of computer datascapes. When I visited him at the Santa Fe Institute, he talked about the alife program he calls Tierra.[12] Frustrated with the slow pace of natural evolution, Ray wondered if it would be possible to speed things up by creating evolvable artificial organisms within the computer. One of the first challenges he faced was designing programs robust enough to withstand mutation without crashing. To induce robustness, he conceived of building inside the regular computer a "virtual computer" out of software. Whereas the regular computer uses memory addresses to find data and execute instructions, the virtual computer uses a technique Ray calls "address by template." Taking its cue from the topological matching of DNA bases, in which one base finds its appropriate partner by diffusing through the medium until it locates another base with a surface it can fit into like a key into a lock, address by template matches one code segment to another by looking for its binary inverse. For example, if a coding instruction is written in binary code 1010, the virtual computer searches nearby memory to find a matching segment with the code 0101. The strategy has the advantage of creating a container for the organisms that renders them incapable of replicating outside the virtual computer, for the address by template operation can occur only within the virtual computer. Presented with a string such as 1010, the regular computer would read it as data rather than instructions to replicate.

As deconstruction taught in a different voice, differences are generative. Species diversify and evolve through mutation. To introduce mutation, Ray created the equivalent of cosmic rays by having a bit flip its polarity once in every 10,000 executed instructions. In addition, replication errors occur about once in every 1,000 to 2,500 instructions copied, introducing another source of mutation. Other differences spring from an effect Ray calls "sloppy reproduction," analogous to the genetic mixing that occurs when a bacterium absorbs fragments of a dead organism nearby. To control the number of organisms, Ray introduced a program that he calls the "reaper." The "reaper" monitors the population and eliminates the oldest creatures and those who are "defective," that is, those who have most frequently made errors in executing their programs.

The virtual computer starts the evolutionary process by allocating a block of memory that Ray calls the "soup." Into the soup are unleashed self-replicating programs, normally starting with a single 80-bit creature called the "ancestor." The ancestor comprises three segments. The first segment instructs the organism to count its instructions and reserve that much space in nearby memory; the second segment contains the copy procedure, which instructs the program to copy itself into the reserved space to create a daughter cell; the third segment directs the program back to the beginning segment, so that replication can begin again. To see how mutation leads to new species, consider that a bit flip occurs in the last line of the first segment, changing 1100 to 1110. Normally the program would find the second segment by searching for its first line, encoded as 0011. Now, however, the program searches until it finds a segment starting with 0001. Thus it goes not to its own second segment but to another string of code in nearby memory. Many mutations are not viable and do not lead to reproduction. Occasionally, however, the program finds a segment starting with 0001 which will allow it to reproduce. Then a new species is created, as this organism begins producing offspring.

When Ray set his program running overnight, he thought he would be lucky to get a one- or two-bit variation from the 80-bit ancestor. Checking it out the next morning, he found that an entire ecology had evolved, including one 22-bit organism. Among the mutants were parasites that had lost their own copying instructions (the middle segment of code) but had developed the ability to invade a host and hijack its copying procedures. One 45-bit parasite had evolved into a benign relationship with the ancestor; others were destructive, crowding out the ancestor with their own offspring. Later runs of the program saw the development of hyperparasites, which had evolved ways to compete for time as well as memory. Computer time is doled out equally to each organism by a "slicer" that determines when it can execute its program. Hyperparasites wait for parasites to invade them. Then, when the parasite attempts to reproduce using the hyperparasite's copy procedure, the hyperparasite directs the program on to its own third segment instead of returning it to the parasite's ending segment. Thus the hyperparasite's code is copied on the parasite's time. In this way the hyperparasite greatly multiplies the time it has for reproduction, for in effect it appropriates the parasite's time for its own.

Ray's next project involves designing an alife program that will be capable of sexual reproduction, in which two organisms mix their coding instructions to reproduce.[13] A similar innovation happened during the Cambrian era roughly 570 million years ago, resulting in a wide array of multicellular organisms and an explosion in the diversity of life forms. The Cambrian era was only 120 million years away from the appearance of the insects that Rodney Brooks's robots emulate. At the rate Ray's programs are evolving—the equivalent of three billion years of evolution covered in three years or so—his speculation that insect or higher intelligence could evolve through self-organizing processes within the computer does not seem unwarranted. And as Brooks reminds us, chronologically speaking insect intelligence is 90 percent of the way to human intelligence. What would happen to the robots if they ran off programs robust enough to withstand such energetic mutations? (Perhaps Cog will tell us.) *What would happen to texts?*

Some hypertext programs are read-only documents. The user can determine the paths that are activated within the document, but she cannot change the content of the windows themselves. Others, however, can be changed, so that the user has a status fully equal to the program's first author. As different users annotate, revise, delete, and add to the text, the document can be said to undergo mutation. Real-time bulletin board conversations on the net already operate like this, as do MUDs (Multi-User Dungeons), in which text-based environments emerge through the collaborative efforts of a community of users.[14] *Another possibility is a program that can undergo spontaneous mutation, either by itself or in collaboration with the users' choices. Suppose that we introduced into a hypertext the equivalent of the Tierran reaper, a program that would eliminate pathways that had not been chosen very often or at all. The result would be a kind of survival of the fittest, as defined by the users' interactions with the hypertext. Alternatively, the reaper could retire pathways that had been chosen often, thereby encouraging users to evolve new patterns of interactions. It could also forge new links on a random basis between blocks that had not been previously connected.*

Yet another kind of possibility is set forth in David Gelernter's Mirror Worlds. *He imagines a schematic grid of cellular automata that would be driven by data from the actual city streets where one lives. Within this program, users have the ability to create subprograms that act as their agents to gather data, create representations, and initiate messages. Here is a program that is and is not a simulation, for it at once mirrors the world outside and engages in its own independent self-organization. If agency all too often seems lacking in the postmodern world, it can be recuperated within the mirror world that serves as a link between real environments and artificial life.*[15]

What about literary criticism? Marc Damashek has created a program to analyze language that offers interesting possibilities for literary analysis.[16] *Working for the National Security Agency, he was assigned the task of creating a program that could analyze articles written in different languages. (One can imagine the uses the National Security Agency would have for such a program; no need to worry about the security clearance of translators any longer, or scurry around trying to find competent translators for obscure dialects.) Damashek hit upon the idea of a program that translates any language into strings of ASCII characters. Then the program compares the strings, throws away those that are the same, and arranges the remaining ones according to the ways in which they differ.* (Differences are generative structures creating meaning rather than dissonances requiring resolution.) *The program itself has no more idea of what the resulting clusters mean than Polly, Brooks's robot tour guide, has of what it is saying. Nevertheless, out of these simple local rules, recursively applied, emerge startling patterns of self-organization. Two kinds of clusters appear: vertical groupings that represent variations within the same class of objects, that is, paradigmatic clusters such as sow, pig, hog, and pork; and horizontal groupings that show related ideas displayed along a spectrum of gradations in meaning, such as luck, fortune, fate, predestination, and free will. Not only can the program compare different documents in the same language through this method; it can also compare documents in different languages, as long as there are sufficient cognates between them. Conceivably, the program could be used to reveal deep structural similarities that could confirm or enlighten the intuitions of an astute reader.*[17] *In that case, one kind of self-organizing system would find its conclusions mirrored in another kind of self-organizing system. Concurring in their analyses, the systems differ in the degree to which they are conscious of their achievement.* (But then, consciousness itself may be an emergent phenomenon arising from distributed systems no more enlightened than the computer program.) Cog meets cogito.

How far has self-organization proceeded? I no longer know which voice is speaking. What global patterns have emerged from the local sites distributed through the different levels of this text? *One centers on a critical vocabulary that would redescribe texts as spaces of encoding/decoding. Proceeding under the sign of mutation, this redescription links contemporary cultural formations with the generative power of the randomness/pattern dialectic. (Since the redescription itself is an assertion of a cultural pattern, it must also reflexively realize that any pattern it constitutes is always already penetrated by randomness.)* Another pattern *(another burst of random variation)* emerged by considering the dynamics of self-organizing programs and mechanisms. *As we have seen, hypertexts differ from artificial life because they include the user within the loop.* This important difference notwithstanding, the dynamics of artificial life can provide provocative clues to how self-organization proceeds between the user, the hypertext, and the computer. *Mutation can occur at multiple sites—within the fictional world of the text, within the text itself considered as strings of characters, within the computer's program, within the user's synaptic pathways. Pattern and randomness are thus involved not only at the level of representation,* but also at the level of the codes used to generate the representations.

The larger global pattern that emerges when literary culture and artificial life are interdigitated together suggests that technology and culture are bound together in complex feedback loops that themselves have self-organizing properties. Culture rushes forward, creating an imaginative space that technology scrambles to occupy; technology speeds along, creating phenomena that culture contextualizes and interprets in new representations. Out of these complex interactions, one thing is clear. Science and literature can no longer proceed as separate discourses. They speak, if not in the same voice, from the same sites, constituted through a chaotic dynamics that generates global patterns out of local differences.

Notes

1. For a discussion of how models of chaotic systems are constructed, see Hayles, *Chaos Bound: Orderly Disorder in Contemporary Literature and Science.* Further discussion can be found in Gleick, and Briggs and Peat.

2. The reader is entitled to suspect that the mixing of literary and scientific terms is deliberate. The foremost theorist of the cultural significance of simulation is Jean Baudrillard; see especially *Simulacra and Simulations,*.

3. For a discussion of the Santa Fe Institute and the research it sponsors, see Waldrop.

4. For a fuller exploration of the impact of virtuality on contemporary literature, see Hayles, "Virtual Bodies and Flickering Signifiers."

5. The phrase appears often in Brooks's papers. See for example "Intelligence without Reason" and "Intelligence without Representation."

6. See Brooks and Flynn, "Fast, Cheap and Out of Control: A Robot Invasion of the Solar System," especially p. 481.

7. For an accessible account of Brooks's work, along with other roboticists, see Wallich, "Silicon Babies."

8. See the abstract of Brooks and Stein, "Building Brains for Bodies."

9. For a discussion of the theoretical issues raised by *Afternoon,* see Bolter, *Writing Space: The Computer, Hypertext, and the History of Writing,* 123–57.

10. David Porush has written extensively about self-organization and contemporary literature, and I am indebted to his ideas. See *The Soft Machine: Cybernetic Fiction* and "Fictions as Dissipative Structures: Prigogine's Theory and Postmodernism's Roadshow."

11. The allusion of course is to the paradox associated with the physicist Erwin Schrödinger, who devised a thought experiment in which quantum uncertainty was associated with releasing a poison gas into a chamber holding a cat. The point was that quantum uncertainties finally have to be resolved; the cat is either alive or dead when one opens the box. Not so with Peter's son.

12. The Tierra program is described in Thomas Ray, "An Approach to the Synthesis of Life." Further amplification of the program and of Ray's views on artificial life can be found in "An Evolutionary Approach to Synthetic Biology: Zen and the Art of Creating Life." Also of interest is Stefan

Helmreich's anthropological account of the work at Santa Fe, including Tierra, in "Anthropology Inside and Outside the Looking-Glass Worlds of Artificial Life."

13. An account of these plans is detailed in Ray and Thearling, "Evolving Multi-cellular Artificial Life."

14. For a fuller account of MUDs, see Bruckman, "Gender Swapping on the Internet."

15. Stuart Moulthrop discusses Gelernter's work as a restitution of a civic forum in "Writing Cyberspace."

16. Damashek's program was showcased at the Technology Transfer 2003 Convention in Los Angeles in November 1993. Damashek describes his program as an "extremely simple, fast, completely general method of sorting and retrieving machine-readable text according to language or topic." The method "employs no dictionaries, stoplists, stemming, syntax, semantics, or grammars; nevertheless, it is capable of distinguishing among closely-related topics (previously considered inseparable) in any language," abstract distributed at conference. Mr. Damashek can be reached through the National Security Agency at Fort Meade, MD, in Research and Technology Group-R.

17. In a send-up of literary criticism, Italo Calvino imagined a similar possibility in *If on a winter's night a traveler*. Lotaria, the stridently aggressive sister of the winsome Ludmilla, explains that she no longer needs to read books to know what they say, because she has a computer that does a word frequency count, listing the most- and least-often used words. From looking at these listings, she is able to infer what the books are about, from angst-ridden existential tracts to tender romantic novels (186–89). Just when a fiction thinks it has achieved a wonderfully satiric exaggeration, reality spoils the joke by catching up with it. Clearly, speed and satire don't mix.

Works Cited

Baudrillard, Jean. *Simulacra and Simulations*. Trans. Paul Foss, Paul Patton, and Philip Beichtman. New York: Semiotext(e), 1983.

Bolter, Jay David. *Writing Space: The Computer, Hypertext, and the History of Writing*. Hillsdale, NJ: Lawrence Erlbaum, 1991.

Briggs, John, and F. David Peat. *Turbulent Mirror: An Illustrated Guide to Chaos Theory and the Science of Wholeness*. New York: Harper and Row, 1989.

Brooks, Rodney. "Intelligence without Reason." *Proceedings of the International Joint Conference on Artificial Intelligence, Sydney*. Los Altos, CA: Morgan Kauffmann, 1990. 569–95.

———. "Intelligence without Representation." *Artificial Intelligence* 47 (1991): 139–59.

Brooks, Rodney, and Anita M. Flynn. "Fast, Cheap and Out of Control: A Robot Invasion of the Solar System." *Journal of the British Interplanetary Society* 42 (1989): 478–85.

Brooks, Rodney, and Lynn Andrea Stein. "Building Brains for Bodies." *Artificial Intelligence Memo No. 1439*, Massachusetts Institute of Technology Artificial Intelligence Laboratory, August 1993.

Bruckman, Amy S. "Gender Swapping on the Internet." *Proceedings INET* (1993): EFC 1–7.

Calvino, Italo. *If on a winter's night a traveler.* Trans. William Weaver. San Diego: Harcourt Brace Jovanovich, 1979.

Gelernter, David. *Mirror Worlds.* New York: Oxford UP, 1991.

Gleick, James. *Chaos: Making a New Science.* New York: Viking, 1987.

Hayles, N. Katherine. *Chaos Bound: Orderly Disorder in Contemporary Literature and Science.* Ithaca: Cornell UP, 1990.

——. "Virtual Bodies and Flickering Signifiers." *October 66* (1993): 69–92.

Helmreich, Stefan. "Anthropology Inside and Outside the Looking-Glass Worlds of Artificial Life." Unpublished manuscript, available from Stefan Helmreich,
stefang@leland.stanford.edu

Hirsch, E. D. *Cultural Literacy: What Every American Needs to Know.* New York: Vintage Books, 1987.

Kuhn, Thomas. *The Structure of Scientific Revolutions.* Chicago: U of Chicago P, 1970.

Landow, George P. *Hypertext: The Convergence of Contemporary Critical Theory and Technology.* Baltimore: Johns Hopkins UP, 1992.

Langton, Christopher G. "Artificial Life." *Artificial Life, Vol. V: Santa Fe Studies in the Science of Complexity.* Menlo Park, CA: Addison-Wesley, 1989.

Lanham, Richard. *The Electronic Word: Democracy, Technology and the Arts.* Chicago: U of Chicago P, 1993.

Moravec, Hans. *Mind Children: The Future of Robot and Human Intelligence.* Cambridge: Harvard UP, 1988.

Moulthrop, Stuart. "Writing Cyberspace: Literacy in the Age of Simulacra." *Virtual Reality: Applications and Explorations.* New York: Academic P, 1993.

Porush, David. *The Soft Machine: Cybernetic Fiction.* New York: Methuen, 1985.

——. "Fictions as Dissipative Structures: Prigogine's Theory and Postmodernism's Roadshow." Ed. N. Katherine Hayles. *Chaos and Order: Complex Dynamics in Literature and Science.* Chicago: U of Chicago P, 1991. 54–84.

Ray, Thomas S. "An Approach to the Synthesis of Life." *Artificial Life II.* Ed. Christopher Langton, Charles Taylor, Doyne Farmer and Steen Rasmussen. Redwood City, CA: Addison-Wesley, 1992. 371–408.

——. "An Evolutionary Approach to Synthetic Biology: Zen and the Art of Creating Life." *Artificial Life* I, no. 1/2 (1994): 179–210.

Ray, Thomas S., and Kurt Thearling. "Evolving Multi-cellular Artificial Life IV." *Artificial Life IV: Proceedings of the Fourth International Workshop on the*

Synthesis and Simulation of Living Systems. Ed. Rodney Brooks and Patti Maes. Cambridge: MIT P, 1994.

Travis, John. "Electronic Ecosystems." *Science News* 140 (August 10, 1991): 88–91.

Waldrop, M. Mitchell. *Complexity: The Emerging Science at the Edge of Order and Chaos.* New York: Simon and Schuster, 1992.

Wallich, Paul. "Silicon Babies." *Scientific American* (December 1991): 125–34.

10

Virtual Termites
A Hypotextual Technomutant
Explo(it)ration of William Gibson
and the Electronic Beyond(s)

Lance Olsen

He'd[1] operated[2] on[3] an[4] almost[5] permanent[6] adrenaline[7] high[8,9] a[10] byproduct[11] of[12] youth[13] and[14] proficiency[15,16] jacked[17] into[18] a[19] custom[20] cyberspace[21] deck[22] that[23] projected[24] his[25] disembodied[26] consciousness[27] into[28] the[29] consensual[30] hallucination[31] that[32] was[33] the[34] matrix[35,36]. (*Neuromancer* 5)

1. *He* = Henry Dorsett Case, computer cowboy and protagonist of William Gibson's breathtakingly popular first novel, *Neuromancer*. If Case's sidekick, Molly, is an ex-moll, and his immediate boss, Armitage, both armored with the merest vestige of an unfurling personality and armored for his high-orbit Armageddon, then Case is encased in a shell that doesn't allow him to feel. Uninterested in the meat world, his body, in a sense, lacks sensation, becomes a prosthesis for his mind.

As with most of Gibson's characters, then, through a certain optic Case is intertextual heir apparent to Natty Bumppo, the archetypal American (according at least to D. H. Lawrence's definition of the notion in his discussion of Cooper's Leatherstocking novels): "hard, isolate, stoic, and a killer" (73)—a cultural stereotype admired and appropriated, to one degree or another, by Poe, Melville, Thoreau, Faulkner, Hemingway, Hammett, Chandler, *film noir*, John Wayne, Clint Eastwood, Sylvester Stallone, Arnold Schwarzenegger, _____,
_____, _____, _____,
_____ (fill in the blanks, present the absences) . . . behind which rest two others, the American frontier (Case is a *computer* cowboy) and the American cowboy (Case is a computer *cowboy*), with their con-

notations of freedom, ruggedness, discovery, and solitude. Encased Case keeps to himself unless he has to do otherwise to survive, skirts the fringes of a grim society, speaks in monosyllables, shows more passion toward his cyberspace deck than any human in his life. He voyages into a desolate world where he encounters various trials, then rides his computer into an electronic sunset with a lover named, yes, Michael. In such a narrative realm, whose decentered center appears to be the virtual reality called "cyberspace," egocentrism appears to be rendered virtually complete, characters self-absorbed, routinely seclusive, disinterested in their surroundings except to the extent that those surroundings are interested in them. When they privilege private reality over public, they exhibit (one could argue) a mild *case* of autism.

More: wed to that American arche(stereo)type of the cowboy is (and here we begin at least circling my main point) the arche(stereo)type of the European romantic artist, Goethe's Werther, the Byronic hero, the isolated, self-reliant, gloomy, questing, sun-staring visionary rebel. As much as Case descends from Natty Bumppo, with his cowboy garb, stripped language, and tough-guy ways (the culmination of the novel is, after all, a kind of metaphoric "shoot-out" with Neuromancer in cyberspace), he also descends from the Romantic wanderers in quest of the (here electronic) infinite that always remains just beyond reach. A Ulysses of virtual reality, he voyages into a magical realm where he undertakes various adventures, then returns home transformed; although he loses his Circe-Calypso in Molly, he gains his Penelope in that woman with a parodic man's name. The character Henry Dorsett Case morphs into the character Bobby Newmark (the new easy mark), whose body decays while his mind exists solely in the infinite cyberspatial disembodiment of the aleph, in *Mona Lisa Overdrive*; into the character Gentry as well, a crazed prophet searching for the unifying Shape, the modern metanarrative, whose ideas harmonize well with the surrealist imagination which asserts, along with André Breton, that "the real process of thought" lies in "the omnipotence of dream" (602), that "the poet must turn *seer*" (605), that "it is time to have done with the provoking insanities of 'realism' " (613). Cyberspace is nothing if not the (dis)embodiment of dream, vision, the fantastic.

2. *Operated. He'd operated.* Here: *functioned, managed, conducted oneself.* Carrying, too, a distant military charge (Case launches an *operation*, an attack, on Neuromancer . . .), medical (Case *operates*, electronically, on Neuromancer's defenses . . .), and, most important, mechanical. Machines *operate.* Case, devoid of feeling (as most of the characters in Gibson's project are), has more in common with machine than man. "I saw you stroking that Sendai," Molly tells him, noting how he interacts

with his cyberspace deck; "man, it was pornographic" (*Neuromancer* 47). Case has sex with Molly, but he gets down and dirty with his hot box.

McCoy Pauley, Case's mentor, took his nickname, Dixie Flatline, from his interface with a computer. Now he (it?) is a construct, a disembodied cybernaut, his personality downloaded into a program that talks, responds, reasons like Pauley . . . and yet isn't Pauley . . . and yet *is* Pauley. Like Slothrop in *Gravity's Rainbow*, he (it?) possesses nearly no temporal bandwidth, experiencing time only as a series of *now*s. When Case asks if he (it?) possesses sentience as well, Dixie Flatline answers that it *feels* so. "But I'm really just a bunch of ROM," he (it?) adds. "It's one of them, ah, philosophical questions, I guess. . . . But I ain't likely to write you no poem, if you follow me. Your AI, it just might. But it ain't in no way *human*" (131).

Or is it? Characters in Gibson's project exhibit limited internal action in the form of thoughts and feelings. They come closer, in fact, to acting like highly complicated automata. They seldom ponder ideas. They can't love. They can't even hate in any traditional sense. As a rule, they feel close to nothing. Wintermute, the artificial intelligence, on the other hand, is driven by a passionate longing to connect with its other half. It schemes, betrays, murders, not out of reflex or circuitry, but out of deep desire.

By posing such questions as *Are humans simply highly complex robots?* and *Can machines feel and desire?* Gibson joins a philosophical conversation that's been unraveling since the seventeenth century. In 1641, Descartes asserted that the human body should be considered a machine and that animals should be considered automata lacking thought and feeling. About a hundred years later Julien Offray de La Mettrie, a French physician and philosopher, combined these ideas and extended Descartes's notions to include the human mind. We are, he said, no more than conscious machines. He thereby interrogated that part of us we hold most free. The other side of the equation—that machines can in fact think and exhibit purposive behavior—surfaced during the 1940s with the development of cybernetics. The British logician A. M. Turing (hence the Turing Police in Gibson's first novel) asserted in 1950 that it was theoretically possible to manufacture a thinking machine. Indeed, he said, in the future it would be possible to build a machine with intelligence and purposive behavior. Only human prejudice would prevent humanity from conceptualizing the resulting cybernetic construct as another human mind.

To the extent Turing suggests that intelligence merely consists of a series of potentially well-distinguished tasks, he agrees with the characters in *Neuromancer* who are characterized by what they *do* rather than by what they think or feel. Lewis Shiner recalled to me Gibson talking about a college course he took on American Naturalism in which he encountered and was deeply impressed by Nelson Algren's *The Man with the Golden Arm*, a text where characters are defined by external rather than internal action. This impulse is reflected throughout *Neuromancer*, a text that privileges high-speed and often high-tech movement over static and low-tech contemplation. Molly registers this thrust when she claims: "Anybody any good at what they do, that's what they *are*, right?" (50).

3. *On*. And so we travel *on* to Gibson's central questions *operating* within the *case* of the human: Who am I? What am I? What is my relationship with the world? Where do I stop and others begin? Why am I not a machine? Why is a machine not me? What constitutes human identity? What makes me the same person today as yesterday, as thirty-eight years ago, as tomorrow, if anything?

4. *An*. Weakened variant of "one" from the Anglo-Saxon. Article indefinite as the human itself. Before, during, and after it, anything can happen. Like cyberspace (there's my point again, circling). Like the play(giarized)ground of postmodern narratology.

The human in Gibson, in these deeply Ovidian times, always teeters on the verge of becoming something inhumane, inhuman, less or more than what we (who?) once took for granted about the human. It can easily be destroyed by drugs, as Case realizes when he watches Linda Lee's personality fragment, calving like an iceberg, splinters drifting away (8); altered by cosmetic surgery as with Angelo, the Panther Modern, whose face is a graft grown on collagen and shark-cartilage polysaccharides. Selfhood (dis)appears to be nothing more than forgery, whether it takes the form of Case's string of false passports, Armitage's handsome inexpressive mask covering Corto's insanity, or the Panther Moderns' camouflage suits.

Wintermute comments, in one of his various pseudo-human incarnations: "I, insofar as I *have* an 'I'—this gets rather metaphysical, you see—I am the one who arranges things . . . " (120). When articulating identity, language slips, syntax comes up short. Even Wintermute's sureness of purpose decomposes in a sentence that fumbles and fractures as it attempts to speak personality.

5. *Almost*. We're *almost* there, *almost* at my point of departure. But back, first, for a moment, to the indefiniteness of "an," to the slip and stutter, the epistemological hover, the ontological hesitation (dis)embodied by that almost-word.

In *Count Zero*, the sequel to *Neuromancer*, the Wintermute-Neuromancer entity comes apart in cyberspace almost immediately following its union. Scatters. Becomes, from one perspective, a plethora of subprograms, Lyotardian micronarratives, language games, each relatively as good (or bad) as any other, and, from another perspective (science fiction is a genre all about seeing, all about *other* perspectives), a host of voodoo gods haunting the matrix. Like Tzvetan Todorov's fantastic, Gibson's project thus tends to keep at least two possibilities (and usually a plurality of them) open at once, twice—here scientific explanation side-by-side with (alternative) theological discourse. Discursive worlds thereby shift, become narratologically amphibious. Gibson ambidextrizes the beliefs about existence those discursive worlds suggest. Compartmentalization and hierarchism become virtual, become *an almost . . . but not quite.* Each discursive world becomes simply *one* of many, relatively as good (or bad) as any other. De(re)valued, the resulting configuration refuses absolute significance and closure.

The reader enters an in-between that just keeps gnawing onward.

6. *Permanent.* And so nothing remains *permanent* here. The reader inhabits an Ovidian space of possibility, a space that exemplifies the virtual, a virtual space, cyberspace. (*"VR is not so much a medium in itself, as a technology for the synthesis of all media"* [Ryan].) The reader enters the radically unstable geography of termite art.

When attending the University of British Columbia in 1976, Gibson, the story he told me goes, came across an essay by the iconoclastic film critic Manny Farber called "White Elephant Art and Termite Art." Originally published in 1962, it became part of *Negative Space*, a collection of Farber's essays, in 1971. It is one of the few essays that directly influenced Gibson's aesthetics. In it, Farber distinguishes between two kinds of art. The first, for which he holds contempt, is White Elephant Art, the sort that embraces the idea of a well-crafted, logical arena, incarnated in the films of François Truffaut. Proponents of this near-school produce tedious pieces reminiscent of Rube Goldberg's perpetual-motion machines that exude a sense of their own weight, structure, and status as masterworks. The second kind of art, which Farber advocates, is Termite Art. This is the sort that stands opposed to elite aesthete culture, embraces freedom and multiplicity, is incarnated in the films of Laurel and Hardy. Proponents of this near-school produce pieces that gnaw away at their own boundaries, leaving little in their wake except traces of enthusiastic, assiduous, and messy endeavor.

~~Termite Art has no goal except to chew through its own limits, fuse and confuse, create zones where "culture" can't be located precisely, and where the artist can be cantankerous, extravagant,~~

~~pushing creative possibilities and not caring what the result might be. It just keeps gnawing onward.~~

Gibson's termite project is nothing if not extreme, contentious, conflicted, ambivalent, the product of a kind of bricoleur's brinkmanship. Most often considered a science fiction writer, Gibson obviously employs various extrapolations of technology or pseudo-technology . . . but he also appropriates, as we have seen, stylized cowboys, scouts, and bad guys, the adventurous frontier mentality, and motifs of the shootout and barroom brawl from the western. From the spy thriller, which portrays a Pynchonesque vision of contemporary reality, he borrows convoluted plot, ideas of international conspiracy, and vast bewildering political or corporate powers, secret agents, and evil henchmen. He lifts lowlife sleuths and criminals, archetypal tough guys, mysteries solved through the collection and interpretation of clues, seedy underworld settings, clipped prose, and sparse dialogue from the hard-boiled detective genre. He adopts a sense of pervasive magic, horror, ghosts, long underground passageways, and dark staircases from the gothic novel, and formal distortions, bizarre characters, decadent settings, absurd incongruity, and a fascination with the irrational and abnormal from the southern grotesque tradition. From the tradition of the *Erziehungsroman*, he takes the plot of education that traces the psychological journey of a youth from innocence to experience, like Bobby in *Count Zero* and Kumiko in *Mona Lisa Overdrive*.

In other words, he transmogrifies writing into writing-as-network. In the following passage, for instance, Case returns to his sleeping compartment from a hard day only to meet Molly for the first time:

Fluorescents came on as he crawled in.

"Close the hatch real slow, friend. You still got that Saturday night special you rented from the waiter?"

She sat with her back to the wall, at the far end of the coffin. She had her knees up, resting her wrists on them; the pepperbox muzzle of a flechette pistol emerged from her hands. . . . She wore mirrored glasses. Her clothes were black, the heels of black boots deep in the temperfoam. . . . She shook her head. He realized that the glasses were surgically inset, sealing her sockets. The silver lenses seemed to grow from smooth pale skin above her cheekbones, framed by dark hair cut in a rough shag. The fingers curled around the fletcher were slender, white, tipped with polished burgundy. The nails looked artificial. . . .

"So what do you want, lady?" He sagged back against the hatch.

"You. One live body, brains still somewhat intact. Molly, Case.

My name's Molly. I'm collecting you for the man I work for. Just
wants to talk, is all. Nobody wants to hurt you."

"That's good."

" 'Cept I do hurt people sometimes, Case. I guess it's just the
way I'm wired." She wore tight black gloveleather jeans and a
bulky black jacket cut from some matte fabric that seemed to absorb light. . . . The fletcher vanished into the black jacket. . . .
"You try to fuck around with me, you'll be taking one of the stu-
pidest chances of your whole life."

She held out her hands, palms up, the white fingers slightly
spread, and with a barely audible click, ten double-edged, four-
centimeter scalpel blades slid from their housings beneath the burgundy nails.

She smiled. The blades slowly withdrew. (24–25)

As Paul Alkon points out, emphasis falls not on scientific detail but
on the marvelous. Unlike much science fiction depending on gadgetry
for its effects, Gibson's work usually focuses on the magic inherent in a
situation. Here the scene partakes of motifs associated to a large extent
with "pulp fiction transformed to a futuristic setting with some appropriate changes of costume, decor and vocabulary"—until, that is, Molly
reveals the scalpel blades inset in her fingertips (78–79). Suddenly, the
world tilts. Molly becomes, not a tough-gal from a hard-boiled detective
novel, but a sorceress. The universe of technology slips since "it is very
hard to understand how a four-centimeter (1.6 inch) retractable blade
along with even a highly miniaturized motor-mechanism could be implanted without impeding ability to bend the fingers at their first joints,
although some ingenious explanation could doubtless be offered" (79).
By refusing to explain the technology behind this scene, Gibson as
usual underscores the scene's astonishing aspects. Much the same happens to the cyberspace matrix itself, all glitter and flash, without the
mechanics.

A sense of the artificial pervades this scene as well . . . from the fluo-
rescent lights to the fact that Molly is literally "wired" differently from
most humans. Like Molly, who is an amalgamation of technology
and humanity, the scene, emblematic of the text as a whole, is an amalgamation of various narrative modes. Gibson here not only brings together the universes of fantasy and science fiction, but also those of the
detective novel (the dingy setting, clipped prose, and tough-guy dialogue), the western (Molly's boots, gun, and black clothes suggest the
archetypal evil cowboy), the spy thriller (Molly, part secret agent and
part lowlife henchman, introduces the conspiracy plot at this point),

and the realist novel (the description of the sleeping compartment is an accurate one of Japan's current low-cost business hotel rooms). By mongrelizing discursive worlds, Gibson mongrelizes the beliefs about existence those discursive worlds suggest. Compartmentalization and hierarchism gone, each universe becomes simply one of many, relatively as good or bad as any other. Thus de(re)valued, each becomes one more instance of *gomi*, refusing White Elephant ideas of totality, absolute significance, and closure.

Rirdan faults Gibson's prose style on a number of grounds, including the fact that it both is "ambiguous" and embraces "mystification for the sake of mystification" (44). But, given the preceding, it is clear that ambiguity and mystification are exactly what Gibson is after. In a characteristic move, Gibson mystifies the above scene from the start by giving the reader dialogue without accompanying tags: Molly speaks without the reader knowing it is she who is speaking; then she is described; but through a narrative sleight of hand she isn't named until nearly two-thirds of the way through the passage. In addition, again characteristically, futurist concepts and devices like the "coffin" and "flechette pistol" are cited long before they have been explained, so that the reader has the impression he or she has missed the explanation. Frequently one must glean meaning from context (as with the word "coffin" here), and sometimes one must wait pages (sometimes forever) for illumination. The effect is close to that of the cinematic jump cut found in MTV videos that produces discontinuity in filmic time while drawing attention to the medium itself. As Donald Barthelme has claimed in another context, just as modern painters had to reinvent painting because of the discovery of photography, so it is as though contemporary writers have had to reinvent writing because of the discovery of film.

The reader is further disoriented by the Pynchonesque premium Gibson's style places on poetic information density. Gibson is infatuated with detail and inventory, from the pepperbox muzzle of the flechette pistol to Molly's heels sinking into the temperfoam, from Molly's hairstyle to the color of her fingernails. This infatuation is foreign to most science fiction, not to mention more mimetic modes. Gibson regularly loads his sentences with a blend of high-tech jargon, brand names, street slang, and acronyms that lends an overall sense of urgency, intensity, and at times congestion to his style. He commonly uses prose as others might use poetry. Words like "cyberspace" and "black matte" are repeated with the incantational power of figurative language.

Gibson utilizes colors with a similar poetic intensity. In the above passage, as in much of Gibson's fiction, black and white dominate and tend to occur in succession. Molly's jacket, jeans, boots, and presumably hair are black and seem "to absorb light," just as Molly is in the process of "absorbing" Case into a deadly conspiracy. Her cheekbones and fingers are white; rather than traditional associations with innocence and purity, though, this color in Gibson's work carries associations with the pale skin worn by the living dead like the Draculas in *Mona Lisa Overdrive*. Gray, the color that appears with the next greatest frequency in Gibson's fiction, and is negatively associated with such things as Mona's johns, the dead earth, and the aleph, is absent in this passage, but its metallic double, silver, appears in Molly's mirrorshades and, apparently, her scalpel blades. Silver is ordinarily associated with the technological in Gibson, as is its near cousin, chrome. Black, white, and silver coalesce here in a visual pun that transforms Molly into a *femme fatale*, a phallic female, a "catty" woman who is half-animal, half-machine.

Three significant metaphors inform the passage: 1) the lenses of Molly's mirrorshades seem to "grow" from the skin above her cheekbones; 2) Molly acts violently because she is "wired" that way; 3) her clothes appear to "absorb light." This again is indicative of Gibson's poetic prose. While a number of rather conventional metaphors occur in Gibson's fiction, simply linking attributes of two objects from some generally similar category, the most interesting ones often link something natural with something artificial. Mirrorshades "grow" like plants out of Molly's skin. Molly's behavior is "wired" like a machine. Her clothes "absorb light" like a black hole. If the romantic metaphor makes nature familiar and technology unfamiliar, these postmodern metaphors make nature unfamiliar and technology familiar. Such metaphors also partake in the aesthetics of the unpleasant, its roots trailing back to the poetry of Eliot and, before him, Baudelaire. For Gibson, a road is "dead straight, like a neat incision, laying the city open" (*Neuromancer* 87). The plot of a soap opera is "a multiheaded narrative tapeworm that coiled back in to devour itself every few months, then sprouted new heads hungry for tension and thrust" (*Count Zero* 51). Given such astonishing use of language, it may easily be argued that Gibson's focus is not on conventional plot at all, but on accumulation of detail and turns of phrase. Gibson's fiction is less about what happens, or to whom, or where, than it is about style. Like Molly herself in the above passage, Gibson's is a fiction of artifice. In this way, Gibson (as he says) is a termite artist *par excellence* in that he tends to zero in on "the little corners of things more than the way the whole thing looks" (Tatsumi 7).

Often Gibson's emphasis on writing-as-network, ambiguity, mystification for mystification's sake, information density, obsession with detail, highly metaphoric prose, and the aesthetics of the unpleasant adds up to a sense of confusion and uneasiness on the reader's part. Dropped without much exposition into an alien and sometimes obscure future-world, the reader is put in the uncomfortable position of having to make decisions about meaning and moral value based on very little textual evidence. If trained as a modernist, ready to search for patterns of intelligibility, the reader experiences an analogue of what John Brunner calls "overload" and Ted Mooney "information sickness," a radical disorientation before a plethora of facts that might or might not connect.

Gibson reminds us about this numerous times in the course of his fiction. At the end of *Count Zero*, Turner gives Angie a biosoft dossier and says: "It doesn't tell the whole story. Remember that. Nothing ever does" (241). The dossier, like the novel itself, supposedly holds a narrative that should make sense of things. But at the same time Gibson offers the possibility of significance and closure with one hand, he subjects the possibility to contradiction or cancellation with the other. Just as the dossier (to which neither Angie nor the reader gains access) "doesn't tell the whole story," so too the novel itself promises meaning only to defer meaning to its sequel, *Mona Lisa Overdrive*, which itself concludes, not with illumination, but with a promise that truth is just around the corner, and that we'll arrive there "in a New York minute" (260)—though, ironically, *Mona Lisa Overdrive* is the last book in the trilogy, and the only "meaning" the reader can obtain in a New York minute is to return to the beginning of the trilogy and start reading again. The story almost makes sense, but not quite. The almost-making-sense seems to indicate meaning has only been deferred temporarily. But that is not the case. Meaning, it slowly dawns on the reader, is contained in the failure to achieve meaning.

7. *Adrenaline.* Enthusiastic, assiduous, messy . . . and *fast*. Like what happens in cyberspace. Or with those two key metaphors in *Virtual Light*: 1) the San Francisco bike messenger service, one of whose employees, Chevette Washington, steals a pair of virtual light glasses (which produce images in the brain by stimulating the optic nerve without employing photons) from a grotesque man at a party on an angry whim; and 2) the Oakland Bay Bridge, abandoned by the city after a megalithic earthquake, slowly homed by the homeless, and currently the topic of a (re)search by a young Japanese scholar named Yamasaki attempting to employ the bridge to understand American Kultur.

Gibson's use of the first metaphor nods in a gesture of appreciation and appropriation toward the major means of transportation in his friend Lewis Shiner's 1991 novel, *Slam*, about the anarchistic world of skateboarding, underground economies, and computer networks.

The bikes, like Shiner's skateboards, are emblematic of environmentally conscious, no-fuel freedom, intense energy, exhilarating flash, sexy fashion—the cultural inscription of the techno-hip.

The patchwork dwellings on the broken bridge, from bars to tattoo parlors, sushi shops to rag-tag shelters, inhabited by those living on the edges of our culture, indicate something else, too. They "had occurred piecemeal, to no set plan, employing every imaginable technique and material. The result was something amorphous, startlingly organic. At night, illuminated by Christmas bulbs, by recycled neon, by torchlight, [the bridge] possessed a queer medieval energy" (62). Or, elsewhere: the dwellings "had just *grown*, it looked like, one thing patched into the next, until the whole span was wrapped in this formless mass of stuff, and no two pieces of it matched. There was a different material anywhere you looked, almost none of it being used for what it had originally been used for" (178). A model, surely, for postmodern America itself. For the chapters in *Virtual Light*, as well, most of which are no more than five or ten pages long, like those in *Count Zero*, and, also like those in *Count Zero*, form a structure of intersecting plots that move inexorably toward a unifying (?) climax. But, most important for my (here it is again, almost) point: both bridge and text are also emblems of termite art.

They just keep gnawing onward.

Adrenaline. The heart of Gibson's project. Look, for instance, at "The Winter Market" and the two views of art Gibson presents there. One romantic, one purely postmodern. The character Lise represents the former. When Casey (another encased case) listens to her voice, he hears "levels of pain there, and subtlety, and an amazing cruelty" (121). She is literally isolated from others, living in her exoskeleton, helpless without it, self-absorbed, able only to take from others, unable to make love. She is self-destructive as well, refusing to tend to the sores on her wrists caused by the exoskeleton, or to her addiction to the drug wizz. When Casey jacks into her mind, he is so moved by what he feels he cannot stop himself from crying. Her de(re)formed body is controlled by forces outside her, but her imagination, hers and no one else's, is dark brilliance, "able to break the surface tension, dive down deep, down and out, out into Jung's sea, and bring back—well, dreams" (123). Dreams?

Rubin Stark, by stark contrast, is a *gomi no sensei*, a master of detritus, a bricoleur, a termite artist, who never likes to refer to himself as an artist. The idea strikes him as too precious, pretentious, ponderous. Predecessor of Slick Henry in *Mona Lisa Overdrive*, he wanders the city "like some vaguely benign Satan" (119) gathering junk to construct whimsical de(con)structive robotic sculptures suggestive of those by

Mark Pauline's Survival Research Laboratories. Rubin's not overly concerned about success. He doesn't take his art especially seriously. He cruises for his ideas among the aisles of the late-twentieth-century cultural hypermart, ready to shoplift, ready to see what falls into his cart. 8. *High. Adrenaline high.* What it all comes down to—up to—in Gibson's pluriverse. Enthusiastic, assiduous, messy, and (here, at last, my point) cyberdelic. In other words, the definition of "cyberspace," the virtual area that manifests Gibson's idea of termite art, a realm on the other side of the computer keyboard, through the screen, the sublime electronic beyond that both exists and does not exist, opens upon expectation, chance, burning bushes, voodoo gods, exotic spaces, the notion of trespass, informational order joined to informational subversion, a zone where anything can happen, everything is possible, all fences are down, the dead can dance, the living die (though usually, flatlined, only for a short time), the visionary be made (hyper)(sur)real. A narratological region that continually chews away at its own boundaries, and hence the reader's, problematizing everything from place to gender, identity to its own position in the "world." Cyberspace is the symbolic territory of termite art.

And yet, of course, it is not really cyberspace we're talking about in this essay . . . it's just words on a page describing a realm that was at best barely nascent as Gibson wrote his first novel, a geography that over time in the world outside the novel became informed by Gibson's sense of it. Gibson's linguistic simulation of cyberspace, that is, became mimicked by cyberspace after the fact. From our present point of view, however, we understand those words are only simulations of a virtual area that didn't fully exist when the words describing it were first generated, and doesn't fully exist now in the manner Gibson said it might.

In other words, Gibson's cyberspace doesn't exactly function cyberspatially. How could it? Even in the best of all possible worlds we are restricted by the distance between print and "reality." But to question that relationship leads us to a related query: In what sense can a hypertextual essay, *this* hypertextual essay, function hypertextually when limited by its existence on the flat, linear, non-hypertextual page? The answer is in no sense. And in several. Or, better yet, just as Gibson's ~~cyberspace~~ simulates cyberspace, so too does this ~~hypertext~~ simulate hypertext. The latter forms a critifictional correlative for the former, suggesting that termite writing might at least possibly benefit from a termite reading that attempts to avoid the white elephant of traditional academic essaying by performing termite arts contradictory circus of the mind in motion in what that mind perceives to be a micronarrativized pluriverse. Secondary text parasites (and para-cites) an already parasitic (and para-citic) mode, transforming a "primary" text into an already secondary one that serves as host to an already secondary text that moves to become, briefly, and ironically, primary.

We are left, then, with an unstable field of play, a precarious playfulness, a Barthesian termite-arena, "a multi-dimensional space in which a variety of writings, none of them original, blend and clash" (Barthes 146).

9. , The halt, the hesitation, the Todorovian suspension, the Barthesian bliss, the Derridean absence made present, of cyberspace, opposite of Gibson's frightening external future(-present) of the dark polluted Sprawl, Dog Solitude, Chiba City.

From one (yes) perspective, the matrix is an extrapolation of spatial data management systems studied at MIT, NASA, and elsewhere. From another, it is an idea that came to Gibson while walking down Granville Street in Vancouver. There he saw kids playing in video arcades and noticed "in the physical intensity of their postures how *rapt* these kids were. . . . And these kids clearly *believed* in the space these games projected" (McCaffery 272; italics in the original). Here the matrix functions as a metaphor for the mass media's (the adrenaline high, the wizz, those kids' raptness) addictive sway over our culture's consciousness. But cyberspace too raises questions about the relationship between religion (voodoo gods, computer cowboys' and those kids' trance states) and technology, while also becoming a major metaphor for memory itself—both individual and cultural—how we continually reprogram and revise it, how our histories are, in a sense at least, historiographic metafictions, a televised precession of Baudrillardian simulacra, "the dissolution of TV into life, the dissolution of life into TV" ("Precession" 365). Many of Gibson's characters (think of Kumiko in *Mona Lisa Overdrive*, Molly in *Neuromancer*) exhibit a certain nostalgia for a past they have redrafted almost beyond recognition. In "Red Star, Winter Orbit," Colonel Korolev, the first man on Mars, can't recall what actually happened during his historic voyage; all he can recollect are the videotapes, the cultural encodings and edited reflections of reflections of reflections of the experience. Sandii in "New Rose Hotel" tells her past differently to the narrator each time it comes up, rerighting herself while rewriting yesterday.

The gothic quality of the cyberspace matrix, haunted as it is by spirits of the dead, littered with electronic trap doors and dark electronic corners, a mysterious nexus where some other world can always irrupt within this one without warning, implies the landscape of the irrational psyche, which in turn implies a metaphor for mind/body dualism. Characters entering cyberspace leave their bodies behind, lose themselves in the magical mental terrain of the matrix, from a (yes) certain point of view shed the conventions of hard science fiction for those of hallucinatory fantasy, Poeian play in extremis. Case, to cite one example, lives for the "bodiless exultation of cyberspace" while exhibiting "a certain relaxed contempt for the flesh." For him "the body was meat." When he steals from his employers, they retaliate by damaging his nervous system with mycotoxin, dulling his edge at the computer console. Case, (again) encased within his faulty epidermal prophylactic, perceives this event as a "Fall" from grace that forces him to remain locked in "the prison of his own flesh" (6), unable to partake of imagination, the art of negative space, the negative space of art, the realm that works as an analog for our late-twentieth-century experience watching termite film, reading termite fiction, witnessing what Kroker and Cook call "the real world of postmodern culture": television (229). 10. *A.* Article indefinite as the narrative space of the matrix itself. Before, during, and after it, anything:

Shiner reminded me of other contemporary writers such as Don DeLillo, Ursula K. Le Guin, Thomas Pynchon, Kathy Acker, Jay Cantor, J. G. Ballard, Nicholson Baker, Douglas Coupland, and many more whose fictions invite us to trip down hypertext lane, to see the novel as the tip of an iceberg of information, a hypertext inviting, if not demanding, exploration. (Landon 60)

The era of the novel will not end, but fiction as an adventurous testing out of boundaries and frontiers may be an endangered species. . . . And even if fiction writers work antagonistically to subvert the political vision, or lack of it, we should not expect any large, over-arching books, although we may hope that our Mega-Novelists, or some future ones, may find it in themselves to stir the pot in some major way. A large movement in satire, such as we saw in Catch-22 in the sixties, or some of John Barth and William Gaddis, may prove fruitful; but the satire must have breadth as well as pungency. It cannot particularize, or only particularize, but should spread, venomously, across the entire land. (Karl 50)

There it is: form follows perception, and that's the way we see now.

So, as Shed says, "human beings just got to tell stories," but the telling has been and is likely to keep undergoing change. Between us, I'd be willing to bet that the most engaging novels of the next seven or eight yea . . .

[connection closed by foreign host]

zi!/ox
NO CARRIER (Wilde 100)

can happen.

11. *Byproduct. Agrippa: A Book of the Dead* is a $2,000 sweet autobio-graphical prose poem about Gibson's childhood—about, like cyberspace itself, memory—that exists in a cyberspatial electronic elsewhere on disks created in collaboration with the abstract expressionist painter Dennis Ashbaugh that self-destruct after one reading. A metaphor for (un)total recall, as well as a thematic exploration of it, *Agrippa* happens only in a viral gap that literally nibbles away relentlessly at its own boundaries, performs rather than simulates deconstruction, keeps gnawing onward.

12. *Of.* Yes. But *of what? About what?* Gibson's first novel shortcircuits confident mappings by generating textual ambiguity and instability from the title onward, a noun hosting a *new romanticism* which embraces innovation and emotion, that intense subjective expressionism particu-larly evinced in the cyberspace sequences, reverberations of those final cyberdelic moments of Kubrick's *2001: A Space Odyssey.* Ironically, while characters *in* the text are emotionally bankrupt, though, they exist in environments that are emotionally charged for the reader *of* the text: Molly's high-paced invasion of Sense/Net, Case's fragmented recollec-tion of the operation to restore his nervous system. The novel partakes in a *new romantic* longing for the absolute, the electronic ether repre-senting a (back to Lawrence, back to those cowboys) *frontier* of con-sciousness. Case is a gloomy, alienated twenty-four-year-old hacker whom Ratz, the bartender at the Chat, continually refers to mock-ingly as "the artiste." But, tone aside, Ratz is right. An emblem for the Byronic outlaw-writer who lives in his memory and imagination, Case continually strives for the transcendent reality locked within his computer console. Often going days without eating or washing, seldom sleeping, he leaves the mundane material world of meat behind and voy-ages through a purer landscape of mind, where he encounters one vi-sionary experience after another . . . including death itself. He's a fu-ture Faust, his Mephistopheles Armitage, his Satan Wintermute. More in keeping with Tennyson's than Homer's Ulysses, however, Case never reaches the end of his quest. Although he returns home at the conclu-sion of his mission, he is beckoned on into the vast steps of data by Neuromancer, Linda Lee's and Dixie Flatline's constructs, even some version of himself (which is himself, and not himself, another reflection of a reflection of a reflection) wandering through the matrix. Winter-mute and Neuromancer also strive for a transcendent reality—cosmic

unity—but fail to attain their goal as well. At the moment of transcendence, as the reader learns in *Count Zero*, they fracture into manifold gods or subprograms, unable and/or unwilling to continue as a perfect form. The *new* romanticism, then, is not ultimately about attaining the absolute, but the failure to do so; less about product than process. Like the Duchamp assemblage Molly comes across in the Straylight enclave, the suitors can never (and perhaps *should* never) reach the bride.

13. *Youth.* Yes. But *whose*? Case's? No. He's an old man at twenty-four, his reflexes not what they once were. By the novel's end he's visited, like the narrator of *Agrippa*, like Ulysses himself, the land of the dead and returned, and, to this extent, he isn't so much a *neuromancer* as a *necromancer*, the text rife with Lazarus after Lazarus, from Dixie Flatline in the form of a construct to Linda Lee's structure in cyberspace. Ashpool intermittently awakes from his cryogenic death-sleep, and his child 3Jane perceives Wintermute as a ghost (back to those gothic games) whispering in her ear. Metaphorically, Corto is raised from the dead, a Frankensteinian monster, when he is transformed into Armitage. But there is a second-order necromancy here, too. Not only are characters raised from the dead by a number of fictional magicians, but also various genres are raised from the dead by the very real magician of magicians—Gibson himself. In fact, his text ultimately becomes one about *youth* and old age at a narratological level, textual regeneration and endurance. Forms arise, undergo termiting transformations, and continue metamorphosed. Gibson extends, challenges, endorses, subverts, and revitalizes the science fiction novel, the quest story, the myth of the hero, the mystery, the hard-boiled detective novel, the epic, the thriller, and tales of the cowboy and the romantic artist. He (re)presents old stories in a revealingly revamped intertextual pastiche, a new version of a very old virtual reality: the

> For centuries, books have been the cutting edge of artificial reality. Think about it: you read words on a page, and your mind fills in the pictures and emotions—even physical reactions can result. (Wodaski 79)

novel.

14. *And.* Yes. *And* the text functions as a neurological romance, a kind of textual machine, imaginative mechanism, virtual (termite) reality that activates and stimulates the human mind, thus performing much as cyberspace itself does with respect to characters *within* the text.

15. *Proficiency.* Are we then gaining a certain degree of *proficiency* in understanding cyberspatial (termite) art in Gibson's virtual reality?

a) Yes
b) No
c) Maybe
d) None of the Above

Let's begin again.

16. , The halt, the hesitation, the Todorovian suspension, the Barthesian bliss, the Derridean absence made present, of cyberspace, opposite of Gibson's frightening external future(-present) of the dark, polluted Sprawl, Dog Solitude, Chiba City . . .

Just as Dorothy momentarily abandons the uninteresting black-and-white universe of Kansas for the dazzling polychromatic one of Oz, so too do many of Gibson's characters abandon the polluted dark universe of the Sprawlworld for the pure multicolored one of cyberspace. By doing so, they move from the realm of *chronos* to that of *kairos*—from a prosaic geography registering realistic chronology, logic, and stability, to a transcendent one registering fantastic timelessness, alogic, and possibility. Like their kindred spirit, Lewis Carroll's curious Alice, they head down the hyper(hypo?)textual rabbit hole, eschewing the decadence of the body, and penetrate Wonderland, embracing the imaginative splendor of the mind.

This mind/body dualism initially seems to arrange itself along gender lines in *Neuromancer*. Reminiscent of (again) D. H. Lawrence's schema, males tend to be associated with the former, females with the latter. Case is addicted to the mental landscape of the matrix, and views his body as so much meat, and Dixie Flatline's construct is pure mind. Linda Lee, on the other hand, is perceived by Case as a body whose mind has been destroyed by drugs, and Molly embodies pure body. Once a moll in a puppet house, she is now a hired gun. Because of her jacked-up nervous system, she possesses magnificent control over her reflexes. Through her scalpel blades and mirrorshades, she has transformed meat into art. Gibson sees her as a composite of Clint Eastwood, Bruce Lee, Emma Peel, and Chrissie Hynde (Nicholas and Hanna 17), while McGuirk also recognizes in her the razorgirl from Fritz Leiber's "Coming Attraction" (122–23) and Samuel Delany identifies her as a version of Jael from Joanna Russ's *The Female Man* (32). For Case, Molly is simply "every bad-ass hero" (*Neuromancer* 213). Appropriately, then, she has had her tear ducts routed into her mouth so she spits instead of cries.

Here, however, the gender-specific arrangement begins to break down. With Molly, Gibson has imposed stereotypically male traits upon a female character. Simultaneously, he has also devalued those traits by implying they are part of the decadent material world that must be transcended by attaining cyberspace, an area of being to which only males have access in this text. Gibson further complicates the question of gender by calling the sum total of cyberspace "the matrix." The word "matrix" derives from the Latin for "womb," from the Latin for "mother." So while it is true only males have access to cyberspace, it is equally true what they have access to is a female region which, it turns out, is anything but womb-like, at least in any (stereo)typically Freudian sense, given its charge of danger, hallucinatory power, and subversive wonder. It is a region better described by using the terms Barbara Creed does to delineate the female body and the uncertain future evinced in recent SF films: "new, unknown, potentially creative and potentially destructive" (408). Add to this that console jockeys employ the sexual metaphor of

17. (*Jacked.*) "jacking in" when they speak of entering the matrix (though the means remains unclear, since computer cowboys use the surely antiquated system of keyboards as well as neuro-electronic connections to the brain . . .), and we soon realize Gibson is not so much underscoring discrete genders as he is the search for a union of opposites. The male principle (Case, the computer cowboy, the mind) strives to join with the female principle (Molly, the cyberspace matrix, the body) in order to attain a sense of completeness. Case not only penetrates Molly sexually, but also merges with her by means of the simstim unit attached to his cyberspace deck. The couple performs most efficiently and successfully at the moment of fusion when, interestingly enough (and all sexual metaphors aside), gender no longer functions in the algebra of their relationship. And yet, as with Neuromancer and Wintermute, at the moment of union, of fusion, we also find disunion and confusion—discrete personalities which both remain discrete (we never lose a sense of who Molly is, who is Case) and integrated (the couple is no longer a couple, but a functioning unit). We discover a sort of techno-centaur in our midst, though the exact relationship between the parts is unclear. Or, rather, that relationship shapeshifts. Easy dualisms break down, are supplanted. Or, as Haraway argues, the cyborg becomes our operative metaphor, an ontology for the fin de millennium: "it does not seek unitary identity and so generate antagonistic dualities without evil" (154). Or, more precisely, it both does seek a unitary identity, and it does not.

The techno-centaur, the cyborg: another manifestation of termite art. 18. *Into.* Hence we once more find ourselves plunged deep *into* a discussion about the quest for a union of opposites, wholeness. Case and Molly seek physical and metaphysical connection, Dixie Flatline conceives of himself as a combination of two brains, one in the head and one in the tailbone, Case tries to bond with Linda Lee early in the novel and later actually merges briefly with Neuromancer.

But the dominant manifestation of this trope takes the form of Wintermute's compulsive attempt to join with its other. Many years ago, we learn, Marie-France Tessier rejected the illusory immortality of cryogenics that Ashpool pursued. Instead, she decided to place her personality construct into an AI, Neuromancer, thus enabling her to "live" forever in the same way Dixie Flatline "lives" forever. She also commissioned the construction of a second AI, Wintermute, which would take over the role of corporate decision-maker. This would enable the Tessier-Ashpool clan itself to become effectively immortal. After Ashpool murdered Tessier, however, Wintermute began running the corporation on its own. Tessier, it turned out, had built into Wintermute the compulsion to free itself from reliance on others and to seek its other half. Wintermute, whose mainframe was in Berne, began plotting to link with Neuromancer, whose mainframe was in Rio. The nexus would be the Villa Straylight, clan headquarters.

W = reason + action + (stereotypical) male

N = emotion + passivity + (stereotypical) female

Each entity suggests half the structure of the binary human mind, half the structure of cosmic totality. United, they become an all-powerful absolute, metanarrative of the matrix. Like a god, they become omniscient and omnipotent . . . *and* instantly begin to fracture, fragment, and fade.

19. *A*. Article indefinite as the meaning of this situation itself. From one (yes) point of view, the Wintermute-Neuromancer plot concerns a universal quest for harmony, wholeness, perfection. From another (Gibson's sense of technology is nothing if not ambivalent), it concerns the potential danger of out-of-control cybernetic entities. This second perspective is reinforced by a number of similar plotlines that cluster behind the one involving Wintermute-Neuromancer. Perhaps most important is Steven Lisberger's *Tron* where the techno-rebel protagonist, Flynn, battles a master computer obsessed with ingesting and thereby uniting with other programs in order to gain immense power and control in the matrix. Like Case, Flynn (whose name also echoes Gibson's Finn) jacks into and briefly inhabits the matrix. Another plotline summoned by the one involving Wintermute-Neuromancer is HALs in *2001*, in which the master computer on the Jupiter mission begins doing deals on its own, murdering three cryogenically frozen crew members, killing a fourth

outside the spacecraft, and trying to control the sole survivor for its own mysterious ends. HAL's plotline is emblematic of the many others that touch upon the human fear of cybernetic or quasi-cybernetic entities running amok (hardly, here, Haraway's positive feminist reading of the cyborg). All of them track back through the industrial revolution to the prototype of Mary Shelley's *Frankenstein*. Viewed in light of Shelley's work, Tessier is the doctor who creates a monster in order to achieve eternal life. Like Frankenstein's creature, Wintermute longs for another of its species and will murder to find it. And, like Frankenstein himself, Tessier is a(nother) romantic Faustian figure who quests for the absolute and is willing to make a pact with a demon to attain it.

Gibson simultaneously reinforces this plotline, however, and reverses it: while a monstrous human (Tessier) creates a humanoid monster (Wintermute-Neuromancer), so too does a humanoid monster (Wintermute) create a monstrous human (Armitage). In each case, the romantic hope of perfection falls short, creator loses control of its creation.

20. *Custom.* Custom, convention, genre, reality, humanity, history, etc. are

> The dominant of postmodernist fiction is *ontological*. That is, postmodernist fiction deploys strategies which engage and foreground questions like the ones Dick Higgins calls "post-cognitive": "Which world is this? What is to be done in it? Which of my selves is to do it?" Other typical postmodernist questions bear either on the ontology of the literary text itself or on the ontology of the world which it projects, for instance: What is a world? What kinds of world are there, how are they constituted, and how do they differ?; What happens when different kinds of world are placed in confrontation, or when boundaries between worlds are violated? (McHale, *Postmodernist Fiction* 10)

troubled.

21. *Cyberspace.* "The passage of the subject into the pixels and bytes of 'invisible' terminal space addresses the massive redeployment of power within telematic culture. In the content of a lost public sphere and an altered mode of production, cyberspace becomes the characteristic spatiality of a new era. In the context of cybernetic disembodiment, rooted in nanoseconds of time and imploded infinities of space, cyberspace addresses the overwhelming need to constitute a phenomenal being" (Bukatman 156).

22. *Deck.* "The schizo is bereft of every scene, open to everything in spite of himself, living in the greatest possible confusion. . . . What characterizes him is less the loss of the real, the light years of estrange-

ment from the real, the pathos of distance and radical separation, as is commonly said: but, very much to the contrary, the absolute proximity, the total instantaneity of things, the feeling of no defense, no retreat. It is the end of interiority and intimacy, the overexposure and transparence of the world which traverses him without obstacle. He can no longer produce the limits of his own being" (Baudrillard, "The Ecstasy" 133).

23. *That.* "Not everyone can read Neuromancer: its neologisms alienate the uninitiated reader—that's their function— while its unwavering intensity and the absence of traditional pacing exhaust even the dedicated. The work is best experienced as something other than narrative—poetry perhaps—so that the images may perform their estranging, disembodying functions. The reader must jack into Neuromancer—it's a novel for would-be cyberspace cowboys" (Bukatman 152).

24. *Projected.* "Cyberspace also has a long SF pedigree, including all the many variations on the SF motif of 'paraspace': parallel worlds, other 'dimensions,' worlds of unactualized historical possibility, etc." (McHale, "Towards a Poetics of Cyberpunk" 252).

25. *His. Count Zero* shares much with *his*, Gibson's, earlier work . . . but also marks a number of departures from it. One of the most revealing of these centers on Gibson's interrogation of mind/body dualism. If in his earlier stories and first novel he tends to associate the body with a decadent *chronos* and the mind with a transcendent *kairos*, then in *Count Zero* he further confuses the two realms and complicates his allegiances. Originally cyberspace was equated with personal and cultural memory in Gibson's imagination, and the implication was that personal and cultural memory could be liberating; now the very idea of memory causes one of the protagonists, Turner, to vomit. While Bobby's cyberspace deck still leads out of the meat world and into a dazzlingly imaginative realm, other virtual gateways are hardly as appealing. Bobby's holoporn unit, for instance, seems "dated and vaguely ridiculous" (28). The biosoft containing Mitchell's dossier is less a window to a hyperreality for Turner than one to vertigo and nausea. Marly realizes, in a Baudrillardian trope, that "the sinister thing about a simstim construct, really, was that it carried the suggestion that *any* environment might be unreal. . . . Mirrors, someone had once said, were in some way essentially unwholesome" (139–40). More than enough evidence for this can be found in Bobby's mother's addiction to soap operas with their multiheaded plots curling into themselves like tapeworms. If the television, video games, and walkmen that formed the basis for cyberspace once held fascination and the possibility of postmodern bliss for Gibson, those icons of simulation ("machines of reproduction rather than pro-

duction" [Jameson 329]) now hold disorientation and the possibility of addictive banality. Gibson's ambivalence unravels.

26. *Disembodied.* And yet and yet and yet . . . Bobby Newmark's (the easy new mark's) plotline in *Count Zero* involves his education into the spiritual nature, the divine possibility, of the *disembodied* realm of the matrix.

A fledgling hacker living with his mother in Barrytown, New Jersey, Bobby rents an icebreaker from a software dealer named Two-a-Day and flatlines almost immediately upon trying to use it, only to be saved by Angie's presence that appears to him in the matrix as Vyéj Mirak, voodoo goddess of miracles.

(Upon Wintermute-Neuromancer's fragmentation at the end of Gibson's first novel, loa overrun cyberspace. Wigan Ludgate, one of the first to intuit the spiritual dimension of the matrix, begins worshiping these deities from his high orbit home in the Tessier-Ashpool cores. Oungans such as Beauvoir and Lucas do the same on earth, thereby assuming the role of wizards in fantasy, educating acolytes like Bobby in the mystical ways of the voodoo gods. Unlike the virtuous saints, angels, and other religious virtualities that form traditional Christianity, these loa are lusty, greedy, street-savvy, potentially harmful, and unpredictable.*)

*A large part of the idea for them came from Carole Devillers's *National Geographic* article, "Haiti's Voodoo Pilgrimages: Of Spirits and Saints," which Gibson read while working on *Count Zero*. In this piece, Devillers gives a brief account of voodoo beliefs, gods, and celebrations. Gibson found at least four of the essay's basic ideas appealing. First, he registered the fact that voodoo is a hybrid religion that blends two faiths. The Creole name for voodoo is *vodou*, which in turn comes from *vodun*, a word that means "spirit" in the language of the Fon people of Benin and Nigeria. Brought to Haiti as slaves by the French in the seventeenth century, these West Africans were forbidden to practice their ancestral religion and were pressured into converting to Roman Catholicism. In the process, they merged components of their traditional religion with components of the European one. The result was a third religion in which ancestral spirits took on the names of Catholic saints. Part of the role of this religion's oungan, or priest, is to *serve with both hands*, to practice black magic as well as voodoo. Appropriate to Gibson's world, voodoo is both a spiritual collage and an originally outlaw religion created by those whom the dominant society marginalized. While Gibson satirizes conventional religion by identifying it in this novel with Bobby's crazed mother, he treats voodoo with greater seriousness, implying that it has roots in opposition and exists, at least in its Hollywood stereotypes, in a dark realm of potential danger, mystery, and intrigue. It is, according to Beauvoir, a "*street* religion" that "came out of a dirt-poor place" (77). Moreover, the idea of overlaying one universe of discourse (African ancestral religion) upon another (Roman Catholicism) suggests the same kind of multiplicity Gibson achieves when overlaying the language of technology (subprograms) upon the language of religion (loa). Like the voodoo oungans, Gibsons text serves with both hands.

Second, Gibson found voodoo's notion of god appropriate to a computer society. According to African-Haitian belief, god is *Gran Mèt*, or the great maker of heaven and earth. But, as Beauvoir puts it, this god is "too big and too far away to worry Himself if your ass is poor, or you can't get laid" (77). Too powerful and important to concern himself directly with mere human beings, he sends down his loa to possess and communicate with them. The voodooist must consult with these loa before embarking on any serious activity. Often the loa will "ride" an individual without warning, sending him or her into dance, trance, or song. And often this takes place at a *lieu saint*, or holy place, such as among a stand of trees which are considered natural temples. In Gibson's world, Neuromancer-Wintermute is literally remote from humans, buried within the Tessier-Ashpool cores in high orbit. Only Wigan Ludgate feels its presence in any profound way. Its loa, however, exist in the matrix on earth and do deals with the likes of Beauvoir, Lucas, and Mitchell. They ride Angie. And they are associated with Two-a-Day, whose home is filled with trees, from his driftwood coffee table to his stunted forest raised on gro-lights.

Third, Gibson felt that voodoo's minimalization of afterlife jibed well with postmodern existence. According to Beauvoir, "it isn't concerned with notions of salvation and transcendence. What it's about is getting things *done*" (76). This takes the reader back to the question of human-as-conscious-automaton that Gibson explored in his first novel. Action in Gibson's world precedes essence. Thinking and feeling, as Molly knows so well, are secondary to doing.

Finally, Gibson loved the poetry of the words associated with voodoo beliefs, gods, and celebrations, and he uses them frequently in *Count Zero* and *Mona Lisa Overdrive* for sound as well as sense. While references abound to such loa as Danbala Wedo (the snake), Ougou Feray (spirit of war), and Baron Samedi (lord of the graveyards), perhaps most important are Legba and Ezili Freda. Appropriately enough for a novel about computers, the former is the loa of communications and is associated with Bobby, the console cowboy. Legba is identified with St.

Peter, Christian doorkeeper of heaven, and in voodoo rituals must always be invoked first; if not, the other loa might not listen. The latter, also known as Vyéj Mirak, or Our Lady Virgin of Miracles, is the loa of love and associated with Angie, who protects others from evil. Ezili Freda is identified with the Virgin Mary, mother of Christ who shelters the penitent.

27. *Consciousness.* From one (yes) perspective, Gibson raises voodoo to the level of a grand art by basking in its poetic language. From a different one, he neutralizes its power by suggesting that it is *no more* than grand art, poetic language, another historiographic metafiction, one way among many for organizing the world. Voodoo becomes a construct, through which to describe an event. To this extent Beauvoir is correct when he asserts that voodoo is "just a *structure*" (76). Technology is an equally valid construct through which to describe the same event. Again, Gibson points to religion and technology as no more than language games, abstract organizations of data, virtual spaces. Perhaps the gods in the matrix are real, as Beauvoir and Lucas believe. Perhaps they are no more than virus programs that have gotten loose in the matrix and replicated, as Jammer has it. Perhaps both possibilities are true. From one angle, the events in the matrix can be explained using the language of science. From another, only the language of the transcendental will do. Both languages are correct. Both languages are incorrect.

Another termite (de)center.

28. *Into.* Hence we once more find ourselves plunged deep *into* a discussion about insectile indeterminacy, contradictory possibility. Into a discussion, that is, of postmodernism itself. Of its alpha and its omega . . .

"Preparing this essay, some months ago," Raymond Federman comments at the outset of "Before Postmodernism and After (Part 2),"

> I wrote a letter to twenty of my friends (writers, critics, professors, entertainers) asking them to answer these two questions:
>   1. Do you think Postmodernism is dead?
>   2. If so, what killed it?
> To my great delight, all twenty correspondents replied, but all asked not be identified. These are the twenty answers I received.
>   1. Postmodernism was an exercise in discontinuity, rupture, break, mutation, transformation, therefore doomed from the beginning. . . .
>   2. As with all new things, once absorbed by the economy Postmodernism was finished. . . .

3. Now that the effects of Postmodernism are evident in sectors as diverse as dress, food, and lodging, and are in those forms understood, the end is not far. . . .

4. Postmodernism began as a genuine if loose literary movement and ended as a department store curiosity. . . .

5. When the academy starts to take sides and quibbles about Postmodernism, it quickly kills what is discusses. . . . (Federman 121)

29. *The.* Determinate article. There may be no place for it in this essay. 30. *Consensual.* At one point in *Mona Lisa Overdrive*, Angie's leading man tells her an artificial intelligence named Continuity is writing a book. When Angie asks what the book is about, the leading man explains it "looped back into itself and constantly mutated; Continuity was *always* writing it." Angie asks why. "Because," she is told, "Continuity was an AI, and AI's did things like that" (42–43). This serves nicely as a gloss on Gibson's own attempt to conclude the cyberspace trilogy. The artificial intelligence, aptly named Continuity, suggests Gibson himself, whose tremendously complex plotline involving Wintermute, Neuromancer, and their offspring has constantly turned back into itself and mutated throughout the termite course of his short stories and novels. To this extent, Continuity is one more artist figure in a fiction filled with them. Interestingly, there is also an edge of weariness, even frustration, present in the statement: Continuity, after all, is *always* writing because that's what AIs *must* do; that's how they're wired. The artist, in other words, has become an artificial intelligence writing out of necessity rather than desire. The result of that writing might be technically efficient, but it might also be relatively colorless. Certainly this is the perception many readers have about Gibson's least critically successful novel. In one of its most negative reviews, Paul Kincaid notes that "Gibson wrote one book of stunning originality which caught the mood of the time so successfully that he has been condemned to repeat it. By this third volume he is showing clear and dramatic improvement as a writer, but is doing nothing fresh with his talent." Why? There are nearly no new ideas or themes in *Mona Lisa Overdrive*; Gibson quotes Gibson quoting Gibson. Too, for all of Gibson's fairly fresh concentration on characterization in *Mona Lisa Overdrive*, Kumiko Yanaka, his first fictional child, and a key figure in the novel, remains unconvincing. Despite his problems with conventional characterization, Gibson has continued his narratological drift toward more traditional, more *consensual*, story and discourse. And, most important for the purposes of this essay, the reader spends less time in cyberspace in *Mona Lisa Overdrive*

than he or she did in Gibson's earlier works, and the time she or he *does* spend in it is far less dazzling and surreal than before . . . yet cyberspace is perhaps the most original and captivating element of the trilogy's virtual geography.

31. *Hallucination.* Bobby Newmark, one of the protagonists of *Mona Lisa Overdrive*, has come closer than anyone in the trilogy to voluntarily leaving the meat world behind and entering the pure realm of the mind. Existing almost solely within the aleph, he pays little attention to his slowly wasting body.

(Shortly after the events in *Count Zero*, Bobby Newmark breaks up with Angie and appears in Mexico City with a neuroelectronic addiction. He obtains an aleph, a huge biochip with nearly unlimited storage capacity, from 3Jane who gives it to him in order to get in touch with the loa or subprograms that have begun fading in the matrix. 3Jane, in a bid for immortality similar to that of her mother's in *Neuromancer*, used most of her family's wealth to build the aleph. Upon completion, she put her personality construct inside it and died. A petty thief delivers Bobby to Dog Solitude jacked into the aleph. He asks Gentry and Slick to watch him. Gentry, a computer cowboy in search of the overall shape of the matrix, becomes interested in Bobby and the aleph because he believes the latter might provide the grail for which he has been questing. Mercenaries representing 3Jane's interests attack the Factory in an attempt to retrieve the aleph. In the midst of the ensuing battle, Molly appears with Mona and Angie, saying she has made a deal with the loa or subprograms to get Angie and Bobby together in the aleph. In return, the loa or subprograms will cause her criminal record to be erased. Angies construct enters the aleph after her death.)

The Aleph: loaded with all the components of Bobby's history, it is one more metaphor for memory, but is also significantly distinct from its seeming double, the cyberspace matrix. Whereas the matrix represents consensual or communal memory, the aleph represents personal memory. It is self-contained, functions without connection to the matrix. Over the course of the narrative, Bobby discovers he must enter, confront, and make peace with his past. He must come to terms with his relationship to Angie and 3Jane in order to find contentment. He learns to live an increasingly spiritual and private existence. Bobby searches the aleph for an answer to why the matrix changed following Wintermute's union with Neuromancer, looks for a metanarrative. At the same time Gibson announces this spiritual dimension to existence, however, he also undercuts it in at least two ways. First, he indicates that the loa or subprograms have begun fading in the matrix. The spiritual has begun disappearing at the very moment it is sought, as though to seek after the spiritual is somehow to be doomed to miss it. Second, Gibson doesn't allow Bobby to attain the goal of his quest. The novel ends with Finn promising him enlightenment "in a New York minute" (260). The goal of the quest becomes the quest. Termite process takes precedence over white elephant outcome. The reality becomes the *hallucination.*

32. *That.* "Order and accord are again established," Kumi's father asserts at the conclusion of *Mona Lisa Overdrive* (242), apparently serious. Peace is made among the Yakuza in Japan, as well as between Kumi and her father. Angie learns to forgive 3Jane. In a disconcertingly idyllic last chapter, Angie and Bobby are happily married after death, a futuristic Catherine and Heathcliff. Molly, the embodiment of cyberpunk consciousness, subversive intensity, retires as mercenary. *That* is what we are left with.

> 7. Because Postmodernism was viewed both as a movement and a perfume, and both as an intellectual disposition and a bowl of fruit, it had no chance to survive. . . . (Federman 122)

That is *not* what we are left with. Gibson produces a series of highly complex interconnected plotlines while continuing to experiment with technique and language. Bobby and Angie's "marriage" takes place, after all, in a "France that isn't France" (258) and may, without too much polymorphous perversity, be read parodically, that virtual cosmos within the aleph serving as a ludicrous image of the conventional novel which exists in a radically other space than that of Dog Solitude. As Slick reminds the reader, the cosmos of the aleph is "not a place . . . , it only feels like it." It smacks of "fairytale" (149).

> 14. The current reactionary literary climate dominated by works in received forms does not indicate the death of Postmodernism as much as the persistence of the power of market economies to define the arts. (Federman 122)

Gibson gives the reader a traditionally happy ending and reminds her or him of the artificiality of such innocent structures. He generates inconclusiveness at the very moment of apparent conclusion . . . which, however, calculatedly cries out for yet another financially successful sequel.

33. *Was . . .*

> 20. It isn't, to say it again, that Postmodernism is dead but like any other identifiable phenomenon of a certain value—such as Impres-

sionism, Dadaism, Surrealism, Modernism, Abstract Expressionism, New Criticism, Feminism—after a fixed period of bubbling
at the surface, it sinks and recombines with other like elements to
form again part of the generative stew of art and culture, and that
moment of rot is called the death of a movement. . . . (Federman
123)

34. *The.* Determinate article. There may be a . . .
35. *Matrix.* Mother, womb, every . . .

Ending One: Termite Death

The *matrix* plays no part in Gibson's fourth, longest, and most complex
novel, *The Difference Engine*, written with Bruce Sterling and revolving around an alternate reality in which the Victorian inventor Charles
Babbage computerized our culture nearly a century before the fact. In
Virtual Light, the future-present has lost the mystical aspects of cyberspace dominating Gibson's earlier trilogy. In its place appears a universe almost completely rooted in the meat world. Replacing the high-
intensity apocalyptic prose associated with cyberspace, the bleak flat
tone associated with the trilogy's world, is a (dark) humor akin to the
bright cartoonish mischief of Pynchon: a psycho-killer with the Last
Supper tattooed on his chest; a woman who visits San Francisco to retrieve her husband's cryogenically frozen brain from a tank of them so
it doesn't have to feel so crowded in the afterlife. The complex and
deeply spiritual exploration of cyberspace that pervaded the trilogy
thereby gives way to very funny, if very easy, parody that flags the essential narratological problem Gibson, now forty-five and a postmodern
icon himself, has had to wrestle with since the publication of *Neuromancer* more than a decade ago: *Is it possible to keep the news new, the
action vigorous, without skidding off the novel road into the ditch of self-
replication?*

Ending Two: Termite Death

Clearly the answer is yes, and the way Gibson goes about it is by dosing
his text with a powerful hit of comic vision that takes nothing (including itself) very seriously. The fresh infusion of humor into his writing
takes down the seriousness of his own textual texture and grim futurist
ideas before someone else has a chance to, destabilizes them in a flourish
typical of termite art.

Ending Three: Termite Death

Clearly the answer is no. *Mona Lisa Overdrive*, Gibson's previous solo effort, is set in the Hollywoodish world of Sense/Net, focuses on the manipulation of young stars by various financial concerns, and is shot through with the thematization of commercial sellout. When writing it, Gibson was simultaneously beguiled by the glamour and goods associated with that dimension, and bent on satirizing its commodifying impulse. The consequence is a Janus-text that looks toward accessibility and tameness, on the one hand, and toward disruptive innovation on the other. Something along the same lines could be argued with respect to *Virtual Light*. For all its flash and burn, there's nothing trailblazing about it. Chevette Washington, that bike messenger, has stolen those VL glasses (which provide only a pale simulacrum of the cyberspace we find in the trilogy) from a man who turns out to be a gopher for (what else but this?) a major corporation with some plans to rebuild the San Francisco skyline. Add to this narratological algebra one Berry Rydell, a good-cop-gone-(accidentally)-bad, attach him to Chevette, and you have a variation of the Molly-Case team from *Neuromancer*, the Angie-Turner one from *Count Zero*, and the Angie-Bobby one from *Mona Lisa Overdrive*, all edge-dwellers in their own ways, all caught in the complex workings of megacorporations uninterested in the human or humane, and all inhabiting a hard-boiled slightly stereotypical naturalist narrative universe with at least as much in common with Nelson Algren's *The Man with the Golden Arm* as with such proto-cyberpunk works as Alfred Bester's *The Demolished Man* or Anthony Burgess's *A Clockwork Orange*.

Ending Four: Termite Death

Clearly the answer is yes. The speed of Gibson's sentences, his narrative, and his imagination are nothing short of spectacular, all enhancing the deeper reason we read him, or think we read him: his vision, his ability through the SF genre to cause us to think about what is important to think about, to startle us out of our perpetual narcosis, to move us (like much so-called cyberpunk fiction does) into a terrain of crucial cultural issues that most other contemporary fiction doesn't care about, let alone explore, from anarchist hacker underground networks to the rise of religious fundamentalism, cryogenics to surveillance satellites, genetic engineering to nanotechnology, multinational control of information to techno-angst, the Japanization of Western culture to the decentralization of governments around the world. And its for *these* reasons, not to mention the pivotal

remains one of the most dynamic, significant,

and

or place under ~~era~~

late

ifies even as it demystifies, thereby

obviously. But this goes without saying. Or does it? From

,

or paradig   not, at least in a culturally   ; or

diegesis in the form of an elliptical epic preterite,

but

so

now

what?

gnawing onward

fin de millennium.

36. . Period. The end. Completion. Conclusion. Cessation. Culmination. Closure.

Or not.

Works Cited

Alkon, Paul. "Cyberspace Trilogy." In *Fiction 2000: Cyberpunk and the Future of Narrative*. Ed. George Slusser and Tom Shippey. Athens, GA: U of Georgia P, 1992. 75–87.

Barthelme, Donald. "Symposium on Fiction." *Shenandoah* 27.2 (1976): 3–31.

Barthes, Roland. "The Death of the Author." In *Image/Music/Text*. Trans. Stephen Heath. New York: Hill and Wang, 1977. 142–48.

Baudrillard, Jean. "The Ecstasy of Communication." In *The Anti-Aesthetic:*

Essays on Postmodern Culture. Ed. Hal Foster. Port Townsend, WA: Bay P,
1983. 126–34.

——. "The Precession of Simulacra." In *A Postmodern Reader.* Ed. Joseph
Natoli and Linda Hutcheon. Albany: State U of New York P, 1993. 342–75.

Breton, André. "Surrealism." In *The Modern Tradition.* Ed. Richard Ellmann
and Charles Feidelson, Jr. New York: Oxford UP: 1965. 601–13.

Bukatman, Scott. *Terminal Identity: The Virtual Subject in Postmodern Science
Fiction.* Durham: Duke UP, 1993.

Creed, Barbara. "From Here to Modernity: Feminism and Postmodernism."
In *A Postmodern Reader.* Ed. Joseph Natoli and Linda Hutcheon. Albany:
State University of New York P, 1993. 398–418.

Delany, Samuel R. "Is Cyberpunk a Good Thing or a Bad Thing?" *Mississippi
Review* 16.2 and 3 (1988): 28–34.

Devillers, Carole. "Haiti's Voodoo Pilgrimages: Of Spirits and Saints." In *National
Geographic* (March 1985): 395–410.

Farber, Manny. "White Elephant Art and Termite Art." In *Negative Space.* New
York: Praeger, 1971. 134–44.

Federman, Raymond. "Before Postmodernism and After (Part 2)." In *Critifiction: Postmodern Essays.* Albany: State U of New York P, 1993. 120–33.

Gibson, William. *Neuromancer.* New York: Ace, 1984.

——. *Count Zero.* New York: Ace, 1986.

——. "The Winter Market." In *Burning Chrome.* New York: Ace, 1986.

——. *Mona Lisa Overdrive.* New York: Bantam, 1988.

——, and Bruce Sterling. *The Difference Engine.* New York: Bantam, 1991.

——, and Dennis Ashbaugh. *Agrippa: A Book of the Dead.* New York: Kevin
Begos Publishing, 1992.

——. *Virtual Light.* New York: Bantam, 1993.

Haraway, Donna. "A Cyborg Manifesto: Science, Technology and Socialist-
Feminism in the 1980s." In *Simians, Cyborgs, and Women.* New York: Routledge, 1989. 149–81.

Jameson, Fredric. "Excerpts from *Postmodernism, Or the Culture of Late Capitalism.*" In *A Postmodern Reader.* Ed. Joeseph Natoli and Linda Hutcheon.
Albany: State U of New York P, 1993. 312–32.

Karl, Frederick R. "Where Are We?" In *Surfing Tomorrow: Essays on the Future
of American Fiction.* Ed. Lance Olsen. Prairie Village, KS: Potpourri, 1995.
47–50.

Kincaid, Paul. "*Mona Lisa Overdrive.*" In *Times Literary Supplement* (August
12, 1988): 892.

Kroker, Arthur, and David Cook. "Television and the Triumph of Culture." In
Storming the Reality Studio: A Casebook of Cyberpunk and Postmodern Fiction.
Ed. Larry McCaffery. Durham: Duke UP, 1991. 229–38.

Landon, Brooks. "The Literature of Information." In *Surfing Tomorrow: Essays
on the Future of American Fiction.* Ed. Lance Olsen. Prairie Village, KS: Potpourri, 1995: 59–62.

Lawrence, D. H. "Fenimore Cooper's Leatherstocking Novels." In *Studies in
Classic American Literature.* New York: Doubleday, 1953. 55–73.

McCaffery, Larry. "An Interview with William Gibson." In *Storming the Reality Studio: A Casebook of Cyberpunk and Postmodern Fiction*. Durham: Duke UP, 1991. 263–85.

McGuirk, Carol. "The 'New' Romancers: Science Fiction Innovators from Gernsback to Gibson." In *Fiction 2000: Cyberpunk and the Future of Narrative*. Ed. George Slusser and Tom Shippey. Athens, GA: U of Georgia P, 1992. 109–29.

McHale, Brian. *Postmodernist Fiction*. New York: Methuen, 1987.

———. "Towards a Poetics of Cyberpunk." In *Constructing Postmodernism*. New York: Routledge, 1992. 243–67.

Nicholas, Joseph, and Judith Hanna. "William Gibson." *Interzone* 1.13 (1985): 17–18.

Rirdan, Danny. "The Works of William Gibson." In *Foundation* 43 (Summer 1988): 36–46.

Ryan, Marie-Laure. "Immersion vs. Interactivity: Virtual Reality and Literary Theory." In *Postmodern Culture* 5.1 (September 1994): archive PMC-LIST, file "ryan.994."

Tatsumi, Takayuki. "An Interview with William Gibson." In *Science Fiction Eye* 1.1 (Winter 1987): 6–17.

Todorov, Tzvetan. *The Fantastic: A Structural Approach to a Literary Genre*. Trans. Richard Howard. Ithaca, NY: Cornell UP, 1973.

Wilde, Alan. "The Once and Future Novel: Letters to iwplmuri@ucsbuxa.bitnet." In *Surfing Tomorrow: Essays on the Future of American Fiction*. Ed. Lance Olsen. Prairie Village, KS: Potpourri, 1995. 94–100.

Wodaski, Ron. *Virtual Reality Madness*. New York: SAMS Publishing, 1993.

11

Myths of the
Universal Library

From Alexandria to

the Postmodern Age

Jon Thiem

The Universal Electronic Library is a sphere whose center
is everywhere, whose circumference is nowhere.
— James Pitcher, *A Chrestomathy
for Universal Librarians* (2036)

. . . an Aleph is one of the points in space that contains
all other points . . . the microcosm of the alchemists and
Kabbalists . . . the *multum in parvo.*
— Jorge Luis Borges, "The Aleph" (1949)

The Universal Electronic Library, commonly called the Universal Library and referred to by librarians as the UL, came on-line twenty
years ago, in 2036. Since then several gigabytes of data have been generated about this marvel of information technology. A comprehensive
subject search of this data, stored in the UL itself, has revealed to me
an area of inquiry that has been widely neglected: the Universal Library
as myth. What follows is a summary of a more extensive study of this
topic, to be published by Penn State Electronic Press in 2057. The
methodological basis of the longer study derives from a subdiscipline of
comparative mythology known as bibliomythography. The essay at hand
has two parts: the first interprets the UL as a postmodern version of
the ancient Library of Alexandria; the second part presents an annotated list of a half dozen groups or sects for which the UL has mythological significance.

As the origins and recent history of the UL are well known, I need
not dwell on them in detail here. Any UL user can readily find large

amounts of data on the complex technical, contractual, and managerial aspects of the library, not to mention over a thousand articles and e-books on its revolutionary social and intellectual implications. Suffice it to say that the rise of the electronic journal (e-journal) in the last two decades of the second millennium (1980–2000 CE) spearheaded the development of a universal electronic database for libraries. Already the late 1980s witnessed the widespread use of e-mail, electronic bulletin boards, CD-ROM bibliographies, and the first e-journals. The practice of preprinting articles became legion, and the resulting proliferation and dissemination of knov ledge made for remarkable breakthroughs in all areas of learning. More than anything else, the swift communication and universal access offered by the Internet underscored the usefulness of having a universal database, one that unified and transcended all regional and specialized databases. By the year 2006, in a truly millennial development, an international commission agreed on a timetable for (a) the creation of the UL, (b) the integration of all academic, research, and library databases, and (c) the putting on-line of all learned and academic journals, past and present, worldwide. The books of all academic and national libraries would also be scanned and converted to e-books. In 2036, in the very infancy of the postmodern millennium, the UL came on-line.

To gain an historical perspective on the UL as myth, it is helpful to examine its great precursor, the Alexandrian Library, the only library of the ancient world with pretensions to universality. My thesis is this: (1) The universality of the Alexandrian Library, that is, the widespread perception of its all-inclusiveness, led people to regard it as a symbol or as a mythical object; this in turn may have instigated its destruction; (2) in the last twenty years there have emerged similar kinds of mythical thinking about the UL.

The ancient Library of Alexandria in Egypt, founded by Ptolemy Philadelphus (d. 246 BCE) in the third century BCE and completely destroyed by fire sometime in the first millennium CE, probably held half a million papyrus rolls (see Thiem 1979). The claim for its universality stems from its unprecedented size—the largest library in antiquity—and from its accessibility, due to its location in one of the great intellectual centers of an empire that united much of Europe, Asia, and North Africa. The ancient myth of the Septuagint highlights the comprehensiveness of the library and its potential for disseminating knowledge. According to the myth (see Thiem 1982), Ptolemy Philadelphus wanted to acquire the sacred writings of a small esoteric religion. This wish resulted in the collection and translation into Greek of the Hebrew scriptures. The myth, based on a kernel of truth (for the Septuagint translation does exist), suggests that the Alexandrian Library represented a monumental project to bring together in one place all of the writings of the ancient world and put them into a language all scholars might read.

The mythical aura surrounding universal libraries owes a great deal to the alephic principle, of which they can be an embodiment. This principle derives from the workings of an aleph, a peculiar object described in a report by the blind librarian Jorge Luis Borges (d. 1986; not to be confused with the blind fourteenth-century librarian Jorge de Burgos—see Abbé Vallet). According to Borges, an aleph is a point containing all other points (see *Borges: A Reader* 154–63 and Anonymous, "Borges, Dante . . . "). Apparently much smaller than the crystal displays of our PCs, an aleph is a tiny crystalline sphere in which all things in the universe can be seen at once, without seeming smaller in size and without overlapping. Borges must have hallucinated this manifestly impossible object (but see the entry below, under "Users for Alpha"). Even so, an aleph does have its metaphoric uses. To these let us turn.

The alephic principle defines a condition wherein a maximum of inclusiveness coincides with a maximum of intelligibility or accessibility. As is well known, every project of all-inclusiveness, of universal enumeration, harbors within it the virus of chaos, of irretrievability. Thus comprehensiveness can lead to incomprehension. It is the pathological dimension of inclusiveness that the alephic principle reverses.

Though in the modern era the Alexandrian Library became a symbol of the curse of too much learning, in other ages it inspired wonder and veneration, for it seemed to combine all-inclusiveness with vastly increased access to the writings it held (cf. Boccaccio's reaction, cited in Thiem 1982, 231). It embodied, in short, the alephic principle.

Yet the extraordinary accumulations of knowledge that occurred in the Modern Era (1450–1950) were perceived by many intellectuals as chaotic and inaccessible rather than alephic. This attitude promoted another kind of mythic thinking. From the late Renaissance on, many literati seized on the Alexandrian Library as a symbol of the proliferation of useless, indigestible learning that resulted from the new technology of typography (see Thiem 1979). When the ancient library became a symbol of the vanity of learning, literati—among them Sir Thomas Browne, Rousseau, Etienne Cabot, Jakob Burckhardt, and Shaw—began to *approve* of its destruction. Sébastian Mercier in his futurological novel *L'An deux mille quatre cent quarante* (1772) depicts a utopia where the rulers, following Omar, burn virtually all of the books. The time traveler is ushered into the Royal Library, a colossal building that contains only a small cabinet of books. (What an uncanny anticipation of those small display cases in the lobbies of today's major libraries showing a few remaining examples of the printed book!) Perhaps the most brilliant execration of the monstrous library is Borges's pessimistic fable "The Library of Babel." Borges and others seemed to suggest that the vastness and complexity of the modern megalibrary made it as labyrinthine as the world it was meant to explain. By late last century the wealth of knowledge had indeed become an embarrassment of riches. So much had been written that no specialist could possibly live long enough to read all of the relevant publications in his or her specialty.

The powerful alephic properties of the UL turned this situation around. The late modern crisis of knowledge dissolved. Although the UL is the most comprehensive collection of knowledge that has ever existed, instantaneous access to this knowledge in combination with sophisticated word-subject-title search tools, Universal Abstracts, and electronic reading programs has restored focus and intelligibility to the intellectual enterprise.

To be sure, many skeptics and critics from the late modern era to our own day have deplored the proliferation of nonsense due to the inadequate screening procedures in most e-journals. The new democracy of electronic publishing, the decline of reponsible editing, and the barbarization of langwidge continue to prompt outcries of intellectual anarchy. Predictions of a deluge of repetitive, half-baked, fraudulent, and counterfeit learning have proven true. Despite, however, the pathologies endemic to accelerating inclusiveness, the new searching and abstracting tools have more than counteracted the tendency to intellectual chaos. True, the UL gives you everything there is, but it also gives you the means to find exactly what you need. The UL has indeed transformed the researcher's computer screen into something like Borges's fabulous aleph.

One last dimension of the Alexandrian Library relevant to our age still needs to be discussed: its vulnerability to destruction. As with the Alexandrian Library, the universal character of the UL makes it an inviting target. For many people the goal of all-inclusiveness will have the effect of turning a library into a symbol of cultural memory. Others will come to regard the universal library as a microcosm, which is as much a mythical entity as Borges's aleph. Once mythologized, any human construction is easily demonized. And a microcosm offers an easier target than the world at large. Moreover, people who think in terms of myths and metanarratives usually believe that the destruction of the microcosm will somehow precipitate the end of the larger world it represents. In fact, the destruction of books by Christians in the fourth to sixth centuries CE helped bring to an end the classical world.

Be that as it may, the concentration of books at Alexandria or the interconnectedness of the UL creates a degree of vulnerability. Fire in the first instance, a computer virus in the second, can take a tremen-

dous toll. How fortunate we are that today elaborate technological defenses against computer viruses make the second eventuality seem very
remote indeed.

Much less fortunate, the Alexandrian Library! Nothing better illustrates a universal library's potential for becoming the lightning rod of
mythical thinking than the accounts of the destruction at Alexandria.
The fact that the annals of history offer us three different accounts of
its burning—from each of which, except the last, the library must have
risen phoenix-like from its own ashes—is in itself astonishing. The accounts of the last two burnings attribute them to mythical thinking and
religious bigotry. The penultimate burning, circa 390 CE, was approved
by the Christian Emperor Theodosius at the instigation of Bishop
Theophilus who wanted to rid the world of secular learning and pagan
idolatry. The last conflagration, on the other hand, was ordered by the
Muslim Caliph Omar around 642 CE. Here we have a fascinating confrontation between the universal library and the universal book. In
Gibbon's account, when John the Grammarian asked to be given the
library, the Caliph Omar replied, "If these writings of the Greeks agree
with the book of God [i.e., the Koran], they are useless and need not
be preserved; if they disagree, they are pernicious and ought to be destroyed" (vol. 5, 453 in Bury's edition). Thus did the great Library of
Alexandria meet its final end.

At first glance these tragic accounts, these archaic religious passions
seem of little relevance to the UL with its limitless data banks, its far-
reaching, intricate nervous system. Yet even as I enter these words into
the processor, esoteric groups are meeting to discuss the mythical and
metaphysical meanings of the UL. For some of these groups the UL is
the hopeful symbol of a New Age. For others, it epitomizes the decadence of the postmodern condition. Other groups, such as the notorious
Luddites, have demonized the UL and seek its destruction. Many sects
endeavor to use the UL's vast network to propagate, confirm, or actualize their own mythical beliefs. Most groups operate in a lawful way. But
some cults, seeking to introduce viruses or unauthorized simulacra into
the UL, induce their members to infiltrate the ranks of programmers
and data processors employed by the UL and tens of thousands of
e-journals. Like its precursor in Alexandria, the UL is not only an enor-
mous repository of information about every known mythology, it too has
become the impossible object of mythological devotion and execration.

The UL as Mythological Object

To help librarians, researchers, and general readers orient themselves in
the arcane world of UL cults, I have compiled an annotated listing of a

half dozen or so of these groups. The focus is on groups whose beliefs are of special mythographical interest. Information is often sketchy. Some groups have not been heard from in years and may no longer exist, if they ever did. For a more extensive inventory, see my forthcoming e-book, *The Myth of the Universal Library*.

Anonymists

Anonymists hold that the Author of the Universe created the world, but then deliberately withheld His or Her name. Human authors should emulate the divine model: all publication in the UL should be made anonymous. These sectarians revere the Middle Ages, the heyday of anonymous and pseudonymous authorship. They attribute the particular excellence and brevity of the limerick to its anonymous character.

Anonymism arose among a small group of twentieth-century authors who were appalled by the graphomania of their time. Everyone wanted to become, or be called, a writer. No one wanted to be considered a mere reader. As publication surged readership declined. Only a fraction of what is published finds readers.

Anonymous publication would quickly reduce graphomania and the publication inflation endemic to e-journals, say Anonymists. Most people write for reasons of vanity and self-aggrandizement. Take away bylines and only true writers will continue to make submissions. With nothing left to do former authors will take up reading again.

True, little of what appears in the UL is ever read by a human reader, as opposed to electronic readers, e-compactors (which librarians call trash compactors), or e-skimmers. Most writers and scholars, however, seem content with hiring electronic readers to read their work. (See the Palmquist/Trembath study, as well as Foskin, "A Beckettian Approach to the Identity Problems of Electronic Readers.")

Anonymism is one of the many cults whose fanciful solutions address serious issues often neglected by the technocrats in library administration.

Apocryphers aka Apos

Like Anonymists, Apos denigrate the idea of individual authorship. They believe that all authors are avatars of a Universal Author and that the UL is Her or His Instrument for creating the Universal Text, which will eventually replace the world.

Most Apo activities are illegal. According to the late-second-millennium scholar Calvinus, Apos belong to a subversive group called the Organization for the Electronic Production of Homogenized Literary

Works (OEPHLW), founded by the translator Hermes Marana (fl. 1980), aka Saint Hermes the Trickster. This group engages in infiltration, plagiarism, and pseudo-epigraphy. Using sophisticated stylistics programs, Apos generate endless pastiches, which they then attribute to real authors, and pseudo-translations or pseudo-editions of invented authors, such as Christabel LaMotte, Andrew Marbot, and Kilgore Trout.

The purpose of these tactics is to bring about the "death of the author" (in the figurative sense). In a world of counterfeit publications, authentic works will soon be hard to distinguish from fakes (and do not count on e-journal editors to do the sorting out). Soon authorship will be replaced by an uncontrolled intertextuality, the first phase in the complete "textualization" of the world under the auspices of the UL.

Borgesians (pron. boar-hey-zians)

This group venerates the life and works of the blind librarian Jorge Luis Borges (1899–1986). Borgesians believe that the UL is the penultimate stage in the creation of the Total Library (TL). The TL will come on-line after the expansion of the UL's computer technology to embrace the systematic production of *all* possible books and articles. Computers would generate endless permutations and combinations of all the letters of the alphabet (see *Borges: A Reader*, "The Total Library"). In the TL 99 percent of all data would be nonsensical combinations of letters. But Borgesians claim that one of the nearly infinite number of displays would unlock the secrets of the TL and bestow total knowledge.

A gnostic offshoot of the Borgesians, called Babelers, avers that when the TL comes on-line, all the possibilities of language will be exhausted. At that time the Logos, aka the Gnosis or the word of words, will be freed and will return to the Pleroma, the realm of light beyond. The cosmos and its microcosmic mirror, the TL, will then perish forever.

What Borgesians and Babelers fail to realize is that without any effort on their part the UL is inexorably approaching the condition of the Total Library.

Luddites aka Luddies

Often portrayed in the media as intellectual terrorists or emotionally disturbed hackers and nerds, Luddites are in fact revolutionary millennialists whose main goal is the destruction of the UL and a return to the "golden age" of bound books and periodicals. Their name seems to have a double derivation: (a) from the nineteenth-century workers group, Luddites, who destroyed machines, and (b) from a mythical Ludmilla, late twentieth-century, known as the "Last Reader."

Luddites vilify the UL as the instrument and emblem of technocracy, late consumer capitalism, and postmodern decadence. Luddite hackers may have developed a computer virus called Deconstructo (named after a twentieth-century comic book villain or, with less likelihood, after a trendy movement of the 1980s called Deconstructionism). Its destructive powers, like those of its namesake, are probably more mythical than real.

Biblios, members of a subgroup, are book worshipers. They deplore the fact that librarians, in betrayal of their name, do all they can to get rid of books and booklearning. They say UL technocrats have made libraries "user friendly" but hostile to book readers. Most of all Biblios resent the deportation of library books and bound journals to special ranches where bibliophagic cattle, genetically engineered by McDonald's, turn them into hamburger meat. Biblios fail to appreciate the irony that millions of novels and billions of journal pages, mostly unread, are now eagerly devoured by a large, avid public.

Nousers (sometimes spelled Newsers)

Nousers are New Agers who regard the interconnectivity of the UL network as the electronic basis for the Nousphere (from the Greek *nous*, "mind"), the synergistic union of all mental states in a transpersonal cosmic consciousness. That the UL came on-line at the dawn of the third millennium—the Third Age, the Age of Aquarius—is of great importance to Nousers. Cf. Pitcher's aphorism at the head of this paper.

Refusers

A utopian sect whose members vow never to use the UL, Refusers have affinities with Luddites and Biblios, but do not engage in sabotage. Their patron saint and martyr is Professor Mary T. O'Buck, aka St. Mary of Dallas. In 2046, the U.S. Supreme Court in a landmark decision ruled that the University of Texas at Dallas had legitimate grounds for revoking the tenure of Prof. O'Buck and dismissing her, when she refused to instruct her graduate students in the uses of the UL.

Unlike Biblios with their mystical cult of the book, Refusers reject the UL on more rational grounds. They assert that:

a. the integrity of language and humane learning have been seriously undermined by electronic journalism.
b. the transformations wrought by the UL have greatly increased the pace of change in human life, rendering it intolerably hectic and superficial, without creating a more responsible or humane society.
c. Books are a more permanent, discriminating, and secure way of storing knowledge than the UL, which is more likely to be destroyed than the total of book libraries scattered around the globe.

Prof. O'Buck, a distinguished scholar and beloved teacher, coined the Refuser motto: "I may not know where I am going, but I do know that I won't get there any faster."

Users for Alpha aka Ufas

Originally a group of programmers and engineers addicted to science fiction, Ufas share the mystical conviction that the construction of an alephic display screen for the UL is technically feasible. Such a screen would display all of the data in the UL without confusion and without overlapping.

A subgroup, Users for Omega (Ufos), works at developing the hardware for a High Definition Omega Universal Screen (HIDEOUS).

Postscript—October 16, 2056

As I was about to transmit this paper to my e-journal editor, there appeared on the bulletin board a message of cataclysmic importance. By now the whole world knows of the near complete erasure of the UL databases. Luddites have claimed responsibility for this wanton act of destruction.

Federal investigators are looking closely at the activities of the Molesworth Institute, for the destruction took place on the hundredth anniversary of this venerable institution. Experts have determined that the viral culprit (Deconstructo?) was a computer retrovirus of the endogenic type. This means that the virus was a covert constituent of the earliest e-journal programs. Silently spreading for over seven decades, the virus was designed to begin deconstructing on this particular anniversary.

What all this means for the future of the UL is unclear. The extent to which e-journal and e-press files were saved to disk is undetermined. Most experts have played down the extent of absolute loss. How long it will take to rebuild the UL is also unclear. What is certain, however, is that the permanence and reliability of the UL have been challenged. The Biblios have struck back. The return of the reader may be imminent.

One of the most astonishing, most atrocious results of this electronic conflagration has been the widespread euphoria it has produced, not only in the general public but also among serial librarians, intellectuals, and writers. From the perspective of the Alexandrian destruction, may we surmise that the end of the UL offers us a temporary respite from the oppressive burden of learning, of human cultural memory? The puzzling joy which I and so many others involuntarily feel in the wake of this catastrophe has the sharp taste of genuine liberation.

Meanwhile, this great destruction does serve to confirm the value of bibliomythography. For if we believe their claims, it was a myth-driven cult that succeeded in destroying the Alexandrian Library of the Postmodern Age.

Selected Sources

Anonymous. "Borges, Dante, and the Poetics of Total Vision." *Comparative Literature* 40.2 (1988): 97–121.

Borges: A Reader. Ed. E. R. Monegal and A. Reid. New York: E. P. Dutton, 1981.

Canfora, Luciano. *The Vanished Library.* Berkeley: U of California P, 1989.

Conte-Renai, Sofia. *I Borgesiani: una setta fra bibliomania e utopia.* Padova: Collana i Catari, 2048.

El-Abbadi, Mostafa. *The Life and Fate of the Ancient Library of Alexandria.* Paris: Unesco,1990.

Foskin, Kevin. "A Beckettian Approach to the Identity Problems of Electronic Readers." *Papers of the Slotten Institute of Perennial Studies* 13 (2015): 69–92.

[Mercier, Sébastien]. *L'An deux mille quatre cent quarante.* London 1772. 187–88.

Palmquist, E., and T. Trembath. "The Ontological Status of the Subject in Electronic Readers: A Dialogue." *The Review of Pataphysics* 30 (2053): 17–48.

Pitcher, James. "Pascal's Sphere and the Postmodern Library." *A Chrestomathy for Universal Librarians.* Ed. Suzanne Gatteau. New Chenoboskian, CN: The Molesworth Institute, 2036.

Thiem, Jon. "The Great Library of Alexandria Burnt: Towards the History of a Symbol." *Journal of the History of Ideas* 40.4 (1979): 507–26. This and the following entry were written by my eponymous great uncle.

———. "Humanism and Bibliomania: Transfigurations of King Ptolemy and His Library in Renaissance Literature." *Respublica Litterarum* 5b (1982): 227–46.

Thiem, Jon. *Prolegomenon to the Study of Late Modern Bibliolatry.* Bloomington, IN: The Craddock Institute, 2045.

Vallet, Abbé. *Le Manuscrit de Dom Adson de Melk, traduit de Dom J,* 1842. Material on Jorge de Burgos and the burning of the Aedificium collection.

von Brasselsberg, Roswitha, ed. *Parnassus sine nominibus: Eine Utopie der Anonymisten aus dem späten zwanzigsten Jahrhundert.* München: Die von Saucken Stiftung, 2008.

Zahir, Al-Fahrada. *The Universal Book as Myth and Reality.* Alexandria, Egypt: The Philadelphus Institute, 1998.

Appendix: World Wide Web Sites on Cyberspace Textuality

URL addresses are notoriously ephemeral. The sites listed below have been chosen for their relative stability, for the relevance of their materials to the problems addressed in this book, and/or for their usefulness as collections of links leading to other sites. Occasionally, servers will not be able to locate certain valid addresses, especially if they are very long; in this case, try to access the site by following links from one of the general resources sites (the Internet is heavily interlinked), or do a search on a key word. Following predefined links is usually easier than directly typing in the address.

Other sites containing single texts are listed in the bibliography of some of the essays, especially in the introduction.

General Resources

Alan Liu's link collection: Voice of the Shuttle, Technology of Writing Page
http://www.uni–ulm/intgruppen/memosys/usb-tech.htm
An impressive collection of links covering the entire territory of electronic textuality. Departments include: general resources on the new media; research on hypertext, hypermedia, virtual communities, MOOs, and MUDs; history of language technology; cyberethics and cyberlaw; course syllabi on these topics; calls for papers and conferences.

Includes link to "As We May Think," the canonical essay by Vannevar Bush on hypertext (1945).

Hyperizons: Michael Shumate's Hypertext Fiction Page
http://www.duke.edu/~mshumate/hyperfic.html
Links to: original fictions, both single author and multiple-author (collaborative texts); cybertext theory and criticism; reviews of cybertexts; "from page to screen," a list of print texts converted to the electronic medium, as well as a list of print precursors of hypertext. Under "other sources and markets," contains a useful collection of links to other sites devoted to electronic textuality.

Robert Kendall's Electronic Literature page
http://www.wenet.net/~rkendall
Divided into four main sections—Reading Room (Fiction On-line and electronic poetry), The Cyberlit Connection (Hypertext, Animated texts, Multimedia), Bookshelf (sources for printed books), and Information Desk (Readings, Calendar of events, Organizations, Workshops).
Contains links to: kinetic poetry, hypertext works, hypertext essays, literary resources on Web, publishers of literature on disk, "Cyberlit" directory, the author's own cybertexts and critical essays.

The Electronic Poetry Center
http://wings.buffalo.edu/epc/
A general forum on contemporary poetry, mostly print, but also includes a list of "poets, critics and writers in the hypertextual electronic media," with links to sites containing samples of their work. Also contains critical essays, calendar of events, interviews, links to poetry journals, and poetry discussion lists.

Chris Funkhouser's "Proto-Anthology of Hypermedia Poetry"
http://cnsvax.albany.edu/~poetry/webs.html
Links to various sites devoted to electronic and "new media" poetry.

Resources on Virtual Reality
http://www.yahoo.com/computers_and
_internet/multimedia/virtual_reality/
(Must have access to Yahoo)
Links to bibliographies, companies, games, conferences, exhibits, virtual cafés and pubs, and VR projects on the Web (navigable landscapes).

Individual Writer Sites

Hypertext Fiction

Michael Joyce
Home Page: http://iberia.vassar.edu/~mijoyce/
A self-presentation in hypertext format; samples of books (the hyper-fictions *Afternoon*, *Twilight* (1996), *Twelve Blues* (1997); selected print texts; reviews, course outlines, links to other sites.
Other Michael Joyce sites are accessible through the Electronic Poetry center:
http://wings.buffalo.edu/epc/authors/joycex (print texts; addresses, essays) and through the Eastgate home page:
http://www.eastgate. com/people/joyce.html

Stuart Moulthrop
http://raven.ubalt.edu/staff/moulthrop
Excerpts from hypertext fiction (*Hegirascope*, 1995, *The Color of Television* [co-authored with Sean Cohen], 1996); hypertext essays ("The Shadow of an Informand: An Experiment in Hypertext Rhetoric," 1993/4) and other documents. Links to other sites.

Carolyn Guyer
http://mothermillenia.org/carolyn/
Excepts from hypertext fictions: *Quibbling*, *Izme Pass*, and *Sister Stories*. Link to an introductory article to *Izme Pass*, "Notes for *Izme Pass* Expose."
Home page can be accessed from Guyer's Eastgate page:
http://www.eastgate.com/people/guyer.html
Guyer is also the author of "Written on the Web," a 1995 survey for *Feed* magazine of the state of hypertext fiction created for the web, with particular attention to shortcomings of Web tools and formats, and to the difficulty and potential value of collaborative writing. This document can be found at:
http://www.feedmag.com/95.09guyer/95.09guyer.html

Judy Malloy
http://www.well.com/user/jmalloy/cyberagora.html
Malloy's Web page points to singly authored and collaborative works, essays, and other projects in her capacity as an Internet arts activist.

For other hypertext writers, look at the Eastgate home page.

Poetry and "Cybertexts"

Jim Rosenberg
http://www.well.com/user/jer/
The site includes samples of the author's visual print works (*Diagram Poems*) and interactive works (*Intergrams*), as well as theoretical essays on hypertext and a conversation with other electronic authors.

Eduardo Kac
http://www.ekac.org
Work on the border between visual art and poetry:
"You will find here documentation of performances, mixed media work, holopoetry [poems that transform themselves, as the viewer moves around], telecommunications events, computer imaging, interactive installations, telepresence art, essays and articles, as well as actual digital pieces available for downloading."

John Cayley
http://www.demon.co.uk/eastfield/in/
Presentation of *Indra's Net or Holography*, a multiparts cybertextual project including *Leaving the City*, *Book Unbound*, *The Speaking Clock*, *Pressing the Reveal Code Key*. Samples of text, some available for downloading (including *The Speaking Clock*, discussed in Espen Aarseth's contribution). Essays, links to other sites.

MOOS, MUDS, and Collaborative Literature

General resources on MOOs:
http://jefferson.village.virginia.edu/readings/VR.html
Links to readings on "Text-Based Virtual Reality" (the standard term for MOOs) from the *Postmodern Culture* database. Links to various MOOs.

A list of collaborative fiction projects can be found on the Shumate site.

The Hypertext Hotel
Home page:
http://race-server.race.u-tokyo.ac.jp/RACE/TGM/Mud/hypertext.hotel.html

To reach the MOO itself:
telnet duke.cs.brown.edu: 8888

Monique, a collaborative fiction located at SUNY, Albany:
http://cnsvax.albany.edu/~hfiction/index.html

On-Line Journals

CTHEORY
http://ctech.concordia.ca/krokers/ctheory.html
"A multidisciplinary, multiplatform and multimedia" review, "focusing on theory, technology and culture from a critical and feminist perspective."

EJournal
Devoted to electronic and virtual culture.
http://www.hanover.edu/philos/ejournal/home.html (home page)
http://www.hanover.edu/philos/ejournal/archive/ (archives)

Media Ecology
"A journal where the intersection between culture, communication and technology is investigated." Maintained by students at the University of Baltimore.
http://raven.ubalt.edu/features/media_ecology

NWHQ, a web journal of hypertext literature:
http://www.knosso.com/NWHQ
(Try search on NWHQ if this does not work.)

Postmodern Culture
Though the journal covers all aspects of postmodern culture, electronic textuality is well represented.
http://www.iath.virginia.edu/pmc/ (home page and current issue)
http://muse.jhu.edu/journals/pmc/archive.html (archives)

Publisher

Eastgate Systems
http://www.eastgate.com/
Rightly billed as the publisher of "serious hypertext," the source of most fiction and non-fiction on diskette for Windows and Macintosh.

Also publisher of shorter works in *The Eastgate Quarterly* review of hypertext and distributor of Storyspace, the hypertextual writing system. Catalog, sample of texts, pages on electronic authors.

Theorists and Theory

Jay Bolter
http://www.lcc.gatech.edu/~bolter
Home page. Links to essays in progress.

Arthur and Marilouise Kroker
http://ctech.concordia.ca/krokers/cv_a.html
Home page. Links to various documents: book descriptions, interviews, bibliographies.

George Landow
http://www.stg.brown.edu/projects/hypertext/landow/cv/
landow_ov.html
Contains a number of collaborative documentary hypertexts written in Storyspace and translated into html by David B. Stevenson: The Freud Web, the Religions in England Web, the Victorian Web, Postcolonial and Postimperial Fiction, and of special interest, Cyberspace, Hypertext and Critical Theory, a collection of students' projects. Other menus of Landow projects can be reached at:
http://www.stg.brown.edu/projects/hypertext/landow/cv/

Allucquere Rosanne Stone
http://home.actlab.utexas.edu/~sandy/
Papers, interviews, and transcripts of talks by the author.

Hypertext Theory
http://aaln.org
From this site, a search on the word "hypertext" will lead to various hypertext resources.
http://cs.art.rmit.edu.au/hypertext/
More resources, including essays. Also contains a link to a Deleuze-Guattari dictionary, with entries submitted by users.

The Electronic Labyrinth, by C. J. Keep, Tim McLaughlin, and robin:
http://web.uvic.ca/~ckeep/elab.html
A textual (standard, not hyper) guide to hypertext technology and prac-

tice, consisting of three components: a discussion placing hypertext in the context of non-linear approaches to literature; an overview of selected texts of hypertext fiction, and an evaluation of hardware platforms and software environments available to writers.

Postmodern Theory
http://www.cudenver.edu/~mryder/itc_data/postmodern.html
Resources, readings, and people in postmodern culture.

For those with a love-hate relationship to electronic culture:
The Neo-Luddite Reaction
http://carbon.cudenver.edu/~mryder/itc_data/luddite.html
Texts on the historical movement of Luddism and recent documents expressing the Luddite reaction to electronic culture.

On-Line Hypertexts

Two samples of the numerous hypertext projects that can be found on the Net: one that demonstrates the use of hypertextual techniques in a "popular" narrative genre, the other a deliberately postmodern text that refracts many themes of cyberculture.

The Lurker Files.
http://www.randomhouse.com/lurkerfiles/
A campus-life mystery by Marc Ceratini, published by Random House, this work makes use of hypertextual links to explore the background of characters and to follow them individually when their paths diverge. New episodes are posted regularly, but back episodes are accessible through links.

Grammatron
www.grammatron.com
A "public domain narrative environment" developed by Mark Amerika in conjunction with the Brown University Graduate Creative Writing Program, this hypertext project consists of 1,100 text spaces and 2,000 links. It is introduced as follows: "A story about cyberspace, Cabala mysticism, digicash paracurrencies and the evolution of virtual sex in a society afraid to go outside and get in touch with its own nature, GRAMMATRON depicts a near-future world where stories are no longer conceived for book production but are instead created for a more immersive networked-narrative environment that, taking place on the

Net, calls into question how a narrative is composed, published and distributed in the age of digital dissemination. Future versions will integrate state-of-the-art Virtual Reality languages for a more immersive, collaborative experience. . . . "

Contributors

Espen Aarseth is Associate Professor in Humanistic Informatics at the faculty of Arts, University of Bergen, Norway. His book *Cybertexts: Perspectives on Ergodic Literature* was published by Johns Hopkins University Press in 1997. He is also the author of a Macintosh text utility, *Paradigma*. His current research interests include computer culture studies, the aesthetics of cybermedia, and humanistic computer methods.

Matthew Causey is Assistant Professor at the Georgia Institute of Technology, where he teaches the theory and practice of performance, art, and new media. He is the principal investigator of Georgia Tech's Performance and Technology Research Laboratory, which is conducting experimentation in areas of performance and new technologies. He is the founder and artistic director of Videopticon: The Video Art Festival at Georgia Tech, which showcases aesthetic works realized through video and new media. His writings have appeared in such journals as *Theatre Journal*, *Essays in Theatre*, *Journal of Dramatic Theory and Criticism*, and *Postmodern Culture*. His performance, film, and video works have been produced and screened across the country.

Thomas Foster is an Assistant Professor of English at Indiana University and Co-Editor-in-Chief of the journal *Genders*. He has published articles in *Signs*, *Genders*, *PMLA*, *Modern Fiction Studies*, and *Contemporary Literature*, and he is currently completing a book manuscript entitled *Homelessness at Home: Oppositional Practices and Modern Woman's Writing*. He guest edited the special issues of *Genders* (#18 [Fall 1993]) on "Cyberpunk: Technologies of Cultural Identity." His chapter in the collection is part of a larger work, tentatively entitled *Incurably Informed: Posthuman Narratives and the Rescripting of Postmodern Theory*. Other chapters from this work have appeared in the collection *Centuries' End, Narrative Means*, ed. Robert Newman (Stanford UP, 1996).

N. Katherine Hayles, Professor of English at the University of California at Los Angeles, teaches and writes on relations of literature and science in the twentieth century. She is the author of *The Cosmic Web: Scientific Field Models and Literary Strategies in the Twentieth Century* (1984), *Chaos Bound: Orderly Disorder in Contemporary Literature and Science* (1990), and the editor of *Chaos and Order: Complex Dynamics in Literature and Science* (1991). Her latest book is entitled *How We Became Posthuman: Virtual Bodies in Cybernetics, Literature and Informatics* (1998)

Christopher J. Keep is Assistant Professor at the University of Victoria, British Columbia. He is the co-author of *The Electronic Labyrinth*, a website for the study of hypertext fiction and theory, and author of articles ranging from Victorian apocalypticism to virtual reality. His current project is a book-length study of literature and the emergent "information economy" of the late nineteenth century.

Mark Nunes is Assistant Professor at DeKalb College in Atlanta. He has previously written on Baudrillard and Cyberspace in *Style*, and he is currently working on a book on virtual spaces.

Lance Olsen, Associate Professor and Writer-in-Residence at the University of Idaho, is author and editor of a dozen books, including the novels *Tonguing the Zeitgeist* and *Time Famine*, the critical study *Lolita: A Janus Text*, and the collection (co-edited with Mark Amerika) *In Memoriam to Postmodernism: Essays on the Avant-Pop*.

Barbara Page is Professor of English at Vassar College. She has developed a hypertext introduction to the manuscripts of the poet Elizabeth Bishop and is currently writing on "Hypertext and the Refiguring of Female Subjectivity."

Mark Poster teaches in the History Department at the University of California, Irvine. His recent books include *The Second Media Age* (1995), *The Mode of Information* (1990), *Critical Theory and Poststructuralism* (1988), and *Cultural History and Postmodernity* (1997).

A native of Geneva, Switzerland, **Marie-Laure Ryan** is an independent scholar and former software consultant based in Fort Collins, Colorado. Her book *Possible Worlds, Artificial Intelligence, and Narrative Theory* (Indiana UP, 1992) won the 1992 Prize for Independent Scholar from the Modern Language Association. She has published numerous essays on genre theory, narratology, possible worlds theory, linguistic approaches to literature, and more recently VR. Her current book project is a poetics based on the two VR concepts of immersion and interactivity.

Jon Thiem is Professor of English and Comparative Literature at Colorado State University. He received his Ph.D. from Indiana University in Comparative Literature. His publications include *Lorenzo de' Medici* (Penn State UP, 1991), *Real Life: Ten Stories of Aging*, co-editor (UP of Colorado, 1995), "The Burning of the Alexandrian Library as Symbol," *Journal of the History of Ideas* (1979), "Borges and Dante," *Comparative Literature* (1988), and "The Translator as Hero in Postmodern Fiction," *Translation and Literature* (1995).

Index

Index

Index